THE STUDENT'S HISTORY OF INDIA

THE STUDENT'S HISTORY OF INDIA

VINCENT A. SMITH

GYAN

Published by

Gyan Publishing House
5, Ansari Road
Daryaganj, New Delhi-110002
Phone: 011-47034999, 9811692060
E-mail: books@gyanbooks.com

Distribution Network
gyanbooks.com
India, USA, Canada, UK, Australia

ISBN: 978-93-7133-179-1 (PB)
First Published, 1915

2nd Impression 2025

Printed at: Gyan Press, Delhi.

THE STUDENT'S HISTORY OF INDIA
Author Vincent A. Smith

W. & D. Downey

GEORGE V, KING-EMPEROR

STUDENT'S HISTORY OF INDIA

BY

VINCENT A. SMITH

M.A. (DUBL. & OXON.), I.C.S., RETIRED
AUTHOR OF 'THE EARLY HISTORY OF INDIA', ETC.

14 MAPS AND 34 ILLUSTRATIONS

1915

BUDDHA

EXTRACT FROM PREFACE TO FIRST EDITION

THIS little book, like its many rivals, is designed primarily to meet the wants of students preparing for the matriculation examination of the Calcutta University, as defined in the latest Syllabus. But it is hoped that other readers also may find it useful as an introduction to the study of Indian history.

Although it would be unbecoming for me to criticize the performances of my predecessors individually, it may be permissible to observe that I have aimed at a standard of accuracy higher than that attained by any of the seven or eight more or less similar books which I have had the opportunity of testing, and that certain inveterate errors continually recurring in text-books will not be found in this work. One such error—the use of the misleading phrases ‘the Pathan empire’ and ‘the Pathan kings’, long since given up by scholars—unfortunately has crept into the official Syllabus. I have done my best to avoid introducing fresh blunders of my own. . . .

Every topic mentioned in the Syllabus is dealt with in this volume, and can be traced with facility in the table of contents and index. The Syllabus is reprinted as Appendix D for convenience of reference. Useful tables have been inserted as required. Many readers, I think, will be glad to find in Appendix A the full text of the Queen's Proclamation, dated November 1, 1858.

PREFACE TO THE FIFTH EDITION

The three earlier revisions of this book were directed almost exclusively to the correction of minute inaccuracies, the paging and bulk of the volume remaining unaltered. On this occasion, while the process of minute correction has been continued and possibly completed, the principal purpose of the revision has been different. When the book was first planned, I was requested to make it small and condensed. Now that it has been widely used for six years, experienced teachers ask that the historical facts should be narrated in fuller detail, that the causes of important revolutions should be clearly explained, that the state of society in different periods should be described, that the story of India under the Crown should be told at greater length, that the narrative should be brought down to the present time, that a sketch of the nature of the sources or original authorities should be supplied, and that the number of maps and illustrations should be largely increased. The advantages to be obtained by adopting those suggestions seem to outweigh the evil of increased bulk. A book as highly condensed as the earlier editions were must be rather dry, and omit so much that the truth is apt to be distorted. On the other hand, the writer of a school history should be extremely careful not to overload his pages. Young students should not be burdened with anything like the mass of detail which is proper in a history composed on a large scale. The author has tried to attain the golden mean by complying to a considerable extent with the suggestions offered, while refusing to insert much matter which some people would prefer to include. Special attention has been paid to simplicity of language and the avoidance of difficult words.

The three notes on the nature of the sources or original

authorities for the history of the Hindu, Muhammadan, and British periods have been inserted by special request, and are designed for the benefit of teachers rather than of pupils.

It may be convenient to specify the principal subjects now treated with fullness greater than before, and the more important additions to the text. They include:

Book I. India in the Vedic age; India of the epics; the rise of Islam; Buddhism; caste.

Book II. The Gupta period; Kumārila-bhatta and Sankarāchārya; the Hinduizing of foreigners; the social condition of the mediaeval kingdoms; the Pāla dynasty of Bengal.

Book III. Description of Vijayanagar; causes of Muslim victories.

Book IV. Administration of Sher Shah; the growth of the Madras and Bombay presidencies; the history of Akbar, with special reference to the Jesuit evidence; the reign of Jahāngīr, as illustrated by his authentic *Memoirs*, now accessible; the reign of Shahjahān, with quotations from De Laët and the recently published *Travels* of Peter Mundy; the life and institutions of Sivājī; the causes of Aurangzeb's failure; the history of the Peshwas; the causes of the decline and fall of the Mughal empire.

Book V. The independence of Bengal under Allahvardi Khan; the Anglo-French wars; Marāthā affairs; Mysore wars; Lord Dalhousie's reforms; dates of the Mutiny, and explanation of its failure.

Book VI. A single chapter of the earlier editions has been expanded so as to form four chapters of the new Book VI, and the narrative has been continued to 1914.

The index has been recast. Many new maps and illustrations have been inserted. The 'Message to his People Overseas' issued by King George V in 1914 is printed as Appendix C.

CONTENTS

BOOK I

PHYSICAL FEATURES: ANCIENT INDIA

BOOK II

HINDU INDIA FROM 600 B.C. TO A.D. 1193: MAHMUD OF GHAZNI

BOOK III

THE MUHAMMADAN CONQUEST; THE SULTANATE OF DELHI (SO-CALLED 'PATHAN EMPIRE') FROM A.D. 1193 TO 1526

BOOK IV

THE MUGHAL EMPIRE FROM A.D. 1526 TO 1761

BOOK V

THE BRITISH OR ANGLO-INDIAN PERIOD; RULE OF THE EAST INDIA COMPANY FROM 1761 TO 1858

BOOK VI

THE BRITISH OR ANGLO-INDIAN PERIOD; INDIA UNDER THE CROWN, 1858-1914

APPENDIX

LIST OF ILLUSTRATIONS

MAPS

BOOK I

PHYSICAL FEATURES: ANCIENT INDIA

CHAPTER I

The geographical foundation of history: the physical features of India.

Geography the foundation of history. 'Geography is', as has been well said, 'the foundation of all historical knowledge.' The history of India, like that of other lands, cannot be understood unless regard is paid to the physical features of the stage on which the long drama of her story has been played, and before we attempt a rapid survey of the actors' deeds we must pause to consider the manner in which the position and structure of India have affected human action.

Exclusion of Burma and Ceylon. The Indian empire as now constituted includes the kingdom of Burma to the east of the Bay of Bengal,. which was annexed in three instalments in the years 1826, 1852, and 1886. Burma, however, which has a history of its own, is not naturally a part of India. Its affairs, therefore, will not be discussed in this book, except incidentally as episodes in the Indian story. The island of Ceylon, on the other hand, although physically an imperfectly severed fragment of the mainland, is not a part of the Indian empire, being administered as a Crown colony under the direction of the Secretary of State for the Colonies. For this reason, and also because the island, like Burma, has a history of its own, the annals of Ceylon do not come within the scope of this book, except so far as they have been affected by the direct action of Indian powers.

Boundaries of India. The India with which we are concerned is the distinct geographical unit bounded on the north by the ranges of the Himalaya and Karakoram, on the north-west by the mountains to the west of the Indus, on the north-east by the hills of Assam and Cāchār, and everywhere else by the sea. The unit so defined includes both a continental area, outside the tropics, extending from the mouths of the Indus in N. lat. 25° on the west to the mouths of the Ganges in about N. lat. 23° on the east, and a triangular peninsular area within the tropics, terminating at Cape Comorin, N. lat. 8° 4′. The northern land frontier measures about 1,600, the north-western about 1,200 and the north-eastern about 500 miles. The length of the sea-coast may be taken as 3,400 miles, more or less.

Physical isolation of India. The leading fact in the position above described as affecting history is the obvious physical isolation of India. In ancient times, when no power attempted to assert full command of the sea, a country so largely surrounded by the ocean was inaccessible for the most part, and could be approached by land through its continental section only. The north-eastern hills and the gigantic Himalayan and Karakoram ranges present few openings at all passable, and none easy of passage for considerable bodies of men. But the hills west of the Indus are pierced by many passes more or less open. The land gates of India are all on her north-western frontier, and this physical fact dominated her whole history for thousands of years.

Isolation destroyed by command of the sea. The command of the sea acquired by the Portuguese at the end of the fifteenth century and ultimately inherited by the British has destroyed the isolation of India. To a modern power possessing an adequate fleet, the sea is a bond of union not a barrier of separation, and so it has come about that India, while still separated from the adjoining continental empires of Russia, Persia, and China by mountain ramparts, is closely bound to the remote island of Great Britain by means of the British control of the ocean routes.

Modern importance of the ports. The ports are now the

main gates, and the north-western passes are but posterns. No hostile force entering India by any of the ancient land routes could hold more than a limited area in the north-west against a power exercising command of the sea. While the traveller from Bombay easily reaches London in a fortnight, Delhi is still almost as far from Ghaznī or Samarkand as it was in the days of Mahmūd and Bābur.

Distribution of the great cities. In former times the great cities and capitals of states were built inland and usually on the banks of rivers, which offered the best means of communication and transport. Now, the position of the greatest cities is determined by the facilities for harbour accommodation, and it is desirable that the capital of the empire should be in close touch with the sea. Bombay owes her modern greatness solely to her magnificent natural harbour, which enables her to deal with the commerce of the world. Calcutta, although not so favoured by nature, is still a great port, and as such was well qualified to be the imperial capital, as it was from 1774 to 1912. The remoteness from the sea is a serious disadvantage to Delhi, the newly appointed official capital.

Want of harbours on the east coast. The lack of good harbours on the eastern coast fit for big modern ships has killed or half killed the ancient towns on that side of India. Ports which were good enough for the tiny vessels of ancient times are of no use for the great steamers of these days. Madras, in order to save herself from ruin, has been obliged to supply natural deficiency by the construction of an artificial harbour at enormous cost. Most of the harbours on the eastern side of India, such as they were, have become so choked with sand and silt as to be almost useless, even for small coasting craft. This physical change has involved the utter ruin of famous old ports, Kāvirīpaddanam, Korkai, and others.

Natural division between north and south. Next in importance to the physical isolation of India, as it existed for countless years, is the natural separation of the north from the south effected by the broad belt of hill and forest running from the Gulf of Cambay on the west to the mouths of the Mahānadī on the east. The country lying between this barrier and the Himalaya, although not altogether devoid of hills, is essentially a plain watered by two river systems, those of the Indus and the Ganges. The parting or watershed of the two systems is marked by the Āravalli (Pāriyātra) hills of Rājputāna. The great plain, formed of silt deposited from the rivers, has been the scene of nearly all the Indian historical events interesting to the outer world. It lies outside the tropics. The peninsular region to the south of the forest barrier lies wholly within the tropics, and until recent times has been so secluded from the rest of the world that the history of its many principalities and powers, excepting some on the coast, has been little known or regarded.

The forest barrier, or Mahākāntāra, and the Narbadā river. The forest barrier itself, Mahākāntāra of old books, used to be a no-man's-land, lying outside the limits of the regularly constituted states, and usually left in the hands of its wild inhabitants. It is now shared by several provincial governments, and is gradually losing its former distinct character. In very early times this forest belt was practically impenetrable at most points, and the slight intercourse between north and south had to be conducted usually either by sea or by a land route along the eastern coast. The forest barrier being broad and ill-defined, a more definite boundary is needed for literary use. Ancient authority, accordingly, warrants the assumption of the Narbadā river as the conventional line dividing the north from the south, and this convention is sufficiently supported by the facts of history to be justified in practice.

Āryāvarta, or Hindustan and the Deccan. The northern plains were called by Hindu authors Āryāvarta, 'the Aryan territory,' and by the Muhammadans Hindustan, 'the Hindu territory.' Modern usage sometimes extends the term Hindustan to the whole of India. The ancients generally designated the whole southern peninsular area by the Sanskrit word *dakshiṇa*, meaning 'south', which is familiar in its corrupt

English form as 'the Deccan'. But the term 'Deccan' is now commonly restricted to the plateau or highlands to the north of the Kistna (Krishnā) and Tungabhadra rivers, which are mostly included in the Nizam's Dominions and the Bombay Presidency. The Far South, or Tamil Land (*Tamilakam*), which comprises the bulk of the Madras Presidency with the addition of the Mysore, Cochin, and Travancore States, is treated as distinct from the Deccan. But historically Mysore has been more closely connected with the Deccan states than with those of Tamil Land.

The historian's three divisions of India. As a matter of fact the three divisions of Hindustan or Aryāvarta, to the north of the Narbadā; the Deccan, between the Tāptī and the Tungabhadra; and the Far South or Tamil Land, from the Tungabhadra to Cape Comorin, usually have had separate histories. The historian of India, therefore, finds it convenient to restrict his main narrative of events before the British period to Hindūstan, which was most in touch with the outer world, and to devote distinct chapters to the account of events in the Deccan and the Far South. Most of the events of at all general interest occurred in one or other of the three regions named above. The affairs of Mahākāntāra, or the central belt of jungle, of the Himalayan slopes and valleys, including Nepāl and Kashmīr, as well as those of the basin of the Brahmaputra, including Assam, ordinarily fall outside of the main current of Indian history. The administrative arrangements of modern India take little account of physical features and natural geographical boundaries.

Basins of the Indus and Ganges. Within the area of Āryāvarta or Hindustan we must distinguish the basin of the Indus and its tributaries, comprising the Panjāb, Sind, Cutch, and Rājputāna to the west of the Āravalli hills, from the basin of the Ganges and its affluents. The history of the countries along the lower course of the Ganges, the modern province of Bengal, is distinct in large measure from that of the countries along the upper course of the same river, now mostly included

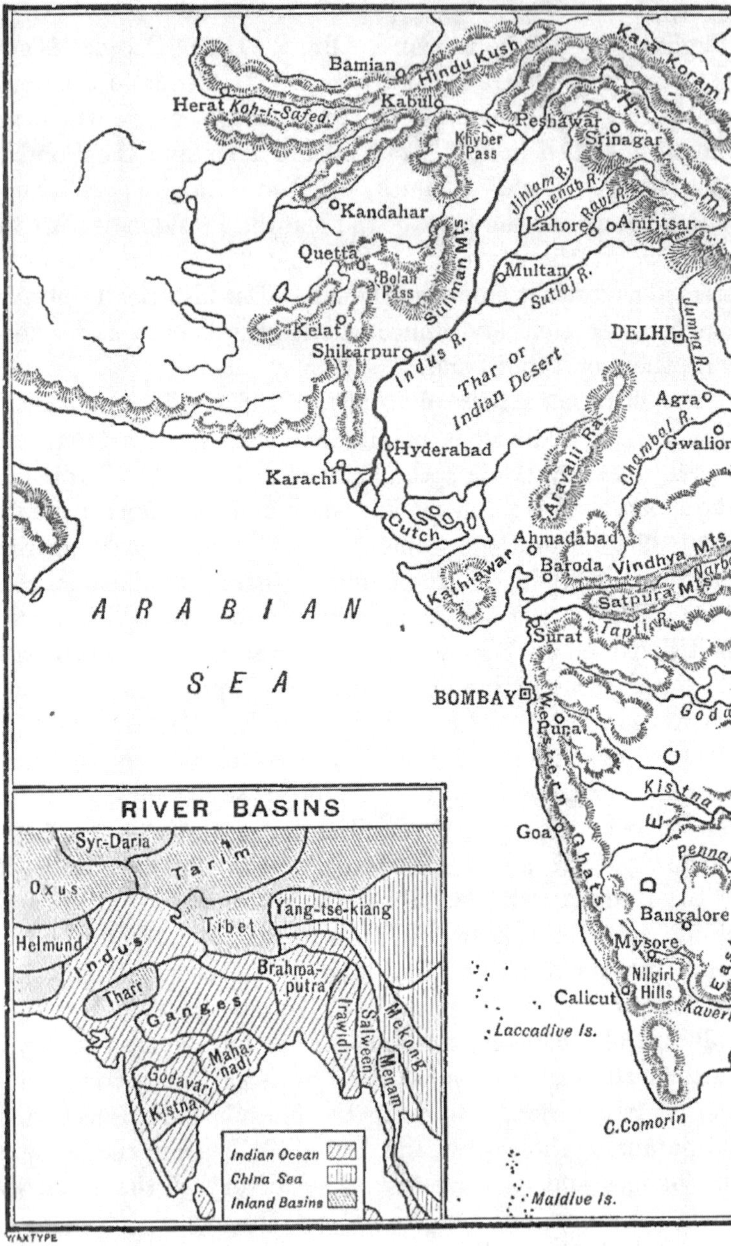

Bamian
Hindu Kush
Kara Koram
Herat
Koh-i-Safed
Kabul
Peshawar
Srinagar
Khyber Pass
Jihlam R.
Chenab R.
Ravi R.
Kandahar
Lahore
Amritsar
Quetta
Bolan Pass
Suliman Mts
Multan
Sutlaj R.
Jumna R.
Kelat
DELHI
Shikarpur
Indus R.
Thar or Indian Desert
Agra
Chambal R.
Gwalior
Hyderabad
Karachi
Aravalli Ra.
Cutch
Ahmadabad
Baroda
Vindhya Mts
Kathiawar
Satpura Mts
ARABIAN SEA
Surat
Tapti R.
BOMBAY
Puna
Western Ghats
Kistna
Goa
Pennar
Bangalore
Mysore
Nilgiri Hills
Calicut
Kaveri
Laccadive Is.
C.Comorin
Maldive Is.
RIVER BASINS
Syr-Daria
Tarim
Oxus
Tibet
Yang-tse-kiang
Helmund
Indus
Brahma-putra
Thar
Ganges
Irawidi
Salween
Mekong
Menam
Maha-nadi
Godavari
Kistna
Indian Ocean
China Sea
Inland Basins

WAXTYPE

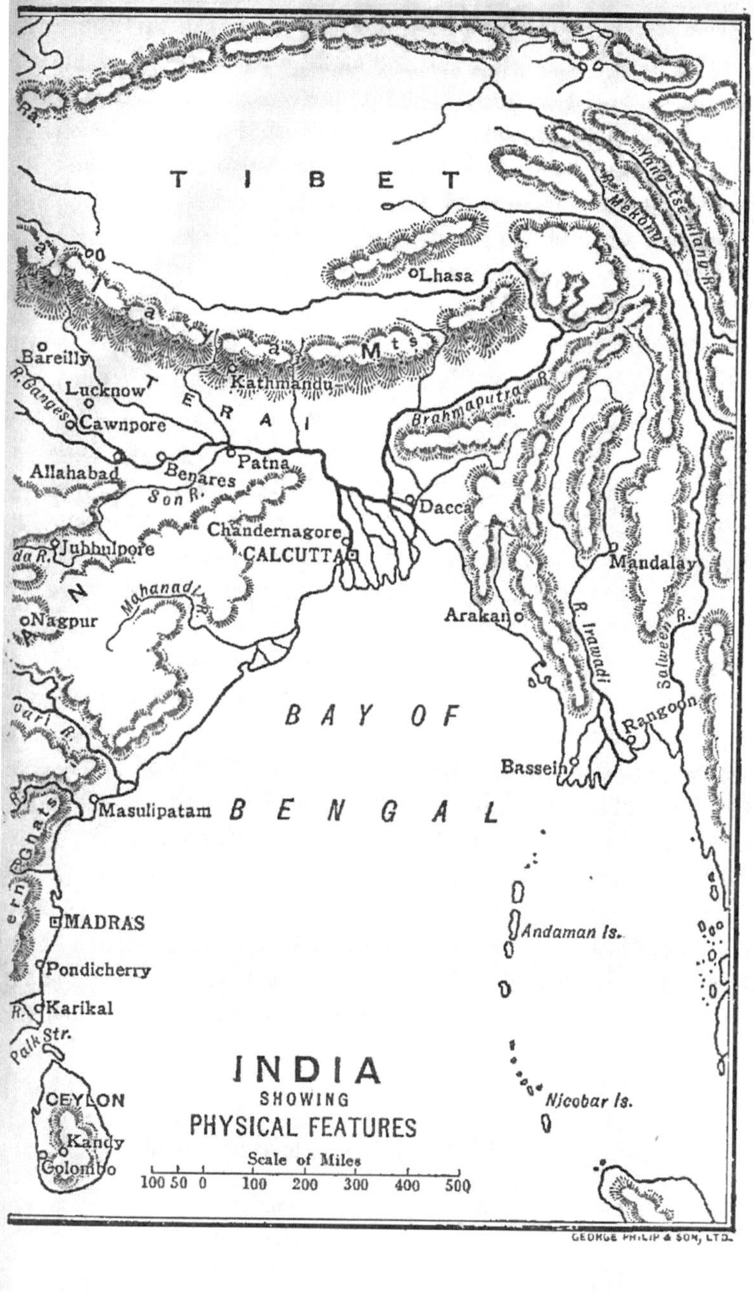

INDIA
SHOWING
PHYSICAL FEATURES

in the United Provinces of Agra and Oudh. South Bihār and Tirhūt, the ancient Magadha and Mithilā respectively, although now under the government of the newly formed artificial province of 'Bihār and Orissa', are associated historically rather more with the upper than with the lower provinces. The outlying peninsula of Surāshtra, or Kāthiāwār, being most easily accessible through Mālwā, was often included in the northern empires of the Gangetic basin.

The 'Lost River'. The extensive desert which now occupies so large an area in Rājputāna and Sind was much smaller in ancient times, when the 'Lost River', the Hakrā or Wahindah flowed through the Bahāwalpur State, and with its tributaries fertilized wide regions now desolate. During the Muhammadan period that river was the recognized boundary between Sind and Hind, or India Proper. It disappeared finally in the eighteenth century, but its ancient channels and the ruins of forgotten cities on their banks may be seen still. Failure to appreciate the enormous scale of the changes in the courses of the rivers of Northern India has caused much misunderstanding of history. In olden days the command of the rivers was as important as the command of the sea is now.

The Western and Eastern Ghāts; the plain of Tinnivelly. The long chain of hills or mountains of moderate height, known as the Sahyādri or Western Ghāts, which extends, with only one short break at Pālghāt, from the Narbadā to Cape Comorin, plays an important part in Indian history. It shuts off from the interior highlands the low-lying fertile strip of land between the hills and the sea, called the Konkans, which has been the seat of trade with Europe since remote ages.[1] The passes, which do not change like rivers, have necessarily deter-

[1] Ancient Hindu authorities name 'Seven Konkans', extending to Cape Comorin. 'The Konkan is now held to include all the land which lies between the Western Ghāts and the Indian Ocean, from the latitude of Damān on the north [20° 25′] to that of Terekhol, on the Goa frontier [about 15° 43′], on the south. This tract is about 320 miles in length' (*Bombay Gazetteer*, 1896, vol. i, part ii, p. ix).

mined the lines of intercourse between the coast and the kingdoms of the interior. The facilities for erecting forts on the flat-topped hills of the Ghāts and Deccan have largely influenced the course of history, especially during the seventeenth and eighteenth centuries, when the Marāthā power was based on the possession of the hill-fortresses. The ill-defined range of the Eastern Ghāts has less historical significance. The arid plain of Tinnivelly and Madura in the south-east of the peninsula is a well-marked natural feature which became the seat of a separate kingdom, that of the Pāndyas, at a very early date.

The temptations of India. The wealth extracted by an industrious population from the teeming soil of the hot northern plains has always been a temptation to the hardy races of the less favoured parts of Asia, and has supplied the motive for innumerable invasions of armies and immigrations of more peaceful settlers. The new-comers, entering from the north, have thence pushed into the less attractive regions of the Deccan table-land, whenever they were strong enough to do so, but none of the invaders from the north were able to establish effective dominion over the extreme south. The riches of Tamil Land—especially pearls, pepper, and spices—always have been sought by foreigners who came by sea, not overland. The eagerness of merchants belonging to European naval states to secure the trade in those precious commodities has resulted in the most wonderful fact of modern history, the conquest of all India by the subjects of an island kingdom in the Far West. The events of 1914 have proved that the union between India and England does not rest merely upon conquest. Community of material interests is hallowed by a common feeling of loyal devotion to the person of the King-Emperor. The sincerity of Indian feeling has been made manifest to the world by the free-will offering of blood and treasure tendered by the princes and peoples of India, and accepted in a spirit of brotherhood by the king, parliament, and people of the United Kingdom.

CHAPTER II

The peoples of India: aborigines; Aryans; Indo-Aryans; Dravidians; foreign elements.

The Stone Age. Poets dream of a golden age when the world was young and men lived in innocent peace and happy plenty. Sober science tells a different tale and teaches that everywhere the earliest men were rude savages, dwelling in caves or huts, ignorant even of the use of fire and the commonest arts of life. Rudely chipped flints or other hard stones were their only tools and are their sole memorial. Later, but still very ancient, men made better stone implements, often exquisitely finished, and learned how to make pottery, at first by hand only, afterwards with the aid of the wheel. India, like other lands, yields many relics of such early men, who had not been taught the use of metals, and are therefore said to have lived in the Stone Age.

The Copper Age. In Northern India the first metal to become known was copper. Hundreds of curious implements made of pure copper have been found in the Central Provinces, in old beds of the Ganges near Cawnpore, and in other places from Eastern Bengal to Sind and the Kurram valley. They are supposed to date from 2000 B.C., more or less. The time when, iron being unknown, pure copper, not bronze, was used to make tools is called the Copper Age.[1] It is possible that some of the *Rigveda* hymns may date from that age, but commentators differ.

The Iron Age. In process of time the use of iron became familiar, having been introduced, perhaps, from Babylonia. Since then men have lived and still live in the Iron Age. The *Atharvaveda*, which, although very ancient, is later in date than the *Rigveda*, seems to recognize the use of iron, which

[1] The use of bronze, an alloy of copper and tin, common in Europe, was rare in India, which had no Bronze Age.

certainly was known to the people of Northern India before 500 B.C., and probably long before that date.

Variety of races in India. How far the existing peoples of India are descended from the ancient men who used stone and copper tools nobody can tell. The most casual observer cannot fail to perceive that the present population of nearly three hundred millions is made up of the descendants of many diverse races, some of which have been settled in the country since the most remote times, while others are known to have entered it at various periods. In the course of ages those diverse races have 'now become so intermixed and confounded that it is impossible to say where one variety of man ends and another begins'.

Two main types. But, notwithstanding infinite crossing, two main types are clearly discernible. The short, dark, snub-nosed, and often ugly type is represented by the Kols, Bhīls, and countless other jungle tribes, as well as by an immense mass of low-caste folk in Northern India. The Southern races also, with certain exceptions, are more akin to this type than to the second, which is tall, fair, long-nosed, and often handsome, as represented by the Kashmīrīs and many high-caste people in the north and some in the south.

Aryans and Aborigines. The people of the short, dark type undoubtedly are the descendants of the older races who occupied the country before the tall, fair people came in. They are, therefore, often called 'aborigines' to indicate that they represent the earliest or original inhabitants, so far as can be ascertained. Attempts, based chiefly upon philology, or the science of language, are sometimes made to distinguish races —Kolarian, Draviḍian, and so forth—among these 'aborigines', but with little success. The tall, fair people certainly came in from the north-west, and the earliest invaders of whom we know anything, the people of the *Rigveda* hymns, called themselves Aryans, or 'kinsmen'. Their blood may be assumed to flow in the veins of certain Brahmans and other classes at the present day, but it is mixed with strains derived from later invaders of similar physical type. The question of the original seat of the Aryan stock, one branch of which entered India from about 1500 B.C. or earlier, has given rise to many theories, which agree only in not being proved. It is, however, safe to say that the Aryan settlers in India were akin to the Persians or Iranians, and probably to many other races of Asia and Europe.

Indo-Aryans. These Aryan settlers in India are conveniently called Indo-Aryans to distinguish them from the continental Aryans on the other side of the passes. The Pārsī or Persian colonies, whose ancestors, fleeing from Muhammadan persecution, reached Western India in the eighth century, may be regarded as Aryans of pure blood. The earliest settlements of the Vedic Indo-Aryans undoubtedly were made in the Panjāb, the 'land of the five rivers', or 'of the seven rivers', according to an ancient reckoning. Thence the strangers spread slowly over Northern India, advancing chiefly along the Ganges and Jumna, but making use also of the Indus route. One section seems to have moved eastwards along the base of the mountains into Mithilā or Tirhūt. The distinctive Brahmanical system was evolved, not in the Panjāb, but in the upper Ganges valley in the Delhi region, between the Sutlaj and Jumna. Manu honours the small tract between the Sarasvatī and Drishadvatī rivers by the title of Brahmāvarta, 'the land of the gods', giving the name of Brahmarshi-desa, or 'the land of divine sages', to the larger region comprising Brahmāvarta or Kurukshetra (Thānēsar), with the addition of Matsya (Eastern Rājputāna), Panchāla (between the Ganges and Jumna), and Surasena (Mathurā). When the treatise ascribed to Manu assumed its present shape, perhaps about A.D. 200 or 300, the whole space between the Himalaya and the Vindhyas from sea to sea was acknowledged to be Āryāvarta, 'the Aryan territory'. The Indo-Aryan advance thus indicated must have been spread over many centuries. As they advanced the Aryans subdued, more or less completely, the 'aborigines', whom they called *Dasyus*, and by other names.

Southern expansion of Aryans checked. The central forest barrier, or Mahākāntāra (*ante*, p. 18), long checked the Aryan advance towards the south, and, indeed, no large body of Aryan settlers can be proved to have passed it. But, in course of time, the ideas and customs of the Aryans spread all over India, even into lands where the people have little or no Aryan blood in their veins. Tradition credits the Rishi Agastya with the introduction of Aryan Hindu institutions into the South.

Aryan languages. The Indo-Aryans spoke a language which in a later literary form became known as Sanskrit, and belonged to the same family as Persian, Latin, Greek, English, and many other Asiatic and European languages. From the early Indo-Aryan speech, Marāthī, Hindī, Bengālī, and other languages of Northern India have been evolved during the course of ages. But multitudes of people who are not Aryan by descent now speak Aryan languages. Community of language is no proof of community of blood.

Immigration from the north-east. Strangers distinct from the Aryans, and belonging to the Mongoloid type of mankind, more or less akin to the Chinese, came down from the north-eastern hills, and are believed to form a considerable element in the population of Eastern Bengal and Assam. This movement from the north-east was of minor importance compared with the Aryan immigration from the north-west.

Dravidians. The people of the south are described as Dravidians because Dravida was the old name of the Tamil country. Some writers extend the meaning of the term Dravidian so as to comprise most of the so-called aboriginal races, even in the north, but such an extension of a purely geographical name is not to be commended. The Southerners undoubtedly include several distinct races, but almost all of the short, dark type. The Tamils are the most important. Learned men have many theories about the origin of these races, which agree only in their uncertainty. No positive assertion on the subject is justified.

Dravidian languages and civilization. The principal languages spoken in the south, namely Tamil, Telugu, Kanarese, Malayālam, and Tulu, which are closely related one to the other, form a group or family totally distinct from the Aryan, and known to philologists as the Dravidian family. It is equally distinct from the Kolarian or Munda family spoken by many of the so-called aboriginal tribes. Tamil, a rich and copious tongue, the most cultivated of the Dravidian group, possesses a fine early literature, perfectly independent of the Sanskrit. Although our knowledge of the ancient life of the Dravidian nations is scanty, enough is known to justify the assertion that they were far from being rude barbarians when Aryan teachers first reached them, several centuries before the Christian era.

The foreign elements of the Indian population. As already observed, the origin of the southern races is not known, and foreign immigration from the north into the south cannot be proved to have taken place on a large scale. The known foreign elements in the Indian population came in mainly from the north-west and settled, for the most part, to the north of the Vindhyas. It will be useful to state briefly what those elements are. The first swarm of immigrants about which anything can be ascertained is that of the Indo-Aryans (*ante*, p. 26), whose movement undoubtedly lasted for centuries.

The Sakas. In the second century B. C. we begin to hear of the Sakas, hordes of nomad tribes from Central Asia, who descended on the Indian plains, formed settlements in the Panjāb, with extensions probably as far as Mathurā, and occupied Kāthiāwār or Surāshtra, of which they became the masters. The ancient Indians having been accustomed to use the term Saka in a vague way to denote all foreigners from the other side of the passes, without nice distinctions of race and tribe, it is possible that many of the people called Sakas may have been akin to the Aryans of the olden time.

The Yuehchi or Kushāns (Kusana). The third recorded inrush of strangers from Central Asia in large numbers began in the first century after Christ. At that time the leading horde was known to the Chinese historians, the principal source of information on the subject, as the Yuehchi, a people probably akin to the Turks, and perhaps to the Aryans. The Kushāns (Kusana), the principal clan or sept among the Yuehchi, founded a powerful empire in Northern India, the history of which will be noticed in Chapter VI.

The White Huns or Ephthalites. Indistinct indications suggest that India may have been invaded by Persians or Iranians in the third century of the Christian era, but the next clearly proved irruption took place in the fifth and sixth centuries, when multitudes of fierce folk from the Asiatic steppes swooped down on Persia and India. The Indians called them all by the name of Hūnas, a term used vaguely like the term Sakas, and covering, no doubt, many different hordes or tribes. European writers distinguish the Indian Hūnas as the White Huns, or Ephthalites, from the other Huns who invaded Europe. As in the case of the Sakas, we cannot say positively whether or not the White Huns were akin to the fair, tall Aryans and Turks, or to the small yellow-faced Mongols. But it is now known that many existing Rājpūt clans and other castes—Gūjars, Jats, Kāthi, &c.—are descendants of either the Hūnas or the Gurjaras or of other similar hordes which followed them. The appearance of the Rājpūts, Jats, and Gūjars indicates that their foreign ancestors must have belonged to one of the fair, tall types of mankind, and not to the yellow-faced, narrow-eyed, Mongoloid type.

Early spread of Islam. A new force which came into existence in the first half of the seventh century ultimately produced enormous effects on the population of India. Muhammad, an Arab of the desert, born about A. D. 570, conceived in middle life the idea of proclaiming a reformed religion which should abolish the rude heathen practices of the Arabs, and be, in his belief, an improvement on the Jewish and Christian religions as known to him. For years he had little success, but he began to acquire political power from the time that he fled from Mecca to Medina in order to escape from the opposition of his hostile kinsmen. The Muhammadan era of the Hijra (often corruptly spelt Hegira), or Flight, dates from A. D. 622.[1] During the remaining ten years of his life, his prophetic teaching, summed up in the phrase, 'There is no God but Allah, and Muhammad is his messenger', made such progress, helped largely by the sword, that Muhammad, when he died in 632, was practically master of Arabia. His position as such brought his successors into conflict with the empires of Persia and Constantinople, resulting in a series of wars, in which the Arabs won marvellous success. Within the short space of eighty years after the prophet's death, the adherents of his religion—Islam—reigned supreme over Arabia, Persia, Syria, Western Turkistan, Sind, Egypt, and Southern Spain. We may say with truth that the rapid progress of the Arab arms was mainly due to the enthusiasm aroused by the prophet's teaching, aided by the weakness of the kingdoms attacked; but no man has ever yet succeeded in explaining how the teaching of a prophet like Muhammad should arouse so quickly the zeal of his followers and make them invincible. The spread of a new religion is one of the mysteries of human nature, which do not yield their secret to attempts at summary explanation.

Muslim element in Indian population. Sind, then regarded as distinct from India proper, was conquered by Muhammad bin Kāsim in A. D. 712, and the occupation of Kābul followed in 870. But the conquest of those outlying territories did not much concern India. The first Indian province permanently occupied by Musalmans was the Panjāb, annexed by Sultān Mahmūd of Ghaznī about 1021. From the closing years of the twelfth century, when the conquest of Hindustan was systematically undertaken, a stream of Muslim strangers began to flow into the plains of India, and continued to flow, with some interruptions, until the eighteenth century, profoundly changing the character of the population over immense areas. The

[1] Hijra dates are denoted by the letters A. H., meaning *Anno Hijrae*, 'in the year of the Hijra'

Muslim immigrants from the north-west belonged mostly to tall, fair races, resembling the Aryans rather than the earliest inhabitants of India.

Lasting effect of the early Aryan immigration. Thus it appears that for thousands of years millions of foreigners, beginning with the Vedic Aryans, and mostly fair-skinned people, have kept pouring into India and mingling their blood with that of the earlier dark inhabitants. The strangest fact in the story is that the most profound effect was wrought by the earliest known swarm of immigrants, the Vedic Aryans, who have stamped an indelible mark on the institutions of India, and given the country as a whole its distinctive character. Sakas, Yuehchi, Hūnas, and many other alien tribes who came in later are now mere names. They have left scarcely a trace of their peculiar institutions or customs, and have been swallowed up in the gulf of Hinduism. The Muslims alone, thanks to their zeal for their religion, have succeeded in keeping distinct and separate. Modern Hinduism, however much it may differ from the religion and social system of the ancient Rishis, undoubtedly has its roots in the institutions of the Vedic Aryans, and not in those of subsequent immigrants. In the next chapter some of the effects of the Aryan occupation will be considered.

CHAPTER III

Early Hindu civilization: the Vedas; *Smṛiti*; the Purānas; the epics; Buddhism and Jainism; caste.

The four Vedas. Although it is true that few of the modern Hindus possess an intimate knowledge of the Vedic literature, and that the Hinduism of recent times has little obvious connexion with the teaching of that literature, it is also true that nearly all Hindus profess to revere the Vedas and regard them, especially the *Upanishads*, in theory as the foundation of their system of life. Some account of the Vedic literature, the gift of the Aryans, therefore, is an indispensable introduction to the history of ancient and modern India.

The word Veda means 'knowledge', and specially the philosophical and religious knowledge which Hindus believe to have been revealed to the most ancient Aryan sages (*rishis*). The books imparting such knowledge are known as 'the four Vedas'.

Contents of the four Vedas. Each Veda may be said to comprise three parts, all ranking as *śruti*, or revelation—namely (1) a collection or collections (*saṁhitā*) of hymns, prayers, invocations, or spells (*mantra*); (2) prose treatises, designed to explain the meaning of the ritual of sacrifice and to serve as text-books for the use of Brahmans (*Brāhmaṇa*); and (3) philosophical discourses (*Upanishad*), chiefly devoted to the exposition of the doctrine of the identity of the world-soul with the individual soul (*ātman, brahma*), and the means of escape from the evils of existence by absorption into the world-soul. Technically the *Upanishads* form part of the *Brāhmaṇas*, which also include supplementary treatises called *Āraṇyakas*, specially designed for the study of advanced students living in the solitudes of forests (*araṇya*). But the matter of the *Upanishads* differs so much from that of the other parts of the *Brāhmaṇas*, that they may be regarded with propriety as forming a distinct section of the Vedas. Some *Upanishads* are presented as chapters of *Āraṇyakas*, while others stand alone. The *Upanishads* are the foundation of the later and more systematic Vedānta philosophy. Their metaphysical doctrine is summed up in the formula *tat tvam asi*, 'thou art that'. They also give the earliest indication of the doctrine of *karma*, so prominent afterwards in Buddhism, and defined by Manu in the words: 'action of every kind, whether of mind, or speech, or body, produces results good or evil, and causes the various conditions of men, highest, lowest, or intermediate'.

The Rigveda and Sāmaveda saṁhitās. The oldest *saṁhitā*, that of the Rigveda (*ṛich* = stanza of praise), comprises 1,017 hymns in praise of the various powers of nature—the sky, fire, winds, and so forth—worshipped as gods. Occasionally the poets rise to a higher level, and dimly perceive 'the only God above the gods'. Some of these hymns must be as old as 1000 B.C., and may be much older. The Sāmaveda *Saṁhitā*, which is merely a book of chants (*sāman*), nearly all taken from the Rigveda, is of comparatively slight importance. The chants relate to the *soma* sacrifices. The *soma* was a plant, the identity of which still is matter of dispute.

The Yajurveda saṁhitā. The Yajurveda *saṁhitā*, existing in two principal forms, the Black and White, is mainly composed of original matter, half in prose, although it includes some hymns, amounting to about one-fourth of the whole, extracted from the Rigveda. It may be described as a book of sacrificial prayers, and its compilation is the work of a period when unduly high value was attached to sacrificial ritual, and 'the truly religious spirit' of the Rigveda had been obscured by formalism. The comparatively late date of this Veda is indicated by the fact that the Hindu holy land, which for the poets of the Rigveda was the Panjāb, the basin of the Indus and its tributaries, is shifted in the Yajurveda to Brahmāvarta or Kurukshetra, in the Gangetic basin, between the Sutlaj and the Jumna.

The Atharvaveda saṁhitā. The Atharvaveda *saṁhitā*, of which about the sixth part is in prose, consists mainly of a collection of spells, charms, and incantations for use in sorcery and witchcraft. Although many of these formulas evidently have come down from extremely remote times, the collection as a whole was not recognized as a Veda until long after the sanctity of the other three Vedas had been established, and its authority still is denied by some of the leading Brahmans of the south. Nevertheless, as early as 150 B.C., the grammarian Patanjali considered it to be 'the head of the Vedas', and the compilation of the work must be referred to a time several centuries before that date, and not later than 600 B.C.

The Brāhmanas, Upanishads, and Sūtras. Although it is impossible to date the Brāhmana treatises with any approach to accuracy, their composition is supposed to have taken place between 500 and 300 B.C. The oldest of the numerous Upanishads, which are of widely different ages, may go back as far as 700 or 600 B.C. The Vedic *sūtras* (about 500–200 B.C.) are compressed treatises dealing chiefly with ritual and customary law in aphorisms, or terse sayings, reduced to the utmost possible limits of brevity. They are classed as *Śrauta*, dealing with ritual; *Gṛihya*, dealing with domestic ceremonies; and *Dharma*, dealing with custom, including law.

The Vedāngas. All the works composed in this strange style are considered to be *Vedāngas*, or members of the Veda, and as such are divided into six groups—namely (1) phonetics or pronunciation (*śikshā*); (2) metre (*chhandas*); (3) grammar (*vyākaraṇa*); (4) etymology (*nirukta*); (5) religious practice (*kalpa*); and (6) astronomy or astrology (*jyotisha*). In ancient times the Vedic literature being taught solely by word of mouth, trained linguistic, grammatical, and metrical skill was needed to secure, as it has actually secured, the correct preservation and transmission of the sacred texts. Astronomical and astrological knowledge was equally necessary to determine the dates of eclipses, the lucky days for ceremonies, and so forth. Thus all ancient Hindu science sprang from religious needs and served religious and ritual purposes.

Uncertain date of Rigveda. The Rigveda, meaning the collection of hymns (*saṁhitā*), is of deep interest to scholars, because it is certainly by far the oldest book in an Aryan language. What its date may be no man can say. Some of the individual hymns may be of immense antiquity, while others may be centuries later. At some particular time they were arranged in a book, but when that was done we cannot tell. Probably it is safe to say that the composition of the hymns ranges between 2000 and 1000 B.C., and that the arrangement of them in a book may be assigned to somewhere about the later date. This utter uncertainty in the chronology makes it difficult to realize the state of society in the age of the Rigveda, or to compare it with that in other lands.

Early but not primitive. The society pictured, although of an early type, is not exactly primitive. The hymns themselves are artificial, literary compositions, arranged by scholars. The language, metres, and style all show a considerable amount of learning. Probably the scholars did not know how to read or write, but that did not prevent them from being learned after their fashion. They had splendid memories.

Social organization. The people were divided into numerous tribes, of which many are named, and each tribe consisted of many families or households, each governed by its head. The Rāja, with the help of the elders, governed the tribe, much as the father managed his family. The several tribes were often at war, one with another, or with the early aboriginal dwellers in India. Their wealth consisted chiefly in cattle, and their principal occupation in peace was tending the kine. But they also used the plough, and were familiar with the crafts of the carpenter, smith, jeweller, and other artisans. They rode in chariots, and fought chiefly with bows and arrows, sometimes also with spears and battle-axes. In short, their mode of life seems to have been in many respects not unlike that of certain tribes on the Afghan frontier in recent times, before firearms came into use.

Diet, &c. Ordinarily the Indo-Aryans used a diet of vegetable food and milk, but they partook of flesh offered in sacrifice, including beef, and so differed widely from modern Hindus. They liked strong drink, of which there were two kinds—namely beer (*surā*), and a liquor made from a plant (*soma*) found formerly in the hills and not certainly identified. They amused themselves largely with gambling.

Religion. They worshipped the powers of nature, conceived as living persons. The hymns accordingly are nearly all addressed to such deities. Indra, the lord of thunder, lightning, and rain, received most homage. Agni or Fire comes next in favour. The Wind, Sun, Dawn, and many other powers or aspects of nature are appealed to. The worshippers tried to get all they could out of their gods, and ordinarily sought from them nothing higher than riches and worldly welfare.

Professor Barnett bluntly observes that 'the Vedic religion, as presented to us in the Rigveda, is not noble'. It seems to me that he is right.

Some of the hymns, presumably included among those comparatively late in date, strike a loftier note, as already observed, and indicate the beginnings of the philosophy worked out in the *Upanishads* and subsequent treatises. Part of the Creation Hymn, the most impressive and readable of the lyrics (x. 129), may be quoted in Professor Macdonell's version :

Non-being then existed not, nor being :
There was no air, nor heaven which is beyond it.
What motion was there ? Where ? By whom directed ?
Was water there—and fathomless abysses ?

Death then existed not, nor life immortal ;
Of neither night nor day was any semblance.
The one breathed calm and windless by self-impulse :
There was not any other thing beyond it.

Darkness at first was covered up by darkness ;
This universe was indistinct and fluid.
The empty space that by the void was hidden,
That One was by the heat engendered.

. . . .

This world-creation, whence it has arisen,
Or whether it has been produced or has not,
He who surveys it in the highest heaven,
He only knows—or e'en He does not know it.

Pānini. The oldest extant Sanskrit grammar, the wonderful work composed in *sūtra* style by Pānini, a native of the Panjāb, was constructed in the first instance, like its numerous lost predecessors, to ensure accurate teaching of the sacred books by highly trained Brahmans. The passion of the ancient writers for brevity is expressed by the saying that the composer of a grammatical *sūtra* would have delighted as much in the saving of a short vowel as in the birth of a son. Pānini's work is so compressed, that although it deals with the whole Sanskrit language, it could be printed in thirty-five small octavo pages. The date of this prince of grammarians is uncertain, some authorities placing him in the fourth century B.C., and others, apparently with better reason, two or three centuries earlier. Yāska, who wrote an etymological commentary on the Vedas, long preceded Pānini.

Smṛiti; Manu, &c. The whole of the *sūtra* literature is regarded as *smṛiti*, or venerable traditional matter, not as *śruti*, or direct revelation, like the Vedas. The six systems of philosophy (*darśana*) were developed from the *Upanishads* in course of time, and the law-books (*dharmaśāstra*) based on the *sūtras*, were composed at various dates by the Brahman teachers of different schools, as manuals of *dharma*, or the Hindu rules of life. The most famous of the *dharmaśāstras* is the *Mānava*, commonly called the Laws, or Institutes, of Manu, a compilation which contains much ancient matter, but is supposed to date in its present form from somewhere about A.D. 200 or 300. This treatise deals with the rights and duties of Hindus in all ranks and conditions of life, and is the foundation of the systems of modified Hindu law now administered by the courts of British India.

The eighteen Pụrānas. The eighteen *Purānas*, which record the story of the gods, interwoven with legends and traditions on many subjects human and divine, are closely connected with the Laws of Manu as well as with the epics. They have been described as being 'the Veda of popular Hinduism', and sometimes are even called 'the fifth Veda'. The *Bhāgavata* and *Vishnu Purānas* exercise the most influence on the religion of the present day. The *Vāyu Purāna*, believed to be one of the oldest of the eighteen, seems to date in its present shape from the fourth century after Christ, but much of its contents may be far older. It is intimately related to the *Harivaṁśa*, which is a supplement to the Mahābhārata. Historical traditions of high value to the historian of northern India are preserved in several of the earlier *Purānas*. This class of works has little concern with the south, which has *Purānas* of its own that are not familiar to most scholars.

The Epics. The two great Sanskrit epics (*itihāsa*), the Mahābhārata and the Rāmāyana, are invaluable as pictures of life in ancient India before the time when authentic history begins. The Rāmāyana, which consists of about 24,000 couplets (*ślokas*), divided into seven books, is essentially the work of a single author, Vālmīki, to which subsequent additions of moderate bulk have been made. The Mahābhārata, more than four times as bulky, and divided into eighteen books, although traditionally ascribed to a mythical author named Vyāsa, really is a collection of many separate poems by various nameless poets of different ages, loosely strung together and appended to an original narrative comprising only about 24,000 couplets. The bulk of the Rāmāyana is believed to have been composed before 500 B.C., but some of the additions seem to be several centuries later. The Mahābhārata, which in its present form is rather 'an encyclopaedia of moral teaching' than an epic properly so called, includes compositions supposed to range in date between 400 B.C. and A.D. 400.

Story of the Rāmāyana. The main theme of Vālmīki's poem is the story of Prince Rāma, son of Dasaratha, king of Ajodhya, who was driven into exile along with Sītā, his faithful wife, in consequence of a palace intrigue. In the course of his wanderings, accompanied by his brother, Lakshmana, in the wild regions of the south Rāma suffered the loss of his consort, who was carried off by the giant Rāvana. But the hero, after many adventures, rescued his wife, and defeated and slew the giant. In the end, Rāma and Sītā, having been delivered from all their troubles, returned to Ajodhya, where Rāma and his loyal brother Bharata reigned gloriously over a happy and contented people.

Story of the Mahābhārata. The subject of the truly epic portion of the Mahābhārata is the Great War between the Kauravas, the hundred sons of Dhritarāshtra, led by Duryodhana, and the Pāndavas, the five sons of Pāndu, brother of Dhritarāshtra, led by Yudhishthira. The poet relates all the circumstances leading up to the war, and then narrates the tale of the fierce conflict which raged for eighteen days on the plain of Kurukshetra, near Thānēsar, to the north of Delhi. All the nations and tribes of India, from the Himalaya to the farthest south, are represented as taking part in this combat of giants. The Pāndava host comprised the armies of the states situated in the countries equivalent to the United Provinces of Agra and Oudh, Western Bihār, and Eastern Rājputāna, with contingents from Gujarāt in the west and from the Dravidian kingdoms of the extreme south. The Kaurava cause was upheld by the forces of Eastern Bihār, Bengal, the Himalaya, and the Panjāb. The battles ended in the utter destruction of nearly all the combatants on both sides, excepting Dhritarāshtra and the Pāndavas. But a reconciliation was effected between the few survivors, and Yudhishthira Pāndava was recognized as king of Hastināpur on the Ganges. Ultimately the five sons of Pāndu, accompanied by Draupadī, the beloved wife of them all, and attended by a faithful dog, quitted their royal state, and, journeying to Mount Meru, were admitted into Indra's heaven.

Episodes of the Mahābhārata. One of the most justly celebrated narrative episodes is the charming story of Nala and Damayantī. The profound philosophical poem, the *Bhagavad-gītā*, familiarly known as the *Gītā*, or 'the Song', which forms the basis of much later pantheistic speculation, and may date from about 100 or 200 B.C., is inserted in the form of a dialogue between Krishna and Arjuna Pāndava, supposed to have been spoken on the eve of battle.

Influence of the epics. These few words, of course, give a very inadequate notion of the contents of the two great *itihāsas*, which are the one department of Sanskrit literature familiar in substance to Hindus of all classes in every part of India. These poems are to India all that Homer's reputed works were to Greece, and, like the Homeric poems, the Mahābhārata and Rāmāyana form inexhaustible treasure-houses filled with material for every kind of literature. The characters in both works supply the Hindu with examples of his highest ideal of man and woman. The hero Rāma, especially, has become the man-God of countless millions and the object of intense devotion.

The Hindī Rāmāyana. In Northern India the popular conception of the perfect man is derived, not directly from the Sanskrit of Vālmīki, but from the *Rāmcharit-mānas*, a Hindī poem on the subject of the Rāmāyana, composed in the sixteenth century by Tulsī Dās. This noble work is an independent composition of the highest merit, and the characters depicted in it 'live and move with all the dignity of a heroic age'.

Social conditions in the epics. The world of the Rigveda (*ante*, p. 34) is so strange and remote that it is difficult to form a distinct picture of it in the mind. The Indo-Aryans of that shadowy time had not yet become Hindus.

When we read the Rāmāyana or the narrative portions of the Mahābhārata we find ourselves on more familiar ground. Whatever may be the dates of composition of the poems, both deal with a thoroughly Hindu India, in which caste was fully developed, and the leading ideas of Hinduism were generally accepted. The heroes and heroines of the stories resemble modern Hindus sufficiently to seem real live men and women, fit to serve as models and exemplars to their descendants. All or nearly all the ordinary features of Hindu life are depicted, and the differences in manners and customs as compared with those of existing society are not very numerous. The incident which is the most shocking to modern Hindu notions of *dharma* is the marriage of Draupadī to five brothers at once. Such a relationship, although still lawful in Tibet and among sundry Himalayan tribes, would be regarded now in India proper as horrible incest. The practice of *svayamvara*, or free choice of her husband by a maiden, is almost equally opposed to existing sentiment. But, as I have said, such cases are rare, and the general impression produced by the poems is that of a picture of old-fashioned Hindu life, such as may be still seen in a purely Hindu native state. The government described in the epics is that of any Rājā in such a state.

Religion. As regards religion and mythology, the Vedic gods and modes of worship had dropped out of sight for the most part. Vishnu in different forms had become the most prominent divinity, the heroes Rāma and Krishna both being treated as incarnations, or descents in human form (*avatār*) of him. Brahmā and Siva also appear, as well as Kuvēra, Ganēsh, and many other minor deities still worshipped. The epic mythology seems thoroughly familiar to every Hindu, and the characteristic Hindu doctrines of *Karma* (*ante*, p. 32) and incarnation are recognized in the poems as freely as they are to-day. The existing Hindu feeling concerning the sacredness of cows was then as strong as it is now. Nobody could imagine Rāma sitting down like a Vedic *rishi* to dine on beef.

Southern literature. The ancient Indian literature and philosophy known generally to the outer world are Aryan in origin and Sanskrit in language, as indicated in the foregoing sketch. But the historian of all India must not forget the fact, already noted, that the Tamil or Dravidian peoples of the Far South possessed an ancient civilization of uncertain origin independent of, and even hostile to, the Aryan system of the north. They produced an extensive literature, chiefly in the Tamil language, which includes epics, lyrics, and philosophical poems. These compositions, although enshrined in the hearts of the southerners, are unfamiliar to readers of other nations. The few European scholars sufficiently versed in the language to appreciate the charms of the Tamil poetry are loud in their praise of its merits, and the translations published justify their verdict. The following extract from Gover's version of a Tamil song may serve as a specimen:

The wise man saith
That God, the omniscient Essence, fills all space
And time. He cannot die or end. In Him
All things exist. There is no God but He.
If thou wouldst worship in the noblest way,
Bring flowers in thy hand. Their names are these:
Contentment, Justice, Wisdom. Offer them
To that great Essence—then thou servest God.

No stone can image God—to bow to it
Is not to worship. Outward rites cannot
Avail to compass that reward of bliss
That true devotion gives to those who *know*.

Buddhism and Jainism. About 500 B.C., a time when speculation was active in several parts of the world, two systems of religious philosophy, which developed into separate religions, took shape in the north of India. These two systems, Buddhism and Jainism, both grew out of Brahmanical Hinduism, as modified by the teaching of reformers of noble Kshatriya, not Brahman birth, who failed to find in the doctrine of the Brahman schools satisfactory solutions of the problems of life. Both of the new systems were preached first, at about the same time, in the same region, namely Magadha, or South Bihār, and the neighbouring districts. Both rely on the support of an organized society of monks or friars, reject the authority of the Vedas and the exclusive claims of the Brahmans, abhor bloody sacrifices, and teach with insistence the doctrine of extreme respect for every form of animal life (*ahiṁsā*). These obvious and real resemblances between Buddhism and Jainism are balanced by differences, equally real, if less obvious. The followers of the two creeds revere distinct saints, study distinct scriptures, and diverge widely in both doctrine and practice. The Jains do honour to twenty-four Jinas or Tīrthankaras; the Buddhists to twenty-four Buddhas. The Jain scriptures are called *Angas* and by other names; the Buddhist books form the great collection known as the *Tripiṭaka*, or 'Three Baskets', dealing with doctrine, monastic discipline, and philosophical comment and speculation. The Pāli books of Ceylon give the Buddhist Canon in its earliest known form. Later developments are dealt with in Sanskrit, Tibetan, Mongolian, and Chinese works. While both Jains and Buddhists profess to venerate the Three Jewels (*triratna*), they use the term in different senses. To the Buddhist the Three Jewels are the Buddha, the Law (*dharma*), and the Order of Monks (*saṁgha*). To the Jains they are Right

Faith, Right Cognition, and Right Morals. The Jains are divided into two great sects, the Svetāmbara, or white-robed, and the Digambara, or nude (lit. 'sky-clad'). The nudity affected by the latter is extremely offensive to Buddhist feeling. The practice of suicide by starvation, which is highly esteemed by the Jains, is strictly forbidden to the Buddhists. These instances will suffice to show that Buddhism and Jainism, notwithstanding their points of resemblance, are radically different. The actual facts of the lives of the founders of the Jain and Buddhist systems are obscured, like those of the founders of all religions, by legends due to the imaginations of pious followers, but the following brief statement may be accepted as authentic :

Life of Mahāvīra. Vardhamāna, surnamed Mahāvīra, a young nobleman of Vaisāli, the modern Basār to the north of Patna, then the chief city of the famous Licchhavi tribe, joined an ascetic order which had been founded by an ancient teacher named Pārsvanāth. Becoming dissatisfied with the doctrine of his masters, he quitted their fraternity when about forty years of age, and, like many another Hindu reformer, set about devising a system of his own and organizing a new society of friars to give effect to his opinions. He spent the remaining thirty years of his life in preaching-tours, wandering with his disciples all over South Bihār (Magadha) and Tirhūt (Mithilā or Videha), until he died at Pāwā or Pāpā in the Patna district. Widely-accepted tradition assigns his death to the year 527 B.C., but the exact year is open to doubt. Some authorities assign the event to 467 B.C. His relationship through his mother with the reigning kings of Videha, Magadha, and Anga (Bhāgalpur) gained for his preaching the advantage of official patronage.

Life of Gautama Buddha. Gautama, surnamed the Buddha, because he claimed to have attained *bodhi*, or supreme knowledge, the secret of existence, was for some years the contemporary of Mahāvīra. His father, Suddhodhana, was a prince or nobleman in the small town of Kapilavastu, situated in the territory of the Sākya clan, which took rank among the Kshatriyas. Hence he is often called Sākyamuni, or the Sākya sage. The land of the Sākyas was the narrow strip of country between the Rāptī river and the mountains, now mostly included in the Nepalese Tarāi and lying to the north of the Bastī District in the United Provinces of Agra and Oudh.

The legends dwell with much play of imagination on the manner in which the young prince became oppressed by sadness and lost all desire for the delights of a court. He became convinced that existence is misery leading to old age, disease, and death, and sought an escape from the endless circle of rebirth. Sitting under a tree near Gayā, he tried to win salvation by the severest penance, but found no peace. At last he saw the light, put away penance as vanity, and, going to Benares, preached to a few disciples his three great principles that 'all the constituents of being are transitory, are misery, and are lacking in an ego, or permanent self (*ātman*)'. His philosophy was based on those doctrines, but as a moralist he taught a lofty system of practical ethics, impressing on men the necessity for personal striving after holiness, and laying special stress on the virtues of truthfulness, reverence to superiors, and respect for animal life. Like Mahāvīra, he wandered for the rest of his life with his disciples through Magadha and the neighbouring kingdoms, and, after a ministry of forty-five years, passed away at the age of eighty at Kusinagara, a small town probably situated near Tribenī Ghāt, at the confluence of the Little Rāptī with the Gandak. The date of his death is uncertain, but there is good reason for believing that the event happened in or about 487 B.C., possibly four or five years later.

Diffusion of Buddhism. From these small beginnings arose the great Buddhist religion, which, after many ages of success in India, slowly died out, and almost completely disappeared from the land of its birth about seven centuries ago. But it still flourishes abundantly in Ceylon, Burma, Siam, Nepāl, Tibet, Mongolia, China, and Japan. The well-organized order of monks and nuns (*saṅgha*) was the most effective instrument in the spread of this religion, which was much helped by the powerful patronage of Asoka.

Buddhism as a religion. Gautama, the Buddha, can hardly be said to have had or to have taught a religion, properly so called. He had a philosophy, the nature of which has been indicated above, although it is impossible here to bring out the full meaning of his principles. He also taught, as others had taught before him, a simple, easily understood *dharma* or rule of life. That rule required his disciples to aim at purity in deed, word, and thought; observing ten commandments—namely not to kill, steal, or commit adultery; not to lie, invent evil reports about other people, indulge in fault-finding or profane language; to abstain from covetousness, and hatred, and to avoid ignorance. But he did not profess to expound the relation of God to man—in fact, without denying the existence of a Supreme Deity, he ignored it. It was the devotion of his followers to the person of Buddha which made Buddhism a religion capable of warming the hearts of men and women. That ardent personal devotion developed early and ended in practically making Buddha a god, instead of a mere dead moralist and philosopher. The primitive Buddhism, which ignored the Divine, was known in later times as the Hīna-yāna, or Lesser Vehicle of Salvation, while the modified religion, which recognized the value of prayer and regarded Buddha as the Saviour of mankind, was called Mahā-yāna, or the Greater Vehicle. Siam, Ceylon, and Burma mostly, but by no means exclusively, follow the primitive Hīna-yāna doctrine; the other Buddhist countries have adopted the Mahā-yāna in diverse varieties, some of which in both doctrine and ritual closely resemble certain forms of Christianity. The Pāla kings of Bengal, from the eighth to the twelfth century, also adhered to Mahā-yāna Buddhism, which, as practised in Bengal and Bihār, was not always easy to distinguish from Hinduism.

Causes of decay of Buddhism. The decay, like the growth, of a religion is a complicated matter not to be described or explained in a few sentences. But we may note that the decay of Buddhism was extremely gradual, spread over many centuries, and that it was not in any large measure the result of active persecution. Undoubtedly, certain kings from time to time did treat Buddhists with cruelty, but deeper causes were at work. The principal cause, perhaps, was the continuous hostility of the Brahmans, who had never lost their influence in India throughout the ages. We can see that the Gupta period was marked by a strong Hindu or Brahmanical revival which was carried further by Kumārila-bhaṭṭa in the eighth century (see *post*, chapter vii). In the end, the Brahmans defeated both Buddhism and Jainism. The Muhammadan conquest at the end of the twelfth century happened to include South Bihār, the province in which Buddhism then had its strongest hold. Muslim violence at that time had much to do with the almost sudden and complete extinction of Buddhism in India proper. The corruptions introduced into the Saṅgha, or monastic order, by the growth of wealth in the monasteries, no doubt had effect in lessening popular respect for the Buddhist teachers. The foreign settlers who entered India in large numbers during the fifth and sixth centuries were not much attracted by Buddhist teaching, while they found it easy to accept more or less fully the Hindu rule of life, and so became converted into Hindu castes, guided by Brahmans. That process will be discussed in chapter viii.

Jainism confined to India. Jainism never attempted distant conquests. Although it became powerful in the south as well as in the north for several centuries, it never spread to any considerable extent beyond the limits of India, and now tends to decline rather than increase in influence. Its followers number about a million and a quarter, and are mostly found among the trading classes of Western India and Rājputāna.

Dravidian resistance to the Aryan religions. The three northern religions—Hinduism, Jainism, and Buddhism—had to fight a hard fight against the native 'devil-worship' of the

Dravidian or Tamil nations in the south, who long resisted Aryan teaching in any form. But ultimately the resistance of the southerners was overcome, and, after the decay of Buddhism and Jainism, Hinduism emerged triumphant, India from end to end becoming the 'land of the Brahmans' and the home of caste, the specially Brahman institution.

Caste. The basis of Hindu society and of Hindu ethics or morals is the institution known to Europeans as 'caste' or 'the caste system'. The word caste is Portuguese; the thing is so peculiarly Indian that it cuts off India from the rest of the world by a barrier far more impassable than deserts, seas, or mountains.

In many countries, ancient and modern, distinctions of classes, often hereditary, may be observed, which more or less resemble the Indian institution of caste. But the resemblance is never very close.

India alone presents now, and has presented for thousands of years, the spectacle of hundreds or thousands of distinct communities each kept apart from its neighbours by strict rules regulating marriage, diet, and every detail of life. Moreover, all these thousands of sections agree in regarding the people of the rest of the world who are not Hindus as mere *mlecchas*—that is to say, outcasts and barbarians. Even kings and viceroys of foreign race are so regarded from the caste point of view.

Origins of the institution. Much ink has been spilled in trying to find the origins of the Hindu caste system and in offering explanations of its unique nature. The results have not been wholly satisfactory. In fact, the subject is too intricate to admit of summary disposal in a few words, and any writer who professes to state in two or three sentences the origins and nature of Indian caste misleads his readers. I will not attempt to perform the impossible, and must content myself with certain brief observations, true as far as they go, which may help the junior student.

We know for certain that the system of castes was well

established in its essential features two thousand four hundred years ago, and consequently that its beginnings must go back to a time many centuries earlier.

It is clear that one reason why the system developed in India so much more fully than elsewhere was the physical isolation of the country (*ante*, p. 16), which forced its inhabitants to work out for themselves their own rule of life (*dharma*). Such isolation of the whole country was repeated on a smaller scale in the interior, where each village community stood for itself. The wide difference in feeling and habits between the Indo-Aryans and the earlier 'aboriginal' inhabitants of other races had a large share in laying the foundation for caste distinctions. The formation of separate castes was helped by diversities in occupation, language, religion, and place of residence. Some castes are in the main trade-guilds, while some are almost identical with religious sects (*sampradāya*). The Brahmaṇs, the most intellectual class of the Indo-Aryans, established their supremacy over Indian minds at a very early date. Those Brahmans had extremely strict notions about ceremonial purity, and an intense horror of defilement. The respect for ceremonial purity, with the corresponding horror of defilement, is really the essence of the caste sentiment. Everybody knows that 'loss of caste' is always due to defilement in some shape or other. The Brahmans set the ideal of *dharma*, or duty, and all other classes of the population tried to live up to that ideal. The nearer a caste comes to the Brahman ideal the higher it ranks, while the farther from that ideal a caste remains, the lower it is in the social scale. So much must suffice concerning the origins and nature of the caste system.[1]

The four varṇas. Brahman theory regards Hindus as divided into four *varṇas*, or groups of castes, according to

[1] In Southern India the castes mostly represent either original tribes or colonies of foreign settlers. Their formation does not depend much on occupation. A Vellāla, for instance, may follow any decent occupation, and the members of the Vellāla caste can do nearly everything needed to keep a village community going.

occupation. The first *varṇa* is that of the Brahmans, the learned, literary class, qualified to direct religious ceremonies and to teach and interpret the sacred scriptures. The second *varṇa* is that of the Kshatriyas, whose business was war and government, with the help of Brahman ministers. The third *varṇa* is that of the Vaisyas, tradesmen and agriculturists. The fourth is that of the Sūdras, the common folk, who were expected to be content with doing service to their betters, the three higher *varṇas*, called 'twice-born' (*dwija*), in virtue of certain ceremonies, not permissible for Sūdras.

Brahman authors expressed the relative rank of the *varṇas* by saying that the Brahmans proceed from the mouth, the Kshatriyas from the arms, the Vaisyas from the thighs, and the Sūdras from the feet of Brāhma, the Creator.

Early Buddhist writers sought to exalt the Kshatriyas to the foremost rank, speaking sometimes of 'base-born Brahmans'; but in the end the Brahmans won, and now their claim to the first place is acknowledged by all or nearly all Hindus.[1]

It is a mistake to translate *varṇa* by the word caste, and to say, as is often said, that originally there were four castes in India. Each *varṇa* always included a multitude of separate castes (*jāti*). The *varṇas* are simply a theoretical grouping of pre-existing castes. Whether a particular caste (*jāti*) should be included or not in a particular *varṇa* is a matter for arbitrary judgement. For example, the modern Kāyasths claim to be Kshatriyas, while other people regard them as Sūdras. The terms Vaisya and Sūdra are not in ordinary use in Northern India, and are to be met with only in books and in discussions about the rank of certain castes. If any province were to be taken, no two people would agree as to the list of castes in it to be assigned to each *varṇa*. The number of separate castes in the whole of India is believed to exceed three thousand.[2]

[1] Exceptions are the Lingāyat sect in the south, and to some extent the Jats in the north.

[2] The word *varṇa* primarily means 'colour', but no one could venture to affirm that the four *varṇas*, in the sense of caste groups, are to be actually

The good and evil of caste. The division of the Hindu population of about two hundred millions into thousands of separate caste compartments, the extreme reverence paid to Brahmans, and the corresponding degradation of the lowest castes, are facts which have obvious inconveniences and disadvantages. The breaking up of the people into so many distinct blocks prevents or obstructs the growth of patriotic or national feeling, checks combination in social and public life, excites sectional jealousies, and is hostile to all modern democratic notions. Hinduism does not profess to regard men as equal. A Brahman cannot possibly look on a Chamār as equal to himself, and can hardly help feeling a certain amount of arrogance. The position of the low castes is depressed by the servility required from them. The inconveniences resulting from the strict enforcement of the rules concerning ceremonial purity are felt daily, and are a serious obstruction to the conduct of business on modern lines. Caste is an old-world institution, constantly clashing with the ideas and requirements of the twentieth century.

On the other hand, Hindu society is built on caste, and if the foundation be dug away the whole structure must fall. The system has succeeded in holding Hindu society together throughout long ages of despotism, each caste being a powerful organization hard to crush. However deficient the members of any one caste may be in sympathy for outsiders, and however devoid of the feeling of general brotherhood, encouraged in different degrees by the Christian and Muslim religions, the caste-followers at any rate hang together and support each other in all sorts of ways. Caste is an extremely conservative institution, and has done much to preserve Hindu tradition. It has also secured the hereditary passing on of arts and sciences from father to son. But it is not easy to reconcile it with the rapid progress in material arts and appliances which marks the present age.

distinguished by four different colours. When a Hindu author assigns the colours white, yellow, red, and black, to the four several *varṇas*, he is merely indulging his fancy without regard to facts.

Ethics or morals. The caste system hinders the acceptance of any universal doctrine of morals. Each caste is a law unto itself, and Hindus readily admit that actions very wrong for one man may be quite right for another. The *Bhagavad Gītā* lays down the Hindu view plainly:

'Better one's own duty (*dharma*), though destitute of merit, than the duty of another well discharged. Better death in the discharge of one's own duty: the duty of another is full of terror' (iii. 35). The sentiment is repeated in a later passage, with the addition:

'He who takes action (*karma*) in accordance with his own nature (*bhāva*) does not incur sin' (xviii. 47). Each caste is looked on as a separate species of mankind, with its own nature, producing action in accord with that nature.

The future of caste. Many changes in the working of the institution have occurred during the long course of ages. For example, the intermarriages between different *varṇas*, as between Brahmans and Kshatriyas, which were not uncommon even in the early centuries of the Christian era, are no longer permitted. The pressure of practical convenience often compels people to evade or defy old-fashioned restrictions. Everybody in India knows how railways, waterworks, and other modern inventions have modified the rules about defilement. But in spite of all changes on the surface, the institution remains substantially what it was in the days of Alexander the Great. So far as I can see, the abolition of caste in India is impracticable, even if it be granted that the evil of the system outweighs the good. Reformers must be content, for many centuries to come, to accept the existence of caste as a fact and make the best of it, by bringing the practice of caste *dharma* into harmony with the conditions of modern life, so far as may be. The British Government acts steadily on that principle. When the authorities thoughtlessly have violated it, as at Vellore in 1806, and in the matter of the greased cartridges in 1857, grave trouble has resulted.

The four stages of a Brahman's life. In theory every

Brahman was supposed to divide his life into four stages (*āśrama*): first, for many years as a student; secondly, as a married householder; thirdly, as a hermit in the forest; and fourthly, as a religious mendicant or beggar. It is hardly necessary to add that this theory was never fully acted on, and that it is wholly unworkable in these days.

Absorbent power of the caste system. The rigid caste system as it exists at the present day takes notice of Hindus only; all outsiders, native or foreign, high or low, being regarded as *mlecchas*, or casteless people. Nevertheless, the system has always shown a wonderful power of absorption, and almost all foreigners resident permanently in India have yielded to its seductions. Yavanas, Sakas, Hūnas, and many other swarms of foreign immigrants have disappeared, losing their separate existence in the sea of caste, either through being admitted into old castes by the help of legal fictions, or through the formation of new castes. Even Islam, the principles of which are utterly hostile to caste distinctions, has been unable to resist the pressure, and multitudes of Indian Muhammadans, like their Hindu neighbours, are fast bound in the trammels of caste, although they do not actually become Hindus, as the descendants of earlier invaders did.

The ascetic orders and caste. The ascetic orders, whether Jain, Buddhist, or orthodox Hindu, usually have been and still are willing to admit to membership persons of almost any caste, and to ignore distinctions of birth among the brethren. Some writers erroneously have supposed Buddhism to have been a revolt against caste, but as a matter of fact the lay Buddhist retained his caste, just as the Jain layman does now. It is, however, true that the free offer of the way of salvation, made to all comers by both Buddhism and Jainism, clashed with the Brahman doctrine that the teaching of the highest truths should be reserved for the highest castes, and so far both religions diminished the importance of caste distinctions. But neither Mahāvīra nor Gautama sought to abolish caste.

BOOK II

SOURCES OF HINDU HISTORY BEFORE THE MUHAMMADAN CONQUEST

Materials exist. In all countries the materials for exact history of remote ages are scanty. People used to think that practically no such materials existed in India, but they were mistaken. Modern research has disclosed the hidden sources of history, and experiment has proved that a fairly consecutive narrative of the story of India before the Muhammadan invasions can be written.

Official annals lost: but traces remain. Although the Brahmans who composed most of the Sanskrit books did not care to write formal literary histories, we must not fancy that the princes of the olden time neglected to record their own lineage and deeds. On the contrary, every Rājā took pains to keep up a record of his genealogy and an exact chronicle of his doings. Owing to the frequent wars and revolutions which have desolated India, those old official records have disappeared almost everywhere. Some, however, have been preserved in Rājputāna, and Colonel Tod has shown, in his immortal *Annals of Rajasthan* (1829), the good use which can be made of the tribal chronicles kept up by official bards. Fragments of the ancient court genealogies and annals obviously are preserved in the prefaces to many inscriptions. In a few cases the body of the inscription recites historical events in some detail. The most notable examples of such documents, perhaps, are the fourth-century inscription of Samudra-gupta at Allahabad and the Tanjore inscriptions of Rājarāja Chola at the beginning of the eleventh century. The lists of dynasties in the Purānas must have come from the same source, the official records of the various states. Although most of those lists have become corrupted in course of time, a few of them are accurate and trustworthy.

Inscriptions. Inscriptions, even when quite short, are often invaluable for fixing dates and the order of succession of kings. They also supply information about details of all sorts.

Coins. The legends on coins supplement the evidence of the inscriptions, and when interpreted by skilled experts, can be forced to yield a surprising amount of information, concerning both political and artistic history.

Tradition in literature. Ancient tradition is recorded in literary works of many kinds. The Buddhist, Jain, and Brahmanical books, intended primarily for religious purposes, are full of references and allusions capable of being used by the historian. Something can be got even out of the grammarians' works, and several plays, notably the *Mudrā-Rākshasa*, throw much light on political and social history.

Buildings and works of art. The testimony of inscriptions, coins, and recorded tradition is supported and amplified by the critical study of the remains of ancient buildings and works of art. Careful examination of the order in which the layers of ruins of different ages lie in excavations on old sites is a great help in fixing the dates of remote events.

Histories. More or less formal Hindu histories are not wholly wanting. The earliest work which can be so classed is, I think, the *Harsha-charita* of Bāna, written in the seventh century, to celebrate the deeds of King Harsha of Kanauj. Works of a similar character—half history and half romance—recount the doings of certain kings of Bengal and the South. The Sanskrit book which comes nearest to the European notion of a regular history is the *Rājataranginī* of Kalhana, a metrical chronicle of Kashmīr, written in the twelfth century by the son of a minister of the Rājā. The Pāli chronicles of Ceylon record versions of early Indian traditions, which deserve consideration, and many other books presenting a certain amount of genuine history mixed with much fanciful legend exist in the literatures of Tibet, Nepāl, Assam, and other border countries.

Summary of indigenous sources. Taken as a whole, the sources of the history of Hindu India, available in India itself, are fairly copious. They may be summed up as, (1) Inscriptions (epigraphic); (2) Coins (numismatic); (3) Buildings and art (archaeological); (4) Tradition, recorded in literature, and (5) Histories, more or less regular, and to some extent contemporary with the events narrated.

Foreign authors. A sixth source is opened up by the writings of foreigners, whose works have proved specially valuable for fixing exact dates. It is difficult, for many reasons which cannot be explained here, to fix dates from purely Hindu evidence. The foreigners, making use of the known chronology of their own countries, often settle problems otherwise almost insoluble. For example, when we know that Chandragupta Maurya was identical with Sandrakottos, the contemporary of Alexander of Macedon, we know approximately when Chandragupta lived, because there is no doubt as to the dates of Alexander. Many other examples might be cited. The foreign authors who help the Indian historian are chiefly the Greeks and Chinese. Some of those authors travelled in India, while others compiled books from the notes of travellers. The Roman authors, who sometimes wrote in the Latin language, usually copied from the Greeks. The Greek notices of India begin with Herodotus and Ktesias in the fifth century B.C. We have next the evidence of the companions of Alexander the Great, late in the fourth century B.C., then the testimony of Megasthenes about 300 B.C., and the observations of the author of the *Periplus of the Erythrean Sea*, or 'Voyage round the Arabian Sea', about A.D. 80. Some of the works referred to are preserved only in fragments.

Chinese evidence. The Chinese evidence is contained both in formal histories and in the accounts written by travellers, especially Buddhist pilgrims. China possesses an immense historical literature of great antiquity. The notices of affairs connected with India in the Chinese histories begin about 120 B.C. The accounts recorded by the Buddhist pilgrims are still more valuable. Fa-hien, the earliest pilgrim (A.D. 399–413), gives much information about the state of India during the reign of Chandragupta II, Vikramāditya. Hiuen Tsang (or Yuan Chwang), perhaps the most learned of the pilgrims, who travelled between 629 and 645, is the most interesting witness of his class, and throws a flood of light on the history of Harsha of Kanauj, and other matters. Many other Chinese pilgrims contribute to the sum total of knowledge.

Muhammadan evidence. From the middle of the ninth century, Muhammadan travellers and historians begin to help. They tell us many things concerning the Hindu dynasties which first met the invaders, and describe the manner of the Muhammadan conquest. Our knowledge of the raids of Mahmūd of Ghaznī is derived wholly from Muslim authors.

Further details will be found in the author's *Early History of India*, 3rd ed. (Oxford, 1914), which gives references.

HINDU INDIA FROM 600 B.C. TO A.D. 1193; MAHMŪD OF GHAZNĪ.

CHAPTER IV

The dynasties preceding the Mauryas: Kosala; Magadha; the Nandas; Alexander the Great.

Beginning of regular history. The preceding chapters have dealt with events which, excepting the foundation of the Jain and Buddhist systems, cannot be dated. Regular history is concerned only with events which can be arranged in order of time and are capable of being dated approximately, if not exactly. In the case of India such history cannot be attempted before about 600 B.C., when we obtain a glimpse of a few definite political facts. But even then, and for nearly three centuries later, our knowledge is extremely scanty, and almost wholly confined to certain states in the Gangetic basin. Nothing is known about the Deccan or the Far South in those early times.

Sixteen northern powers. The most ancient Buddhist books give a list of sixteen states or tribal territories which existed in Northern India about the time of the rise of Buddhism or a little earlier. These extended from Gāndhāra, the country of the Gāndhāras, on the extreme north-west of the Panjāb, including the modern districts of Peshāwar and Rāwalpindi, to Avanti, or Mālwā, with its capital Ujjain, which still retains its ancient name unchanged. Among these sixteen states two are prominent in tradition—namely Kosala, or the territory of the Kosalās, and Magadha, or the territory of the Māgadhās.

Magadha. The kingdom of Magadha (S. Bihār), approximately equivalent originally to the Gayā and Patna Districts south of the Ganges, is mentioned in the Mahābhārata as having attained the rank of a paramount power under King Jarāsandha. The earliest capital was the hill-fort of Rājagriha or Rājgir (Girivraja). The most ancient king who can be approximately dated was Sisunāga (about 600 B.C.), but nothing is known about him or his next three successors.

Bimbisāra ; Ajātasatru ; Darius. Bimbisāra, or Srenika, the fifth Saisunāga king, is credited with the foundation of New Rājgir, the outer town at the base of the hill, and with the annexation of the small kingdom to the east, Anga or Champa, roughly equivalent to the Bhāgalpur District, and probably including Monghyr (Mungir). This annexation was the first step in Magadha's progress to greatness during historical times. After a reign of twenty-eight years Bimbisāra abdicated in favour of his son Ajātasatru, or Kuniya, who would not await the course of nature, and cruelly starved his father to death. Gautama Buddha is said to have met Ajātasatru and reproved him for his crime. A fort built by this king at Pātali, to check the incursions of the Licchhavis of Vaisāli from the north side of the river, developed into the magnificent city of Pātaliputra, the modern Patna and Bankipore.

About 500 B.C., in the reign of either Bimbisāra or Ajātasatru (for dates are uncertain), Darius, son of Hystaspes, king of

Persia, sent an expedition commanded by Skylax of Karyanda, to explore the rivers of the Panjāb. The admiral reached the sea, and the Indus valley became a province of the Persian empire, to which it yielded a large revenue. Indian archers were included in the Persian army defeated at Plataea, in Greece, in 479 B.C. The Persians probably ruled the Indus region for many years, but how or when they lost control of it is not known.

Kosala. Bimbisāra of Magadha was married to the sister of Prasenajit, king of Kosala, who naturally went to war with Ajātasatru when he murdered his father. The war was waged with varying fortune, but ultimately peace was made and Prasenajit gave a daughter to Ajātasatru in marriage. Some three years later, Virūdhaka, Crown Prince, rebelled against his father Prasenajit, who fled to the capital of his former enemy of Magadha, but died before he entered the gates. Virūdhaka succeeded to the throne of Kosala, and is remembered as the author of a cruel massacre of the Sākyas, the kinsmen of Buddha. After his time the kingdom of Kosala was overshadowed by the growing power of Magadha. At an early date Kosala had absorbed the smaller kingdom of Kāsi or Benares, and when at its greatest extent included the whole of Oudh, and all the country between the Ganges, the Gandak, and the mountains. The capital was the city of Srāvasti, on the upper course of the Rāptī, probably the modern Saheth-Maheth in Northern Oudh. The whole of this territory passed under the rule of Magadha, but we cannot fix the date.

The 'Nine Nandas'. Mahāpadma Nanda, the son of the last Saisunāga king, Mahānandin, by a Sudra woman, usurped his father's throne, and is said to have been succeeded by his eight sons. The dynasty of two generations is therefore known to tradition as that of the Nine Nandas. Mahāpadma was reigning when Alexander the Great was in India, and the invader was told that the king of Magadha possessed an army of 200,000 infantry, 20,000 cavalry, 2,000 chariots, and 3,000

ALEXANDER THE GREAT (THE TIVOLI HERM)

or 4,000 war elephants; but he was so unpopular that there was reason to believe his army would not support him. Alexander did not get the chance of testing the accuracy of this information, as his own troops refused to plunge farther into unknown country.

Alexander the Great. Alexander, king of Macedon, in the north of Greece, in the course of the years from 334 to 331 B.C. had conquered Asia Minor, Syria, Egypt, and Persia, defeating the Persian monarch, Darius Codomannus, in three pitched battles, and taking his place. Having resolved to conquer India, he crossed the Indus at Ohind in February or March, 326, and was hospitably received by the king of Taxila, then a great city, the ruins of which are traceable near Hasan Abdāl, in the Attock District, Panjāb.[1] The Rājā of the country between the Indus and the Jihlam or Hydaspes river, whom Greek and Roman writers call Porus, tried to stop the invader, but was defeated in a battle near Jihlam. Alexander then pushed on eastward, passing Siālkōt, across the rivers of the Panjāb, until he came to the last of them, the Biās or Hyphasis, when his European troops refused to go on, and he was obliged to turn back, and retrace his steps. Meantime his officers had built near Jihlam a fleet of about 2,000 vessels, on which he embarked part of his army. The rest marched along the banks of the Hydaspes and other rivers, and after ten months the whole force, fighting its way, reached the mouths of the Indus. The courses of the rivers have changed so much that it is not possible to trace the stages of Alexander's voyage and marches from north to south through the Panjāb and Sind. The fleet sailed round by sea to the Persian Gulf, and Alexander himself led a division of his army through Balochistan or Gedrosia. After much suffering and heavy losses, he met his fleet, and brought what was left of his army into Persia. He had previously sent another

[1] Excavations now (1914) in progress are yielding remarkable and unexpected results. The earliest part of the site is believed to be of immense antiquity.

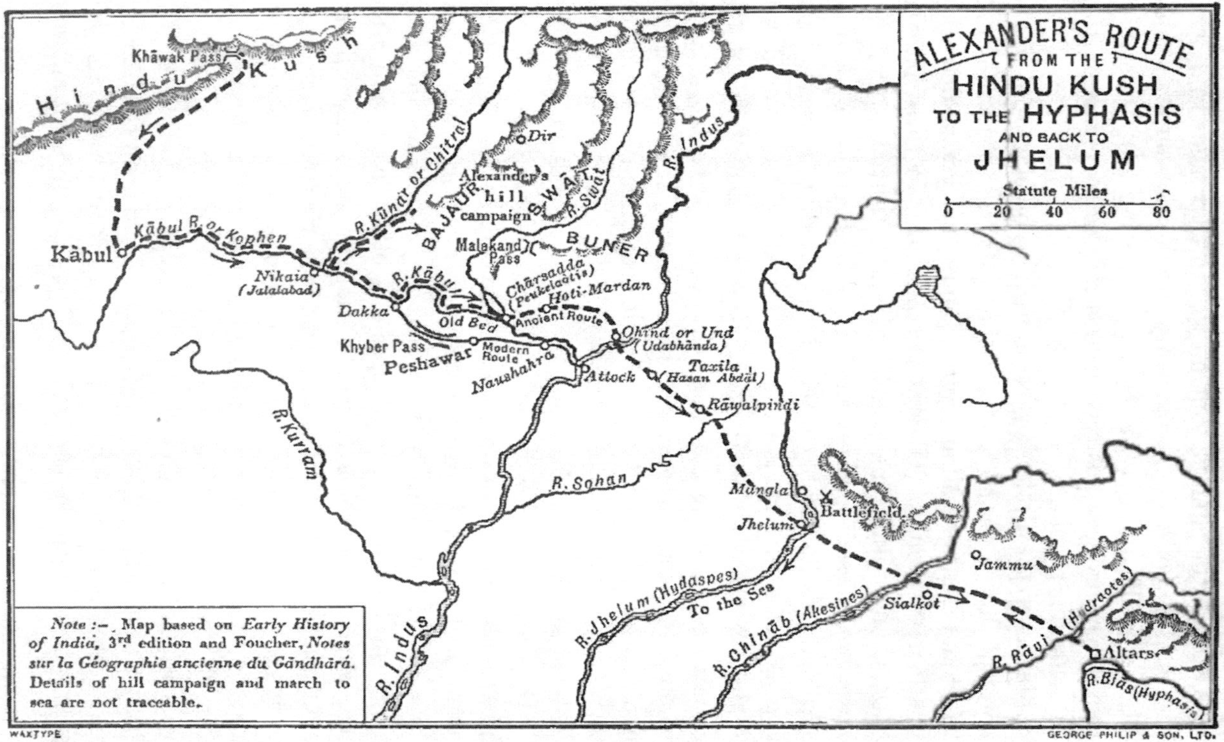
ALEXANDER'S ROUTE
(FROM THE)
HINDU KUSH
TO THE HYPHASIS
AND BACK TO
JHELUM
Statute Miles
0 20 40 60 80
Hindu Kush
Khāwak Pass
Kābul
Kābul R. or Kophen
Nikaia (Jalalabad)
R. Kūnar or Chitral
Dir
Alexander's hill campaign
BAJAUR
SWAT
R. Swat
BUNER
Malakand Pass
R. Kābul
Chārsadda (Peukelaōtis)
Hoti-Mardan
Ancient Route
Old Bed
Dakka
Khyber Pass
Peshawar
Modern Route
Naushahra
Attock
Ohind or Und (Udabhānda)
Taxila (Hasan Abdāl)
Rāwalpindi
R. Indus
R. Kurram
R. Sohan
Mangla
Battlefield
Jhelum
R. Jhelum (Hydaspes)
To the Sea
R. Chināb (Akesines)
Sialkot
Jammu
R. Rāvi (Hydraotes)
Altars
R. Biās (Hyphasis)
Note :— Map based on Early History of India, 3rd edition and Foucher, Notes sur la Géographie ancienne du Gāndhārā. Details of hill campaign and march to sea are not traceable.
WAXTYPE
GEORGE PHILIP & SON, LTD.

division back to that country by the Mūla Pass route. In June, 323 B.C., Alexander died at Babylon, aged thirty-two. No other man in the history of the world ever accomplished so much in so short a time and at such an early age.

He had intended to annex the Panjāb and Sind to his empire, but his premature death made the task impossible—no other hand could wield the sceptre of universal dominion. The empire fell to pieces and was carved into kingdoms by his generals, none of whom was strong enough to hold the distant Indian provinces. In three or four years all traces of Macedonian rule in the Indus valley had disappeared, and the local powers were left to their own devices. Indian writers do not mention Alexander's raid, for our knowledge of which we are indebted to Greek authors. The Macedonian invasion had practically no effect on Indian institutions. The Greek influence which made itself felt in certain respects afterwards came from the Bactrian kingdom, and still later from the Asiatic provinces of the Roman empire.

CHAPTER V

The Maurya empire: Chandragupta; accounts of India by Greek writers; Asoka and his successors.

Chandragupta Maurya. About the time of Alexander's death, or a little later, a revolution took place in Magadha, which cost the unpopular Nanda king his throne and life. A young man named Chandragupta, who is said to have met Alexander, and seems to have been related to the Nanda royal family, assembled a force of robber clans from the north and seized the kingdom of Magadha, the capital of which was then Pātaliputra, the modern Patna. His agent in effecting the revolution was Chānakya, also called Kautilya or Vishnugupta, a wily Brahman, who became his minister. An ancient treatise called *Arthaśāstra*, attributed to Kautilya, gives precise details of the systems of government in the small Hindu kingdoms of Northern India as worked before Chandragupta made himself the master of them all. The accession of Chandragupta may be dated in 322 B.C., but at this period it is impossible to fix dates with absolute precision. The family name Maurya is supposed to be derived from Murā, the mother of Chandragupta. The line of his successors down to about 184 B.C. is spoken of as the Maurya dynasty.

The first emperor of India. Before the time of Chandragupta India had been parcelled into a multitude of small states, some monarchies, some tribal republics, which were continually fighting among themselves, and owned no allegiance to any overlord. But the new king of Magadha, a stern and masterful man, was determined to bring his neighbours into subjection. In the course of a reign of twenty-four years he carried out this plan and made himself the sovereign of at least all Northern India. He is the first historical person who can be described as Emperor of India, but, of course, his rule did not extend to the Far South. Its exact limits southwards are not known.

Seleucus Nikātor. When Alexander's empire was finally partitioned in 321 B.C. among his generals, one of them, Seleucus, surnamed Nikātor, 'the Victorious,' obtained as his share Syria, Asia Minor, and the eastern provinces. After a prolonged struggle with rivals he was crowned king at Babylon in 312 B.C., and is known to historians as king of Syria. Seleucus thought that he would like to recover Alexander's conquests. About 305 B.C. he crossed the Indus with the intention of subduing the country. But Chandragupta was too strong for him, and Seleucus was obliged to retreat, surrendering all claim to the satrapies or provinces west of the Indus. Those provinces passed under the sway of Chandragupta, who thus ruled the countries now called Balochistan and Afghanistan, as well as all Northern India. Seleucus was content to take five hundred elephants as compensation for three rich provinces, and concluded a matrimonial alliance with Chandragupta, probably giving a daughter to the Indian king.

Megasthenes, and Greek accounts of India. Soon afterwards the Syrian monarch sent an envoy named Megasthenes to the court of Chandragupta at Pātaliputra. That officer lived there a long time and spent his leisure in compiling a careful account of the geography, products, and institutions of India, which continued to be the principal authority on the subject for European readers until modern times. Although his book has been lost, copious extracts from it have been preserved by other writers, which give the pith of the work. Our knowledge of the system of government in the time of Chandragupta is derived largely from Megasthenes. His statements disclose a well-ordered State, governed by a stern, capable despot, who did not hesitate to shed blood, and consequently lived in daily fear of assassination. But, so far as appears, Chandragupta died in his bed. According to some traditions he was a Jain, abdicated, and starved himself to death. His empire certainly passed undiminished to his son and grandson.

The army of the Mauryas. The main instrument of authority was a powerful standing army of paid soldiers equipped from government arsenals, and, as usual in ancient India, comprising the four arms of infantry, cavalry, chariots, and elephant corps. The war elephants numbered 9,000, attended by 36,000 men, the cavalry were 30,000, and the infantry 600,000. The chariots kept by Mahāpadma Nanda numbered 8,000, and Chandragupta's force in that arm, of which the strength is not stated, probably was still greater. The four arms were administered by four Boards; transport, commissariat, and army service were the business of a fifth Board, and a sixth attended to admiralty affairs.

The capital and civil administration. The capital city, Pātaliputra, situated on the northern bank of the Sōn, which then joined the Ganges below the city, was strongly fortified, and administered by a Municipal Commission composed of six Boards or *panchāyats*, consisting each of five members, and charged with various duties. The other great cities of the empire probably were governed on similar lines. The general civil administration also was effective. Elaborate rules providing for the proper treatment of strangers show that the empire had constant dealings with foreign states. The mainstay of finance was then, as now, the land revenue, or Crown rent, generally amounting to one-fourth of the gross produce. Like the modern Government of India, the king levied water-rates, and assessed land at rates varying with the mode of irrigation. The subject of irrigation was carefully attended to by a special department, as it is now by the Canals branch of the Public Works staff. Besides the land revenue and water rates, many other taxes and cesses were levied, among the most profitable to the treasury being the tax on goods sold.

Revenue and criminal law. The revenue and criminal law was severe and sternly administered. Theft was ordinarily punished by mutilation, which was also the penalty for wilful false statements made to revenue officers, and for sundry other crimes. Evasion of the town duty on goods sold was punishable with death, which was inflicted without scruple for many offences. But this severity, if repugnant to modern feeling, had the good effect of maintaining order. Judicial torture for the purpose of extracting confessions was recognized and freely used, the principle laid down being that 'those whose guilt is believed to be true shall be subjected to torture', of which there were eighteen kinds, including seven varieties of whipping. A regular system of excise was in force, the drinking-shops being under official supervision, as they now are.

Reign of Bindusāra. About 298 B.C. Chandragupta either died or abdicated, and was succeeded by his son Bindusāra Amitraghāta. No record of the events of his reign has survived, but the history of Asoka shows that Bindusāra certainly maintained and probably enlarged the empire inherited from his father.

Asoka—273 or 272 B. C. Asoka, or to give him his full name, Asoka-vardhana, was viceroy of Ujjain at the time of

Sārnāth Capital (Asoka Period)

his father's death, if Buddhist tradition may be believed. The Buddhist monks pretend that Asoka in his youth was cruel and wicked, attaining the throne by the murder of ninety-eight out of ninety-nine brothers. But there does not seem to be any truth in these tales, because Asoka's inscriptions prove that long after his accession he had brothers and sisters living for whose welfare he took anxious care. His inscriptions, which are numerous, are the best authority for the events of his reign. The coronation of Asoka (about 269 B.C.) did not take place until four years after his accession. The delay may or may not have been due to some dispute about the succession.

War with Kalinga. Some eight years after his coronation, Asoka went to war with Kalinga, the country on the coast of the Bay of Bengal between the Mahānadī and Godāvarī rivers. After hard fighting he overcame all resistance and conquered that kingdom. But he was horrified at the suffering caused by his ambition, and has recorded his 'remorse on account of the conquest of the Kalingas, because, during the subjugation of a previously unconquered country, slaughter, death, and taking away captive of the people necessarily occur, whereat His Majesty feels profound sorrow and regret'. Asoka's first war was his last, and for the rest of his life he devoted himself to winning 'the chiefest conquest, the conquest by the Law of Piety or Duty (*dharma*)'.

Asoka's devotion to Buddhism. This sudden change in his feelings seems to have been due to his acceptance of the teachings of Buddhism, to which, as the years went on, he became more and more devoted, even to the extent of assuming the robes and vows of a monk.

Asoka is said to have convened at his capital a council of Buddhist monks to reform the church and revise the scriptures. As a means of diffusing a knowledge of the Buddhist *dharma*, or moral law, he engraved a series of edicts on rocks and stone pillars throughout his dominions, which have been deciphered by European scholars during the last eighty years.

These records, which are found in Orissa, Mysore, the Panjāb, on the Bombay coast, and in other places, prove that Asoka ruled all India, except the extreme south below the fourteenth parallel of latitude.

FACSIMILE

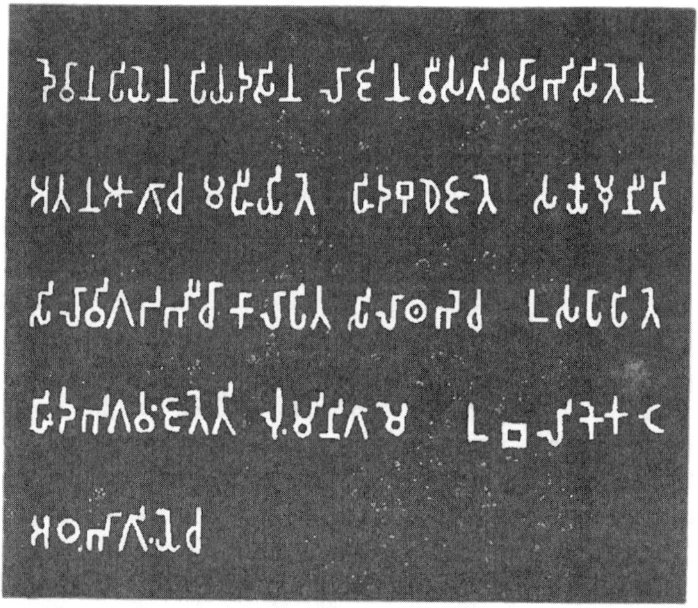

TRANSLITERATION

1. Devānapiyena piyadasina lājina vīsativasābhisitena
2. atana āgācha mahīyite hida budhe jāte sakyamunīti
3. silā vigaḍabhīchā kālāpita silāthabhecha usapāpite
4. hida bhagavaṁ jāteti luṁminigāme ubalikekaṭe
5. athabhagiyecha

ASOKA'S INSCRIPTION AT RUMMINDEI

Asoka's teaching. One of these inscriptions, on a rock in Mysore, may be quoted as giving a short summary of his moral teaching. It runs: 'Thus saith His Majesty :— " Father and mother must be obeyed ; similarly, respect for living creatures must be enforced; truth must be spoken. These are the virtues of the Law of Piety (*dharma*), which must be practised. Similarly, the teacher must be revered by the pupil, and proper courtesy must be shown to relations. This is the ancient standard of piety—this leads to length of days, and according to this men must act."'

Censors were appointed to enforce obedience to these rules with all the power of the government, and the moral regulations were supplemented by works of practical piety. Banyan trees for shade and mango trees for fruit were planted along the high-roads, wells were dug, rest-houses were built, watering places were prepared for travellers, and abundant provision was made for the relief and cure of the poor and sick. All the forms of Indian religion were treated with respect, and the emperor enjoined his subjects to abstain from speaking evil of their neighbour's faith. Everybody, however, whatever his creed might be, had to obey the regulations of the government concerning his conduct. Men might believe what they liked, but must do as they were told.

Asoka's missions. The emperor organized a system of missions to carry his teaching to all the protected states on the frontiers of the empire, including the Himalayan regions, to the independent Tamil kingdoms of the Far South, to Ceylon, and to the Greek monarchies of Syria, Egypt, Cyrēnē (west of Egypt), Macedonia, and Epirus, thus embracing three continents, Asia, Africa, and Europe. The statement of some authorities that missionaries were sent also to Burma does not seem to be correct. The leading missionary to Ceylon was Mahendra (Mahinda), the brother, or, according to others, a son, of Asoka. In this way, Buddhism, which had been merely the creed of a local Indian sect, became one of the chief religions of the world, a position which, in spite of many ups and downs, it still holds. This result is the work of Asoka alone, and entitles him to rank for all time in that small body of men who may be said to have changed the faiths of the world. The numerous and wealthy Buddhist

ASOKA PILLAR

monasteries founded in the time of Asoka and in later ages did much to spread Buddhism, and no doubt looked after the education of the young, as the monks now do in Burma.

The later Mauryas. In or about 232 B.C. the great Asoka passed away, the most notable figure in the early history of India. One tradition asserts that he died at Taxila, but nothing is known with certainty concerning his latter days or his death. Inscriptions prove that he was succeeded in the eastern part of his dominions by his grandson Dasaratha, and, according to tradition, the western provinces passed under the rule of another grandson, Samprati, who favoured the Jain religion. The names of five later members of the dynasty are recorded, but nothing is known about their reigns. It is clear that these princes must have enjoyed only limited power, and that the empire could not be held together after the removal of Asoka's controlling hand. The last of the Mauryas, Brihadratha, was slain, in or about 184 B.C., by his commander-in-chief, Pushyamitra Sunga.

Sunga Kānva and Āndhra dynasties. Very little is on record about the Sunga dynasty founded by Pushyamitra, which is said to have lasted for a hundred and twelve years. The great grammarian, Patanjali, was a contemporary of Pushyamitra, in whose time a Greek king, most likely Menander, invaded India.

The Sungas were succeeded by the Kānva dynasty, to which forty-five years are assigned by the lists in the Purānas. The last Sunga was killed by an Āndhra prince, about 27 B.C. But the Āndhra dynasty had been established some two centuries earlier, probably soon after the death of Asoka, and had acquired a wide dominion extending across the Deccan from sea to sea. There is no distinct evidence that the Āndhras held Magadha, and the history of the dynasty is extremely obscure.

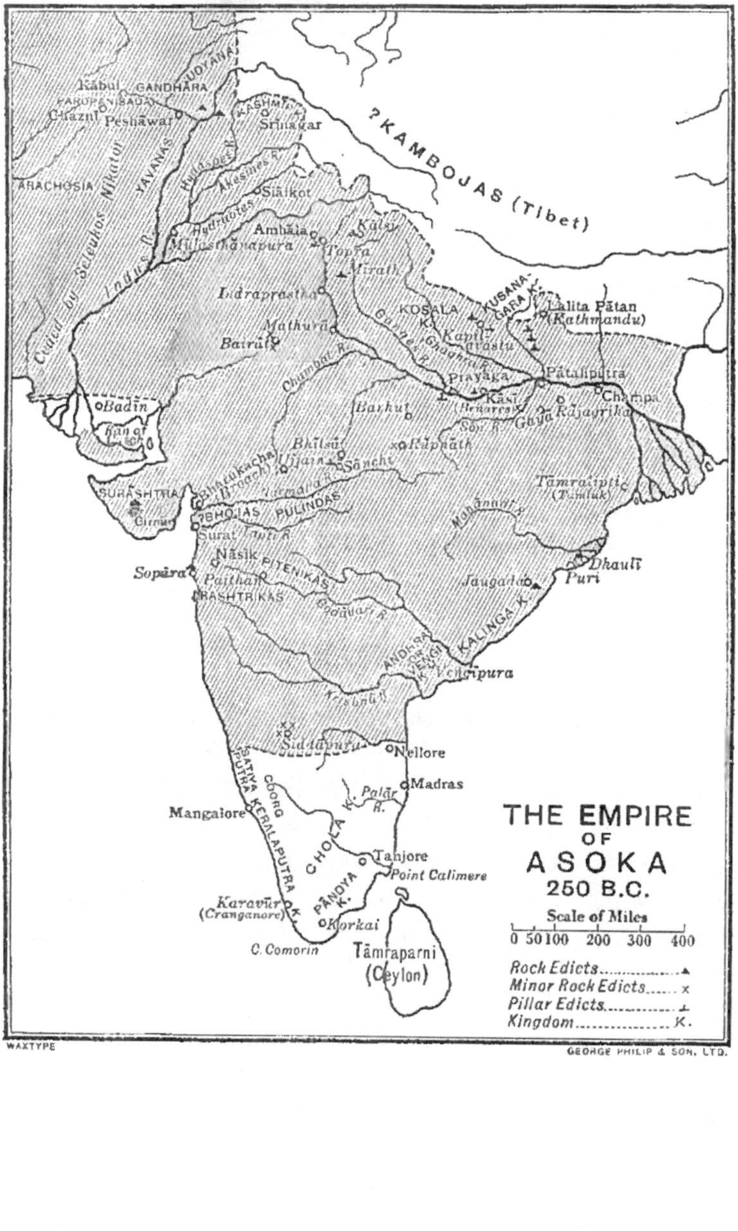

WAXTYPE GEORGE PHILIP & SON, LTD.

The Kings of Magadha.

		Approximate dates, mostly not exact.
		B.C.
Sisunāga	acc.	600
Bimbisāra	acc.	528 (Prasenajit of Kosala contemp.)
Death of Mahāvīra	?	527
Ajātasatru	acc.	500
Death of Gautama Buddha	?	487
The Nine Nandas	acc.	371
Campaign of Alexander the Great		326–325 (date exact).
Chandragupta Maurya	acc.	322
Invasion of Seleucus Nikātor		305
Embassy of Megasthenes		303
Bindusāra	acc.	298
Asoka	acc.	273
Coronation		269
War with Kalinga		261
Death of Asoka		232
Other Mauryan kings		232–184
Sunga dynasty		184–72
Invasion of (?) Menander	?	155
Kānva dynasty		72–27

CHAPTER VI

The foreign dynasties of the north-west: the Kushān (Kusana) empire; Kanishka; the Saka era; art and literature.

Bactrian, Indo-Greek, and Indo-Parthian kings. Parthia, the country south-east of the Caspian Sea, and Bactria, the country between the Hindu Kush mountains and the river Oxus, which had been both included in the kingdom of Seleucus Nikātor, became independent monarchies under kings of Greek descent about the middle of the third century B.C., when Asoka was emperor of India. He probably continued to hold the provinces west of the Indus—the modern Balōchistan and Afghanistan, which had been ceded to his grandfather by Seleucus. After Asoka's death no Indian sovereign could retain those distant dependencies, which were broken up into a multitude of principalities governed by Greek kings, whose names are known from coins. One of these kings, Menander, lord of Kābul, appears to have invaded India about 155 B.C., reached Oudh, and met the army of Pushyamitra Sunga. Parthian princes also governed parts of the frontier regions after 140 B.C. About that date Mithradates I of Parthia had annexed the Western Panjāb, and united it for a time with the Parthian empire, which included Persia.

Saka and Kushān invasions. From about the middle of the second century B.C. the nomad and pastoral tribes of Central Asia for some reason or other, probably a change of climate, were obliged to leave their home territories and move to the south and west in search of pasturage for their herds and subsistence for themselves. These wild people overwhelmed the Greek kingdom of Bactria and set up governments of their own. The earliest swarm was known to the Indians by the name of Sakas. They made their way into Sīstān on the Hilmand river, west of Kandahār, which was consequently called Sakastān, or the Saka country. Saka rulers also established themselves in Surāshtra or Kāthiāwār, and probably at Taxila and Mathurā. Another horde of nomads, called Yueh-chi by the Chinese historians, descended through Bactria and Kābul to India. The leading clan of this horde was named Kushān or Kusana. About the middle of the first century after Christ the Kushān chief, known to historians as Kadphises II, conquered the various Indo-Greek and Indo-Parthian princes on the frontier and made himself master of a large part of North-western India, where his coins are found abundantly.

Kanishka. His successor seemingly was Kanishka, son of Vajheshka, also a Kushān, but of a family other than that of Kadphises II. Recent researches have made it probable that Kanishka came to the throne in A.D. 78, and reigned for more than forty years, until about A.D. 120, but it is possible that his true date may be some years later. His capital was Purushapura (Peshāwar), from which he ruled Kābul, Kashmīr, and all Northern India, perhaps as far as the Narbadā. In his later years he favoured Buddhism, and, like Asoka, assembled a council of Buddhist monks, which prepared authorized commentaries of the scriptures. He spent many years in war on the other side of the difficult Pāmīr passes, and, after the death of the Chinese general, Pan-chao (A. D. 102), is believed to have annexed Kāshgar and Khotan, now in Chinese Turkestan. He is said to have been smothered by discontented officers. During his long absence India seems to have been governed, first by Vāshishka and then by Huvishka, presumably his sons, whose dates, consequently, overlap those of Kanishka. About A. D. 120 or 123 Huvishka succeeded to the sole government, certainly of India, and probably of the whole empire. He was a powerful king, and is known to have founded a town in Kashmīr and a monastery at Mathurā. In or about A. D. 140 Huvishka was succeeded by Vāsudeva I, during whose reign the empire began to break up. Scarcely anything is known of the history of Northern India from his time to the rise of the Gupta dynasty in A. D. 320. There is reason to hope that the chronology of Kanishka, his predecessors and successors, will soon be settled definitely. Until that is done, an important section of the history of India must continue to be vague and confusing.

The Saka era. Opinions differ, but it is probable that the Saka era of A. D. 78 dates from the accession or coronation of Kanishka, the Saka king. Indian authors use the term Saka vaguely to denote all foreigners from beyond the passes, and would have had no hesitation in calling a Kushān a Saka. In later ages the era was known as that of Salivahana.

Buddhist architecture and art. Both Kanishka and Huvishka were great builders, and spent much money on Buddhist monasteries and *stūpas* at Mathurā, Peshāwar, and other places, of which some traces still exist.[1] Ever since the time of Asoka, India had been filled with magnificent Buddhist

[1] The remains of Kanishka's huge *stūpa* at Peshāwar were excavated in 1908-9, and a remarkable relic casket was found bearing the image of the king and an inscription. An inscribed portrait statue of Kanishka, lacking the head, was found at Māt near Mathurā in 1912.

buildings. The monasteries were often huge structures built of timber on brick foundations, several stories high and splendidly decorated. The *stūpas* were domed cupolas,

BUDDHA (GRAECO-BUDDHIST)

generally constructed of brick, designed either to enshrine relics or to mark some holy spot. The larger ones were often surrounded by richly carved stone railings with highly ornamented gateways, and no expense was spared in the adornment of the buildings in every possible way. The best

THE GREAT STŪPA, SĀNCHĪ, RESTORED

preserved example is the great *stūpa* at Sānchi in Bhopāl. The finest carved railing was that which surrounded the *stūpa* of Amarāvatī on the Kistna river in the Guntūr District, Madras. In and about the Peshāwar District the remains of numerous *stūpas* and monasteries of Kushān age exist, and multitudes of well-executed sculptures resembling in style the Graeco-Roman work of the first three centuries of the Christian era have been found. The Buddhists also were fond of hewing chapter-houses, or churches, out of the solid rock. The best examples of these are at Kārlē and other places in the Bombay Presidency. The practice lasted for many centuries, and some of the cave-temples were excavated for Jain and Hindu worship. The Jains also built *stūpas* exactly like those of the Buddhists.

Two famous Buddhist teachers, Nāgārjuna and Asvaghosha, as well as a medical author, Charaka, are reputed to have lived in Kanishka's time.

CHAPTER VII

The Gupta empire: the Hūnas or White Huns; reign of Harsha; state of civilization; Chinese pilgrims; Kālidāsa.

The Gupta dynasty. The next prominent dynasty of which records have been preserved is that of the Guptas. A Rājā of Pātaliputra, who took the name of Chandragupta (I), enhanced his power at the beginning of the fourth century by marrying a princess of the influential Licchhavi clan of Vaisāli in Tirhūt, and formed a considerable kingdom extending along the Ganges to Prayāg or Allahabad. In 319–20 he established the Gupta era to commemorate his coronation.

Samudragupta. The founder of the Gupta empire is a dim figure, hardly more than a dated name. His son and chosen successor, Samudragupta, stands forth as a real man—scholar, poet, musician, and warrior. The early years of his vigorous reign were devoted to the thorough conquest of Upper India, that is to say, the country now known as the United Provinces

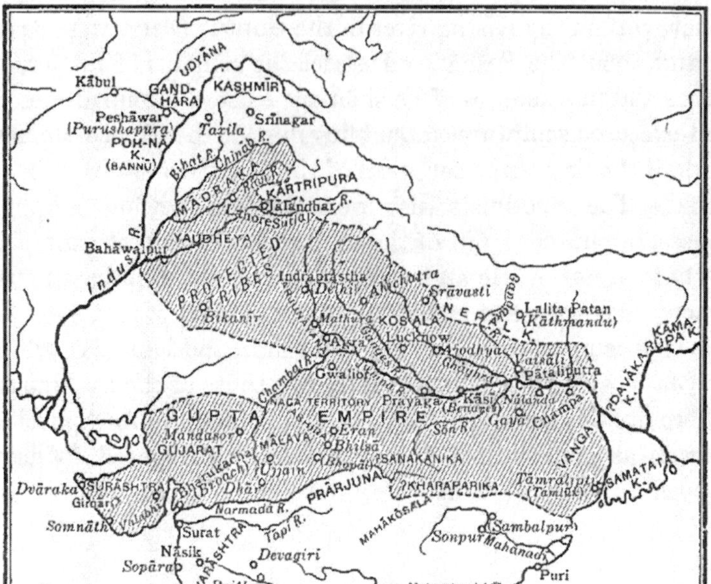

The Conquests of SAMUDRAGUPTA, 340 A.D. and the GUPTA EMPIRE, 400 A.D. (Travels of Fa-hien)

WAXTYPE

GEORGE PHILIP & SON, LTD.

of Agra and Oudh with the Central India Agency and Bengal, but not including the Panjāb. When that conquest was finished, he turned his arms against the south. Marching across the wild regions of the tributary states of Orissa, he advanced by the road of the eastern coast until he reached about the latitude of Nellore. He then turned westwards and came home through Khāndēsh. He did not try to annex the realms beyond the Narbadā. He was content with receiving the humble submission of the vanquished princes and bringing home a huge store of golden booty. Having thus proved his title to be Lord Paramount of India, he celebrated the horse-sacrifice (*aśvamedha*), lawful only for a king of kings. Extant medals testify to the liberal share of his bounty then bestowed on the Brahmans. When he died his dominions comprised all the most populous and fertile regions of Northern India, extending from the Hooghly on the east to the Sutlaj and Chambal on the west, and from the Himalayan slopes on the north to the Narbadā on the south. Beyond those limits of his direct government he controlled the wild tribes of the Himalaya and the Vindhyas, as well as the free clans of Rājputana and Mālwā, while his ambassadors had dealings with the rulers of Ceylon in the Far South and of the Scythian kingdom on the Oxus in Central Asia. His empire was far greater than any that India had seen since the days of Asoka, six centuries earlier. The elegant inscription at Allahabad which records the conquests of Samudragupta tells also of his personal qualities, and its evidence as to his musical skill is confirmed by the medals which exhibit the king in the act of playing the Indian lute (*vīnā*). Pātaliputra apparently continued to be the capital of the immense empire won and held by Samudragupta.

Chandragupta Vikramāditya. The next king, Chandragupta II, surnamed Vikramāditya, who annexed Mālwā and Ujjain to his empire, probably is the original of Rājā Bikram, famous in legend. He dispossessed the Saka rulers of Surāshtra, who used the Persian title of Satrap, and are called the

Western Satraps by modern writers. Chandragupta II seems to have made Ajodhyā his capital. His reign (about 375 to 413) may be regarded as marking the climax or highest point attained by the imperial Guptas, a singularly able line of kings.[1]

Kumaragupta, Skandagupta, and the Huns. His successor, Kumāragupta I (413–55), was troubled towards the end of his reign by irruptions of a fresh horde of Central Asian nomads, the White Huns or Ephthalites, who overcame the next king, Skandagupta, and broke up the Gupta empire, about A. D. 480. For a short time Northern India became a province of a huge White Hun empire, which embraced forty countries, extending from Persia on the west to Khotan in Chinese Turkestan on the east. In India the tyranny of the Hun chief, Mihiragula, becoming unbearable, he was defeated by Narasimha Bālāditya, a Gupta king, and Yasodharman, Rājā of Mālwā, in or about A. D. 528, and forced to retire into Kashmīr. The nomad immigrants, known collectively to Indians as Huns, but comprising various tribes, settled in large numbers in the Panjāb and Rājputāna, and caused great changes. But history is silent as to details of events in the sixth century. It was certainly a time of confused warfare, and there was no paramount power.

The Vikrama era. The popular belief which associates the Vikrama era of 58–57 B. C. with a Rājā Vikramāditya or Bikram of Ujjain at that date is erroneous. There was no such person then. It is, however, true that the earliest known use of the era was in Mālwā and probably it was invented by the astronomers of Ujjain. The first name of it was the Mālwā era. The term *Vikrama-kāla* used in later times must refer to one or other of the many kings with the title of Vikramāditya or Vikrama, who was believed to have established the era. The king referred to may be presumed to be Chandragupta II,

[1] The phrase 'Guptas of Kanauj' is an ancient error; Kanauj never was the Gupta capital. The designation of the Western Satraps as 'the Shah kings' is another 'vulgar error', based on an old misreading of coin legends.

Vikramāditya, who conquered Ujjain about A.D. 390. The Gupta and Saka eras changed their names similarly, becoming known in after ages as the Valabhī and the Sālivāhana eras respectively.

Reign of Harsha of Kanauj. At the beginning of the seventh century a strong man arose, Harsha, Rājā of Thānesar, who, in the short space of six years (606–12), made himself master of Northern India as far as the Sutlaj, fixing his capital at Kanauj, and became the paramount power even over Surāshtra and Gujārāt in the west, and Assam and Bengal in the east. The equally vigorous ruler of the Deccan, Pulakesin II Chalukya (608–42), prevented him from extending his dominions south of the Narbadā. Harsha died in 647, and his death was followed by another dark period of anarchy and confusion.

Chinese pilgrims; Fa-hien. Our knowledge of events in the Gupta period and age of Harsha is largely derived from the narratives of Chinese Buddhist pilgrims, who crowded into India as the Holy Land of their faith, and eagerly sought for Buddhist books, relics, and images. The earliest of these pilgrims was Fa-hien (399–413), who came overland through Khotan and returned to China by sea. He remained for six years in the dominions of Chandragupta II Vikramāditya studying Buddhist literature, and was much pleased with the country. Pātaliputra was still a flourishing city, with numerous charitable institutions, including a free hospital. In Mālwā the penal code was mild, and the people were not worried by official regulations. Order was well preserved, and the pilgrim was free to pursue his studies in peace. Although the Gupta king was himself an orthodox Vaishnava Hindu, Buddhism flourished and was fully tolerated.

Hiuen Tsang, or Yuan Chwang. Hiuen Tsang, or Yuan Chwang, the prince of pilgrims (629–45), came to India overland by the road to the north of the Taklā Makān desert, and then through Samarkand, returning by the Pāmīrs and Khotan —a terribly long and arduous journey both ways. He visited almost every part of India, and recorded his experiences in a book of inestimable value. He became a personal friend of King Harsha, who, in his latter days, took a fancy to Buddhism. The king was a vigorous despot, keeping his dominions in order by personal supervision exercised during constant touring, interrupted only by the rains. The penal code was rather more severe than in the days of the Guptas, and the roads were not quite so safe, but the country seems to have been fairly well governed.

Buddhism was still strong, although orthodox Hinduism was gaining way. The king favoured all the Indian religions, doing honour in turn to Siva, the Sun, and Buddha, with a personal preference for the last-named. The pilgrim attended a strange assembly held at Kanauj, the capital, for the purpose of disputations on religious subjects, at which twenty tributary Rājās were present, including the rulers of Assam in the east, and Surāshtra on the west. Pātaliputra was in ruins. No record of the fall of the ancient imperial city has survived, but it can hardly be doubted that the disaster was a consequence of the Hun wars. Harsha lavished his favours on Kanauj, an old city between the Ganges and Jumna, which he made the seat of his government, filling it with splendid buildings. The Kanauj assembly moved on to Prayāg (Allahabad), where the sovereign ceremoniously distributed the wealth of his treasury to people of all denominations on the ground at the junction of the Ganges and Jumna where the great fair is now held annually. Harsha was in the habit of making such distributions every five years, and the celebration in which Hiuen Tsang assisted was the sixth of the reign.

The Gupta period a golden age. The Gupta period, and more especially the fifth century, may be justly regarded as the golden age of Northern India. Powerful and long-lived kings of exceptional personal ability made extensive conquests and established a well-governed empire, in which the energies of gifted men had free scope. The kings maintained a splendid court, and gathered round their throne men of eminence in every branch of knowledge, on whom they bestowed liberal patronage. Literature, art, and science were alike cultivated with success and distinction.

Literature: Kālidāsa. The name of Kālidāsa, whose activity may be referred to the reign of Kumāragupta I, in the first half of the fifth century, enjoys unquestioned pre-eminence. Unanimous opinion proclaims him as the chief of Sanskrit dramatists and poets. The *Ṛitu-saṁhāra*, or 'Cycle of the Seasons', and the *Meghadūta*, or 'Cloud Messenger', both charming descriptive poems of a lyrical character, seem to be among his early works. The heroic epic entitled *Raghuvaṁśa*, or 'The Race of Raghu', a product of his more mature genius, gives eloquent expression to the Hindu national ideal. *Śakuntalā*, acclaimed by all critics as the best of his three dramas, and one of the most interesting plays in the literature of the world, has succeeded in delighting alike European and Indian readers.

Sculpture, painting, and architecture. The sculpture of the Gupta age, the excellence of which was not fully recognized until recently, may be reasonably considered the best of all Indian sculpture, but, of course, tastes differ. Although no examples of Gupta painting have survived in Northern India, the power of the artists of the fifth and sixth centuries is proved by the beautiful frescoes of the Ajanta caves in the west and of Sīgiriya in Ceylon. The accident that the Gupta empire was mostly made up of those provinces which were continually overrun by Muhammadan armies and permanently occupied by Muslim governments explains the rarity of Gupta buildings. Muhammadan Sultans and Padshahs seldom spared a Hindu edifice. But the little that has survived suffices to prove that the architecture of the Gupta period was worthy of the sculpture which adorned the buildings.

Coins and music. The only Hindu coins possessing any considerable artistic merit are certain pieces struck by Samudragupta and Chandragupta II. We have seen how Samudragupta practised and patronized the art of music.

Science. Mathematical and astronomical science was largely

Seated Buddha, Sārnāth (Gupta Period)

advanced by Āryabhata (born A. D. 476), who taught the system studied at Pātaliputra, which was based on the works of Greek authors.

Causes of intellectual activity. It is impossible to go further into details or to mention less famous names, but what has been said is enough to show that every form of mental activity made itself felt during the Gupta period. The intelligent patronage of a series of able and wealthy kings for more than a century had much to do with the prosperity of the arts and sciences. A deeper cause was the conflict of ideas produced by the active intercourse between the Gupta empire and the great powers of both East and West. Many embassies to and from China are recorded, while communication with the Byzantine Roman empire through Alexandria in Egypt was made easy by the conquests of Chandragupta II in the closing years of the fourth century. Although the works of the Gupta authors and artists are thoroughly Indian in subject and treatment, it may be doubted if they would ever have been produced but for the stimulus given to Indian minds by their contact with the ideas of strangers.

Religion : Sanskrit. When the *Travels* of Fa-hien (399–413) are compared with those of Hiuen Tsang (629–645), it becomes clear that during the interval between the two pilgrims Buddhism had declined, while Brahmanical Hinduism had advanced. The Gupta kings, who were officially Vaishnava Hindus, showed a wise tolerance for other creeds. Some of them, indeed, took a lively interest in Buddhist teaching. But, as the years rolled on, the influence of Buddhism slowly faded away, and that of orthodox Brahmans increased. That change was accompanied by a freer use of Sanskrit, the language of the Brahmans, in books and inscriptions, and by the disuse of the Prakrit dialects.

Harsha and Bāna. The revival of Hinduism, with the parallel decay of Buddhism, continued in the seventh century, during and after the reign of Harsha, who was a zealous patron of Sanskrit literature, although personally inclined to Buddhist doctrine. The king is the reputed author of a play called *Ratnāvalī* and other works. The most famous author of his day was his friend Bāna, who celebrated the deeds of his royal patron in the *Harshacharita*. The book is of high value as history, but the fantastic, involved style of the composition is annoying to most readers.

Kumārila-bhatta and Sankarāchārya. The Hindu reaction against Buddhism was carried further early in the eighth century by Kumārila-bhatta, an Assamese Brahman, who taught the Mīmānsa philosophy, and is popularly supposed to have led an active persecution of Buddhists. The reality of the alleged persecution is doubtful. About a century later, Sankarāchārya, a Nambudri Brahman of Malabar, taught a form of Vedāntist philosophy, which still has great vogue. He travelled throughout India and established many *maths*, or monasteries, several of which still exist, the principal one being at Sringēri in Mysore. Professor Barnett observes that, 'the religious attitude of Sankara is summed up in a fine verse ascribed to him':

Though difference be none, I am of Thee,
  Not thou, O Lord, of me;
For of the Sea is verily the Wave,
  Not of the Wave the Sea.

Gupta Dynasty.

Dates (nearly exact).

		A.D.
Chandragupta I	acc.	320 (Gupta era, 319–20)
Samudragupta	acc.	330 or a little later.
Temporary conquest of South		347–50
Chandragupta II, Vikramāditya	acc.	375
Conquest of Mālwā and Surāshtra . . .		395 (Fa-hien's *Travels*, 399–413)
Kumāragupta I	acc.	413
First Hun invasion . .		450 (? Kālidāsa)
Skandagupta, Vikramāditya .	acc.	455
Hun wars, to about . .		480 (Āryabhata born, 476)
Other Gupta kings, from about		480
Defeat of Mihiragula the Hun		528

Skanda-gupta's Pillar, Bhitarī

Reign of Harshavardhana (Śīlāditya)

Accession	606
Conflict with Pulakesin II .	620 (Brahmagupta, astronomer, 628)
Assembly at Kanauj, almsgiving at Prayāg . . .	643 (Hiuen Tsang, Chinese pilgrim)
Death	647 (or late in 646).
Usurpation by Harsha's minister	647–8

CHAPTER VIII

The Muhammadan conquest of Sind: the rise of the Rājpūts; some Rājpūt kingdoms.

New grouping of powers after Harsha's death; the Rājpūt period. It is impossible to narrate in detail the histories of the many powers which emerged in India when the anarchy and disturbance consequent upon Harsha's death in A. D. 647 began to settle down. In some cases the story of a single dynasty would be enough to fill a volume. Most of the new states took shape during the eighth and ninth centuries under chiefs belonging to various Rājpūt clans, who claimed to be the successors of the Kshatriyas of ancient times. The whole period between the death of Harsha and the Muhammadan conquest of Hindustan at the close of the twelfth century, comprising about five and a half centuries, may be called the Rājpūt period, and we must consider who the Rājpūts were, and how they come so much into view at this particular time. But in this chapter we shall confine our attention to the affairs of Northern India before the time of Mahmūd of Ghaznī.

Muhammadan conquest of Sind. The new powers, as has been said, almost without exception were Rājpūt. The principal exception was Sind. An ancient Sūdra dynasty, with its capital at Aror (Alor), had ruled the country from the Salt Range to the sea. In the seventh century the sceptre passed into the hands of Chach, a Brahman. But meantime the Arabs, full of enthusiasm for the Muhammadan religion, then just started on its victorious career had occupied

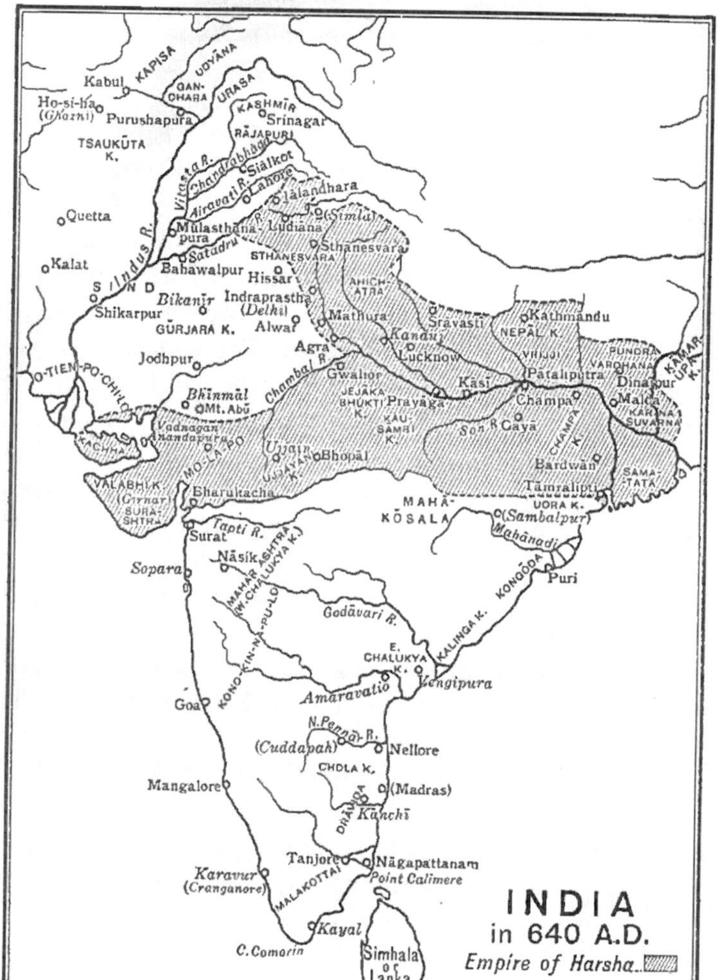

INDIA in 640 A.D.

Empire of Harsha

WAXTYPE — GEORGE PHILIP & SON, LTD.

Balōchistān (Makrān). In A.D. 712, under the command of a general named Muhammad, son of Kāsim,[1] they invaded Sind, slew the reigning king, Dāhir, son of Chach, and established a Muslim state which endured for centuries. The boundary between it and India proper was the 'Lost River', the Hakrā (*ante*, p. 22). The Muhammadan occupation of Sind did not much affect interior India, and the serious Muslim attack on the countries east of the Indus did not occur until nearly three centuries later.

The rise of the Rājpūts. Most of the existing Rājpūt clans trace back their pedigrees to the eighth or ninth century, but no farther, and the reason seems to be that their ruling families became prominent about that time. Multitudes of foreign settlers, Hūnas, Gurjaras, and others, who had taken up their abode in the Panjāb and Rājputāna during the fifth and sixth centuries (*ante*, p. 80), became Hinduized in the course of two or three generations, and were then recognized as Hindu castes. War and government being the business of a Kshatriya, the chiefs and their kinsmen, when they adopted the Hindu *dharma*, or rule of life, were considered Kshatriyas, while the humbler folk took rank in castes of less degree.

How foreigners became Hinduized. Several causes made it easy for the new comers to become Hindus quickly. The invaders must generally have arrived without their womankind. When they settled down in India they married Hindu wives, who naturally continued to follow their old customs which they taught to their children. The men, being far away from home, could not possibly keep up the mode of life to which they had been used in Turkistan. They thus readily dropped into the ways of their wives, children, and neighbours. In order to be a good Hindu it is not necessary to hold any particular creed. All that is needed is to follow the Indian *dharma*, or rule of life, which may be defined roughly as reverence for Brahmans, respect for the sanctity of cows, and scrupulous care about diet and marriage. In the course of a

[1] Not 'Muhammad Kāsim'.

generation or two the descendants of the original invaders began to adopt the Hindu *dharma*, and so became Hindus. The Brahmans were then ready to find everybody a suitable place in the caste system. The ruling classes, as stated above, were treated as Kshatriyas, while the common people were recognized as castes included in either the Vaisya or the Sudra group. The Central Asian tribes which entered India during the fifth and sixth centuries do not seem to have possessed any organized or well-defined religion of their own, which could hinder their acceptance of Hindu belief and practice.

Exactly the same process has often been observed going on in modern times. In the wilder parts of the country, multitudes of so-called 'aboriginal' tribes gradually slide into Hinduism, almost without knowing it. Superintendents of the census profess to distinguish among such tribes between Animists, or the worshippers of sundry spirits or demons, and Hindus, but in reality no line can be drawn separating the two, because the tribesmen continue to mix up 'animist' rites with the worship of the regular Hindu gods. Even after the lapse of many centuries it is still possible to trace 'Scythian' customs in the practice of high-caste Rājpūt clans.

Foreign origin of some clans. It has been proved that the Parihār Rājpūts of the present day are descended from the Gurjaras, who came into India as foreigners, and it is, of course, obvious that Gūjars are the same as Gurjaras. But the Parihārs count as Kshatriyas or Rājpūts because they were a ruling clan in ancient days, while the Gūjars, who represent the rank and file of the old Gurjaras, now form a large middle-class caste, much inferior in social standing to Rājpūts. There is reason to believe that many other famous Rājpūt clans originated in the same way from the ruling septs of foreign tribes.

Aboriginal origin of other clans. Another group of Rājpūt clans has been formed by the promotion of the so-called aborigines. For instance, the famous Bais clan of Oudh is closely connected with and seems to be descended from the

Bhars, who are now represented by a numerous caste of very low rank, and the Chandēls of Bundelkhand are similarly associated with the Gonds of the Central Provinces. While the Rājās and the kinsmen of Rājās of aboriginal blood are universally acknowledged to be Kshatriyas, the other members of the old tribes now form all sorts of lower-grade Hindu castes. Very often the clans of aboriginal origin had a standing feud with neighbours of foreign, or Scythian, origin, as the Chandēls had with the Parihārs, but, of course, this arrangement did not always hold good. Rājpūt clans of all sorts combined occasionally to resist the Muhammadans.

Kingdom of Kanauj or Panchāla. In A.D. 880 the most powerful state in Northern India was that of Panchāla or Kanauj, then ruled by Rājā Bhoja Parihār, whose Gurjara ancestors had been masters of a large kingdom in Rājputāna. At the beginning of the ninth century one of those princes occupied Kanauj and made it the capital of his dynasty. For fifty or sixty years after the middle of the ninth century the kings of Kanauj governed a dominion rivalling that of Harsha in extent. It included Kāthiāwār or Surāshtra, and extended from the boundary of Magadha (South Bihār) to the Sutlaj. Unluckily, hardly anything is known about Rājā Bhoja's method of government, or the state of the country in his time.

Pāla dynasty of Bengal. At the same time the so-called Pāla kings were lords of Bengal and Bihār and enjoyed great power. They were often at war with Kanauj, and early in the ninth century Dharmapāla was strong enough to depose a king of Kanauj and replace him by another. At that moment the Pāla sovereign was the most powerful monarch in Northern India.

Chandēl dynasty of Jejākabhukti. Another important kingdom was that of the Chandēls of Jejākabhukti, the modern Bundelkhand. The capital was Mahoba (now in the Hamīrpur District) and the strong fortress of Kālanjar (now in the Bānda District) gave much importance to the Rājā. This kingdom, separated from that of Kanauj by the Jumna, was at the height of its grandeur in A.D. 1000.

Rājā Bhoja of Dhārā. Many more Rājpūt kingdoms, Gwalior, Chedi, and others, played a part in the history of the times, but are too numerous for mention. The learned Rājā Bhoja, of Dhārā in Mālwā, who was a Pawār Rājpūt, and reigned from about A. D. 1018 to 1060, must not be confounded with Rājā Bhoja Parihār of Kanauj mentioned above. Rājā Bhoja of Dhārā was a liberal patron of Sanskrit learning, and his name has become proverbial as that of the model king according to the Hindu standard.

CHAPTER IX

The kingdoms of the Deccan and the Far South.

The Deccan and the Far South. Before proceeding to narrate the story of the Muhammadan conquest of the Panjāb we shall turn aside for a moment to bestow a passing glance on the kingdoms of the Deccan and the Far South, which, for the reasons explained in chapter i (*ante*, p. 18), were rarely in touch with the North.

The Āndhras, and the Chalukyas of Vātāpi. The Āndhra dynasty (*ante*, p. 70) held the Deccan until about A. D. 236. The next dynasty of which we know anything substantial is that of the Chalukya Rājpūts, which established itself at Vātāpi (Bādāmi) in the Bijāpur District. The most notable prince of this line was Pulakesin II (608–42), who has been mentioned (*ante*, p. 81) as having successfully opposed the attempt made by Harsha to intrude on the south. His capital, probably then at or near Nāsik, was visited by the Chinese pilgrim Hiuen Tsang, in A. D. 641, who noted that the king was a Kshatriya by caste and that his people had a high and warlike spirit. Pulakesin, relying on his brave soldiers and mighty elephants, received loyal service from his subjects and treated neighbouring countries with contempt. Learning was prized. The kingdom contained more than a hundred Buddhist monasteries with more than five thousand residents, but votaries of the Hindu gods were also numerous.

In the following year, 642, this proud monarch was humbled and deprived of his kingdom by the Pallava king of Kānchī (Conjeeveram). Thirteen years later the Chalukya line was restored, and lasted for a century longer. The kingdom of the Eastern Chalukyas of Vengī between the Godāvarī and Krishnā (Kistna) rivers, an offshoot of the Western Chalukya monarchy, lasted for about four centuries from A. D. 615. In the end it became merged in the Chola kingdom of the south.

The Rāshtrakūtas. In the middle of the eighth century the sovereignty of the Deccan passed to the Rāshtrakūtas, a Rājpūt dynasty of uncertain origin, whose capital, at first at Nāsik, was transferred to Mānyakheta, now Mālkhed, in the Nizam's dominions. The Rāshtrakūta kings acquired great power, and were regarded as the leading princes in India by Muhammadan writers of the ninth and tenth centuries. In fact, Amoghavarsha, who reigned in the ninth century for more than sixty years, was reckoned to be the fourth among the great kings of the world, the other three being the Khalīf of Baghdad, the Emperor of China, and the Emperor of Constantinople (Rūm). The rank and power of the Rāshtrakūta prince were largely due to his immense wealth, acquired apparently by commerce. The members of his dynasty were always on the best of terms with the Arab rulers of Sind, with whom no doubt the Indian kingdom did profitable trade. The Gurjaras of Rajputāna and Kanauj, on the contrary, were as hostile to the Arabs as they were to the Rāshtrakūtas, who actually captured Kanauj in A. D. 916. Amoghavarsha was a great patron of the Digambara Jains.

The Chalukyas of Kalyāni. In 973 the Rāshtrakūtas had to give way to the second Chalukya dynasty of Kalyāni, which lasted for more than two centuries, and was engaged in constant wars with the neighbouring powers.

The Hoysala and Yādava dynasties. When Muhammadan armies entered the Deccan, at the close of the thirteenth and the beginning of the fourteenth century, the Mysore country was held by the Hoysala dynasty, and the western side of the

Deccan was under the rule of the Yādava kings of Deogiri. The Hoysala capital, Dorasamudra, was captured by Malik Kāfūr and Khwāja Hājī in 1310, and reduced to ruins by Muhammad bin Tughlak in 1327. Rāmachandra, the Yādava king, was forced to submit first to Alā-ud-dīn, and then to Malik Kāfūr, purchasing his life by payment of enormous treasures. His son Harapāla, who tried to shake off the foreign yoke, was defeated in 1318 by Kutb-ud-dīn Mubārak, who barbarously caused him to be flayed alive.

Religion. During the centuries summarily noticed in the preceding paragraphs, many changes occurred in the religious condition of the kingdoms on the Deccan table-land and in Mysore. Buddhism, which had never obtained very wide acceptance in Southern India, slowly declined, and can be hardly traced after the twelfth century. Jainism, which, according to tradition, had been introduced into Mysore in the days of Chandragupta Maurya, continued to be popular for many ages. As already observed, the religion of Mahāvīra was specially favoured by Amoghavarsha Rāshtrakūta in the ninth century. The conversion of Bittiga or Vishnu, Hoysala king of the twelfth century, from Jainism to Vishnuism, under the influence of the famous reformer Rāmānuja, testified to the growth of orthodox Hinduism, and contributed to the decay of Jain influence. We hear from time to time of fierce conflicts between the adherents of rival creeds, and occasionally of violent persecutions.

Art and literature. Some of the best paintings in the caves of Ajantā date from the time of the first Chalukya dynasty in the sixth and seventh centuries. The marvellous rock-cut Kailāsa temple at Ellora, one of the wonders of the world, was executed under the orders of Krishna I, Rāshtrakūta, in the latter half of the eighth century. The rule of the Hoysala kings of Mysore is memorable for the erection during the twelfth and thirteenth centuries of many magnificent Hindu temples, covered with elaborate ornament and adorned by multitudes of fine statues. Sanskrit literature was cultivated with success at many Rājās' courts, but no great original work of general fame was produced.

The three kingdoms of the Far South. From very ancient times the Far South, or Tamil Land (*Tamilakam*), was shared between three Dravidian kingdoms: (1) the Pāndya, corresponding with the Madura and Tinnevelly Districts, (2) the Chera or Kerala, in the Malabar region, and (3) the Chola, on the Madras or Coromandel coast.[1] These kingdoms kept up a brisk trade with the Roman empire in the early centuries of the Christian era, and possessed an advanced civilization of their own, with institutions quite different from those of the Aryan north. Very little is known about their political history before the ninth century.

Chola supremacy. In the tenth and eleventh centuries the Chola kingdom, under Rājarāja and his successors, became the leading power in the south, and maintained a strong fleet, which ventured across the Bay of Bengal and annexed Pegu. The Chola kings ordinarily were zealous devotees of Siva, and some of them are said to have cruelly persecuted the Jains. Such persecution seems to have had a good deal to do with the gradual decline of Jainism in Southern India. When the Muhammadans came, at the beginning of the fourteenth century, the power of all the old Dravidian kingdoms had become much weakened. Even Madura, the Pāndya capital, was held by Muhammadan governors from about 1311 to 1358. During the fourteenth century the new Hindu state of Vijayanagar arose and dominated the whole of the Far South until its fall in 1565.

The Pallavas. Between the fourth and eighth centuries the ancient Dravidian states were disturbed and overshadowed by an intrusive and vigorous dynasty of uncertain origin, the Pallavas, who made Kānchī (Conjeeveram) their capital, and attained the maximum of their power in the seventh century, when they destroyed Pulakesin II, Chalukya, as already stated.

[1] The word Coromandel is a corruption of *Chola-maṇḍala*, 'Chola territory'.

CHAPTER X

The Muhammadan conquest of the Panjāb: Sultan Mahmūd of Ghaznī.

Muhammadan invasion; Amīr Sabuktigīn. Towards the close of the tenth century the Hindu Rājpūt states of Northern India, which had enjoyed long immunity from foreign attack, were disturbed by the intrusion of Muhammadan invaders through the north-western passes. About A. D. 962, Alptigīn, a Turk, who had been a slave in the service of the Sāmāni king of Khurasan and Bukhāra, established himself in practical independence as master of a small principality with its capital at Ghaznī, between Kābul and Kandahār. When he died he was succeeded by his son Ishāk. After a few years, in A. D. 977, Sabuktigīn, who also had been a slave, became chief of Ghaznī, and, like his predecessors, bore the style of Amīr. Subsequently he received the title of Nāsir-ud-dīn from the Khalīfa.

Wars between Sabuktigīn and Jaipāl. In A. D. 986–7, Amīr Sabuktigīn began to make raids into the territory of Jaipāl Rājā of the Panjāb, whose capital was at Bathindah, now in the Patiāla state. A year or two later the Indian king retaliated by invading the Ghaznī territory, but lost most of his army from the excessive cold, and was forced to purchase peace. Jaipāl, having broken the treaty, was promptly punished by a fresh invasion, in the course of which the Amīr reduced to subjection the Lamghān territory between Peshāwar and Kābul. Jaipāl then organized a great league of Hindu princes, including the Rājās of distant Kanauj and Kālanjar, and made a final effort to save his country by leading the allied army of 100,000 men into the dominions of the Amīr. A fierce battle, probably fought somewhere in the Kurram valley, ended in the total rout of the Hindus. The invaders, eaters of meat, inured to war, and bound together by fierce religious fanaticism, were too much for the Hindus.

Sultan Mahmūd of Ghaznī. In A. D. 997 (A. H. 387), the

crown of the Amīr Sabuktigīn descended, after a short interval of dispute, to his famous son Mahmūd, then twenty-six years of age, the first Musalman chief who enjoyed the title of Sultan. Mahmūd, urged by religious zeal and love of plunder, vowed to carry on what he considered to be a 'holy war' against the idolaters of India, and to lead an expedition into that land each year. To the best of his ability he kept his vow, and, in pursuance of it, is computed to have made fifteen or, according to some authorities, seventeen expeditions of which the more important will now be noticed.

Defeat and Death of Jaipāl, A. D. 1001. During the course of his second expedition the sultan met Jaipāl on the plain near Peshāwar, on the 27th of November, A. D. 1001, and utterly defeated him, taking him and his family prisoners. After a while the Rājā was released, but on return to his own country, committed suicide by fire, and Ānandpāl, his son, reigned in his stead. The Peshāwar territory was annexed by the sultan.

Capture of Multān. Mahmūd's fourth expedition (A.H. 396 = A. D. 1005–6) was directed against Multān, but before he captured that city the invader attacked Ānandpāl, 'stretching out upon him the hand of slaughter, imprisonment, pillage, depopulation, and fire, and hunted him from ambush to ambush.'

Rout of Ānandpāl and his son. The sixth expedition (A. H. 399 = 1008–9) was aimed specially against Ānandpāl, who, following his father's example, organized a league of the Hindu powers, including the Rājās of Ujjain, Gwalior, Kālanjar, Kanauj, Delhi, and Ajmēr, and assembled a greater army than had ever taken the field against the Amīr Sabuktigīn. The hostile forces watched each other in the plain of Peshāwar for forty days, the Hindus meantime receiving reinforcements from the powerful Khokhar tribe. The sultan was obliged to be cautious, and formed an entrenched camp. Thirty thousand Khokhars by a sudden rush stormed it, and in a few moments had slain three or four thousand Musalmans. Victory seemed to be in the grasp of the Hindus, but at the critical moment, the elephant carrying Ānandpāl turned and fled.[1] The Indians, thinking this accident to be a signal of defeat, gave way and broke. The Musalman cavalry pursued them for two days and nights, killing 8,000 and capturing thirty elephants and enormous booty.

Capture of Kāngra. This decisive victory was followed up by the capitulation of the fort of Kāngra, also known as Nagarkot or Bhīmnagar, where treasure of immense value was taken. 'Among the booty was a house of white silver, like to the houses of rich men, the length of which was thirty yards, and the breadth fifteen. It could be taken to pieces and put together again.'

Expedition against Kanauj and Mathurā. One of the most celebrated of Sultan Mahmūd's raids was that which is reckoned as the twelfth, and had for its object the conquest of Kanauj, the imperial city of Northern India. The sultan started from Ghaznī in October, passed all the rivers of the Panjāb, and crossed the Jumna on December 2, A. D. 1018. He captured the forts which obstructed his path, and was preparing to attack Baran, the modern Bulandshahr, when the local Rājā, Hardatt by name, tendered his submission, and with ten thousand men accepted the religion of Islam. The holy and wealthy city of Mathurā having been taken, 'the sultan gave orders that all the temples should be burned with naphtha and fire, and levelled with the ground'.

Conquest of Kanauj. In January, A. D. 1019, the ever victorious invader appeared before Kanauj. The Rājā, Rājyapāl Parihār, fled to the other side of the Ganges, and allowed his capital to be occupied without serious resistance. The seven forts, or lines of fortification, guarding it fell in one day, and were given over to plunder. Rājyapāl submitted, and the city, as a whole, seems to have been spared, although the temples were destroyed, many of the inhabitants slain, and much plunder was acquired. Mahmūd then advanced through the Fatehpur District and entered the hills of Bundelkhand

[1] Al Utbi says that the Hindu leader was Brahmanpāl, son of Ānandpāl.

before he returned to Ghaznī at the beginning of the hot season.

Death of Rājyapāl. The submission of Rājyapāl to the foreigner angered the neighbouring Hindu princes, who under the leadership of Vidhyādhara, son of Ganda, the Chandēl Rājā of Kālanjar, and the chieftain of Gwalior, attacked Kanauj, and slew Rājyapāl. He was succeeded by Trilochanpāl.[1]

The vengeance of the sultan. Mahmūd, who regarded the king of Kanauj as his vassal, was furious when he heard the news and determined to punish the audacious Hindus. Again leaving Ghaznī in the autumn of 1019, he forced the passage of the Jumna in spite of the opposition of Trilochanpāl, and advanced into the territory of Ganda Chandēl, who had assembled a huge army. Even Mahmūd's stout heart quaked, and 'he regretted having come thither'. But during the night the courage of Ganda failed, and he shamefully stole away with a few followers, leaving his camp and 580 elephants a prey to the sultan, who, 'loaded with victory and success, returned to Ghaznī'. In 1021–2 Mahmūd once more entered the Chandēl dominions, and invested the famous fortress of Kālanjar, now in the Bānda District, which was held by the Rājā. Again Ganda feared to fight, and was content to buy peace. The sultan, laden as usual with 'immense riches and jewels, victoriously and triumphantly returned to Ghaznī'.

Expedition to Somnāth. The most adventurous of Mahmūd's expeditions was that against the shrine of Somnāth at Prabhāsa in the south of the Surāshtra peninsula. Starting from Ghaznī in the middle of December, A.D. 1023 (10th Shabān, A.H. 414), and marching through difficult country by way of Multān, Ajmēr, and Anhilwāra in Gujarāt, he arrived at his destination in the beginning of March, A.D. 1024 (middle of Zī-l-ka'da).[2] Overcoming a fierce resistance, he stormed

[1] These kings of Kanauj had no connexion with the Pāla kings of Bengal, as a certain text-book alleges them to have had.

[2] According to other authorities Mahmūd left Ghaznī in 1024, and sacked Somnāth in the beginning of 1025. The exact chronology of the early Muhammadan history of India is not easy to settle.

the Hindu fortress which stood on the sea-shore and was washed by the waves. A dreadful slaughter followed, the magnificent temple was laid low, and the sacred *lingam*, one of the twelve most holy ones in India, was smashed, parts of it being taken to Ghaznī, and cast down at the threshold of the great mosque to be trodden underfoot. The gates now lying in the Agra Fort, brought from Ghaznī in 1842 as being those of the temple of Somnāth and made the subject of a silly proclamation by Lord Ellenborough, are Musalman work and never came from a Hindu temple. The sultan's army suffered severely on its return march through the Sind desert, but enjoyed compensation in the vast treasure plundered from the shrine, which was estimated to exceed two millions of *dīnārs*.

Death of Sultan Mahmūd : his patronage of scholars. The last of Mahmūd's Indian expeditions took place in A.D. 1027, when he attacked the Jats near Multān, and is said to have fought them on the rivers with a fleet of boats constructed for the purpose. During the rest of his life he was occupied with troubles at home. He died in April, A.D. 1030 (A.H. 421). Sultan Mahmūd is famous for the magnificence of his court and buildings and for his patronage of numerous Persian poets, especially Unsari and Firdausi, although it is true that the latter, the author of the epic poem called *Shāhnāma*, did not consider himself well treated by the sultan, who bears the reproach of avarice. Alberūnī, a mathematician and astronomer of profound learning, accompanied Mahmūd to India, and wrote in Arabic a valuable account of the country and its institutions, which he completed in the year of his patron's death.

Destruction of Ghaznī. The wars and dynastic troubles in the kingdom of Ghaznī which followed on the death of Mahmūd do not concern India and need not be related. It will suffice to say that the cruelties practised by Bahrām, one of his successors, on a chieftain of Ghor, an obscure principality in the mountains to the south-east of Herat, were terribly avenged by that chieftain's brother, Alā-ud-dīn Husain, who, in A.D. 1150 (A.H. 544), sacked Ghaznī for seven days and nights and destroyed all its splendid buildings, except the tombs of Sultan Mahmūd and two of his descendants.

The Province of Lahore. This disaster did not immediately deprive the dynasty of Ghaznī of the Indian province of Lahore, or the Panjāb, which had been annexed by Sultan Mahmūd. Khusrū Malik, the last prince of the house of Sabuktigīn, a weak and pleasure-loving man, retained possession of Lahore until A.D. 1186 or 1187 (A.H. 582 or 583), when he was expelled by Shihāb-ud-dīn, the Ghorī, otherwise called Sultan Muizz-ud-dīn, Muhammad, son of Sām. Khusrū Malik was shut up in a fortress and put to death fifteen or sixteen years later. The student should remember that the province of Lahore was the sole permanent possession in India acquired by Mahmūd, who made no attempt to hold the regions in the interior which he overran in the course of his raids.

Sultan Mahmūd of Ghaznī.

	A.D.
Accession	997 or 998
Defeat of Jaipāl	1001
Defeat of Ānandpāl	1005–6
Defeat of Brahmanpāl (or Ānandpāl)	1008–9
Capture of Kanauj	Jan. 1019
Rout of Ganda Chandēl	1020
Somnāth expedition	1024 or 1025
Last Indian expedition	1027
Death	1030 (Alberūnī)

CHAPTER XI

Hindu civilization on the eve of the Muhammadan rule in Hindustan.

Survival of the Hindu kingdoms. The forays of Sultan Mahmūd, destructive though they were of life and property, did not shatter the Hindu kingdoms of the interior, which survived the passing storms, and were left free to conduct their affairs in their own fashion. The Panjāb alone had become a Muhammadan province. So far as appears, no considerable body of foreigners settled in India, excepting Sind and the Panjāb, for about six centuries, from A.D. 600 to 1200, in round numbers. The serious efforts of the Musalmans to establish a permanent Indian dominion did not begin until the closing years of the twelfth century.

Great Hindu powers of the twelfth century. At that time the great Hindu powers of Northern India were no longer the same as they had been in the tenth century (*ante*, p. 92), and may be named as (1) the Gaharwārs of Kanauj, (2) the Tomaras of Delhi, (3) the Chauhāns of Sāmbhar and Ajmēr, (4) the Pālas and Senas of Bihār and Bengal, and (5) the Bāghelas of Gujarāt. Of course, there were plenty of other kingdoms, but those mentioned were the principal.

The Gaharwārs of Kanauj. The Parihār dynasty of Kanauj was ruined by Mahmūd, and soon faded into obscurity. Towards the end of the eleventh century another Rājpūt clan, of 'aboriginal' origin, the Gaharwārs, afterwards known as Rāthōrs, occupied Kanauj and founded a new dynasty, which attained considerable power under Govindachandra and his successors during the twelfth century. Rājā Jaichand (Jayachchandra), the last of them, famed in song and legend, who fell in the struggle with the Musalmans, was the grandson of Govindachandra.

The Tomaras of Delhi. Delhi, including under that name a series of cities built under different names by many kings, but excluding the legendary Indraprastha of the *Mahābhārata*, is one of the most modern of Indian capitals, and, according to the best authority, was not founded till A.D. 993. Ānangapāla, a Tōmara chief in the middle of the eleventh century, was the first prince to beautify the newly founded city with handsome buildings. He erected a group of twenty-seven fine temples, from the materials of which the Kutb mosque was built a century and a half later, and set up beside them the famous and ancient iron pillar, which was removed from its original position, perhaps at Mathurā. Ānangapāla and his successors made Delhi the centre of a kingdom of moderate extent. The common belief that the Tomaras also held Kanauj is an error.

The Chauhāns of Sāmbhar and Ajmēr. After about a century of Tomara rule, Delhi was annexed by Vīsaladeva (Bīsal dēo), the Chauhān Rājā of Sāmbhar and Ajmēr in Rājputāna, who thus became a powerful prince. His nephew was the famous Prithirāj, who distinguished himself by carrying off the daughter of Rājā Jaichand of Kanauj about 1175, by defeating Parmāl, the Chandēl Rājā of Mahoba in 1182, and finally by his gallant leadership of the Hindu host against the Muhammadans a few years later. Most historians state that the mother of Prithirāj was a daughter of Ānangapāla, Rājā of Delhi, but she seems really to have been a princess of the Chedi kingdom in the south.

The Pālas of Bengal and Bihār. Harsha, when at the height of his power, appears to have enjoyed full dominion over Western and Central Bengal. After his death in 647, that country, like the rest of his empire, fell into disorder. Very little is known about its history for nearly a century. About 730 or 740, the people of Central Bengal established order by electing as their king one Gopāla, the first of the dynasty known to history as the Pālas. Towards the end of a long reign he annexed South Bihār. The second king Dharmapāla, and the third, Devapāla, whose reigns covered about a century, raised Bengal to the rank of one of the great powers of India. We have seen (*ante*, p. 92) how Dharmapāla was able to pull down one king of Kanauj and set up another in his place. All the members of the dynasty were devoted adherents of Buddhism in its later forms. Early in the eleventh century, two kings, Mahīpāla I and Nayapāla, were zealous enough to send missionaries to Tibet in order to revive Buddhism in that country. The last powerful king of the line was Rāmapāla (about 1084–1130), who conquered Tirhūt or North Bihār. The Pālas, after enduring the ups and downs of fortune for about four centuries and a half, were finally uprooted by the Muhammadan conquest in 1197.

The Senas of Eastern Bengal. In the first quarter of the twelfth century the greater part of Bengal was formed into a separate kingdom by Vijayasena, whose successors are known as the Sena kings. The Senas greatly reduced the power of the Pālas, who, however, usually retained possession of South Bihār and sometimes held North Bihār or Tirhūt. At the time of the Muhammadan conquest in A.D. 1197–1200, the Pāla capital appears to have been either Mungir (Monghyr) or the town of Bihār, while the Sena capital was at Nūdīah (Nuddea, Navadwīp), in Bengal. The Senas were orthodox Hindus. Ballāla Sena is famous in the traditions of Bengal as the king who is believed to have introduced the system of caste rules known as 'Kulinism' among the Brahmans, Baidyas, and Kāyasths. After the Muhammadan conquest Sena princes continued to rule Eastern Bengal from Bikrampur near Dacca.

The Bāghelas of Gujarāt. During the twelfth century the kingdom of Gujarāt attained to great power under the rule of the Chaulukya or Solankī kings, Siddharāja and Kumārapāla, and it is even alleged that the authority of the latter extended as far east as the Ganges. Towards the end of the same century the throne passed from the Chaulukyas to a Bāghela dynasty. Rājā Vīradhavala of that dynasty was strong enough to repel an attack on his country led by Muhammad of Ghor, defeating the Musalmans with great slaughter.

General condition; architecture; literature. The states above described were independent one of another, frequently at war, and not subject to any controlling power. They rarely could combine, and when a confederacy was formed in a desperate emergency, it was loosely held together and easily dissolved. Many of the Rājās' courts were splendidly appointed, and in the principal cities handsome buildings were numerous. The Pālas were the only considerable princes who continued to profess and support Buddhism; in all other provinces either Jainism or Hinduism prevailed, and

PILLARS, JAIN TEMPLE, OSIA (10TH OR 11TH CENT.)

the doctrine of Buddha was little regarded. The Buddhist buildings of the Pāla dynasty in Bihār have nearly all been destroyed, but many Hindu and Jain temples of the period

A TIBETAN LAMA

survive elsewhere. The beauty of the Jain temples of Mount Ābū, built in the eleventh and twelfth centuries, is unsurpassed, and the Hindu temples erected by the Chandēl kings at Khajurāho, a little before and after A.D. 1000, are among the best examples of Indian architecture. The venerated temple of Jagannāth at Puri in Orissa, built by order of

Anantavarman Cholaganga in the closing years of the eleventh century, is inferior in merit as a work of art. In the ninth century, during the reigns of Dharmapāla and Devapāla, two Bengal artists, Dhīmān and his son Bitpālo, or Vitapāla, attained high fame as painters, sculptors, and bronze-founders.

Literature was encouraged by many Rājās. For instance, Rājasekhara, the dramatist, graced the court of two Parihār kings of Kanauj; Bhoja Pawār of Dhārā, himself an author, was always surrounded by a crowd of scholars; and Vīsaladeva, the Tomara ruler of Delhi, both produced and patronized poetry. Kalhana, who wrote the *Rājatarangiṇī*, a Sanskrit metrical chronicle of Kashmīr, in 1149, was the son of a minister at the Srīnagar court. The *Gīta Govinda* of Jayadeva was composed shortly before the Muslim conquest of Bengal.

The foundations of vernacular literature were laid during this period by the bards, among whom may be mentioned Chand Bardāi, the author of the *Chand Rāisā*, an epic in ancient dialects of Hindī, dealing with the exploits of Prithirāj and other chieftains. The poem, in the shape generally known, has been immensely expanded by later additions. The manuscript of the work in its original form is said to be still preserved in the Jodhpur state.

BOOK III

THE MUHAMMADAN CONQUEST; THE SULTANATE OF DELHI (SO-CALLED 'PATHAN EMPIRE') FROM A.D. 1193 TO 1526.

SOURCES OF INDO-MUHAMMADAN HISTORY

Muhammadan histories numerous. Muhammadan literary men, unlike the Brahmans, had a strong liking for the writing of histories, which, consequently, exist in great numbers, in Arabic, Persian, and Turkish. Every Indo-Muhammadan dynasty, I think, has been treated in at least one formal history. The modern writer, therefore, when undertaking to tell the story of Muhammadan rule in India, turns first to the history books. Inscriptions, coins, and the evidence to be deduced from the remains of ancient buildings or works of art, are of much less importance than they are for the Hindu period, although they still afford evidence of much value about details, and often settle doubtful dates.

Most of the histories dealing with India were written in Persian, and many of them have been printed and translated into English or other European languages. But many exist only in manuscript, and there is room for more good translations.

Elliot and Dowson. The best view of the Muhammadan sources of Indian history is to be obtained from *The History of India as told by its own Historians*, by Sir H. M. Elliot and Professor John Dowson (8 vols., London, 1867–77). Sir E. C. Bayley's volume on the *History of Gujarāt* (London, 1886) is a supplement to the work of Elliot and Dowson. The labours of those gentlemen are invaluable. The editors were pioneers in the subject, and naturally could not attain perfection, especially in the earlier volumes, but the errors in detail are as nothing compared with the benefit conferred on students by such a library of translations. Unfortunately, the book is now scarce and expensive.

It would take up too much space to enumerate individual works. The authorities for Akbar's reign are specially good, and are mostly accessible in one or other European language. The substance of the Jesuit accounts will be found in Mr. (Sir) E. D. Maclagan's admirable treatise, 'The Jesuit Missions to the Emperor Akbar' (*J. As. Soc. Bengal*, Part I, vol. lxv (1896), pp. 38-113).

Firishta. Elphinstone relied principally on Firishta or Ferishta, a careful compiler who wrote in the seventeenth century. The best translation is that by Briggs, which is most cheaply accessible in the reprint issued by Cambray & Co. (Calcutta, 1908–10, 4 vols.) But the rendering by Briggs is far from being perfect, and is spoiled by the insertion of passages which are not in the original.

Royal memoirs. The memoirs written by various kings form an exceptionally interesting section of the Muhammadan histories. We have a short tract by Fīrōz Shah Tughlak of the fourteenth century (Elliot and Dowson, vol. iii), and *Memoirs* written or dictated by Tīmūr, Bābur, and Jahāngīr. No use should be made of the edition of Jahāngīr's *Memoirs* translated by Price in 1829, which is mostly fiction. The only genuine form of the *Memoirs* is that translated by Rogers and Beveridge (*R. As. Soc.*, 2 vols., 1909, 1914), which is a work of high value. Jauhar's *Private Memoirs of Humāyūn* (transl. Stewart, 1832), and the *Life and Memoirs of Gulbadan Begam*, Akbar's aunt (transl. Beveridge, *R. As. Soc.*, 1902), are nearly as intimate as the works written by sovereigns in person.

State papers. In all European countries the mass of original state papers relating to the centuries during which Musalman rule lasted in India is enormous. Very few of such documents have escaped Indian revolutions and white ants. Such as exist chiefly concern the reign of Aurangzeb. A manuscript in London contains a collection of small slips of brown paper forming what may be called the Court Circular of about thirty years of Aurangzeb's reign. His correspondence has been preserved in large quantity, but has never been properly edited. A good Persian scholar well read in history might employ several years to advantage in bringing out a critical edition and partial translation of Aurangzeb's correspondence. The task would be a difficult one (see Sarkar, *Hist. of Aurangzeb*, vol. ii, 1912, p. 309). We also possess some of the letters issued in Akbar's name, and preserved by the Jesuits, besides a good many written by his secretary, Abūl Fazl. A few *farmāns* and other official documents of various reigns have escaped destruction.

Inscriptions. A list of the published Muhammadan inscriptions of India, compiled by Dr. Horovitz under the title *Epigraphia Indo-Moslemica*, has been printed (Calcutta, 1912, Superintendent of Government Printing, India).

Coins. The Indo-Muhammadan coins have been fully discussed in the official catalogues of the collections in the British Museum, Indian Museum, Calcutta, and the Lahore Museum.

European travellers. Numerous European travellers throw an immense amount of light on Indo-Muhammadan history. One of the best of them, the Frenchman Bernier, wrote a formal and excellent narrative of the war of succession by which Aurangzeb won the throne. His book, in English, has been reprinted, with notes by Mr. A. Constable and the author of this history, by the Oxford University Press (1914). A small cheap book by Mr. E. F. Oaten, entitled *European Travellers in India during the Fifteenth, Sixteenth and Seventeenth Centuries* (London: Kegan Paul, Trench, Trübner & Co., 1909), gives a serviceable list and summary of the principal works, many of which are rare and costly. The writings of De Laët and

Manrique, published in the reign of Shahjahān, deserve modern editions. De Laët's valuable little Latin book was partly translated by Lethbridge in the *Calcutta Review* for 1873. Manrique, who wrote in Spanish, has never been translated.

Modern histories. No good critical modern history of Musalman rule in India exists. It is no disparagement of Elphinstone's justly admired work, first published in 1841, to say that it is no longer adequate. Professor Stanley Lane-Poole's *Mediaeval India under Mohammedan Rule*, 712–1764 (Unwin, 1903), is the best sketch, but does not pretend to be more. *The History of Aurangzīb, mainly based on Persian Sources*, by Professor Jadunath Sarkar (vols i, ii, Calcutta, 1912) at present only comes down to the beginning of the War of Succession. The work promises to be of much importance.

The later Mughals. The late Mr. William Irvine, best known as the editor of Manucci, had purposed to write in great detail from the original authorities a history of the decline and fall of the Mughal empire from the death of Aurangzeb in 1707 to the capture of Delhi by Lord Lake in 1803. But he was never able to complete his design, and had to be content with the publication of fragments in various periodicals. References to his more important papers are as follow:

(1) *J. A. S. B.*, vol. lxv, Part I, pp. 136–212; the reigns of Bahādur Shah to Jahāndār Shah, inclusive;

(2) Ibid., vol. lxvii, Part I, pp. 141–66; the reign of Farruksīyar. Both papers give full lists of authorities, and are the most satisfactory statements on the rather dreary subject;

(3) 'The Emperor Aurangzeb Alamgir, 1618–1707,' in *Ind. Ant.*, 1911, pp. 69–85. This paper settles many doubtful points in the chronology of the reign.

Mr. Irvine contributed to vol. ii of the 'Indian Empire' in the new edition of the *Imperial Gazetteer*, 1908, chapter x, a summary of the history of Muhammadan India, which is generally, although not perfectly, accurate. He also published in 1903 a treatise on the army of the Mughals, based on a paper contributed in 1896 to the *J. R. A. S.* for 1896, pp. 509–570. Mr. Irvine aimed in all his publications at the compilation of an exact chronicle filled with minute details.

CHAPTER XII

Muhammad of Ghor (Ghorī): conquest of Hindustan, Bengal, and Bihār: Kutb-ud-dīn Ībak; the so-called 'Pathan dynasties'; the Mongol (Mughal) invasions; end of the Slave Kings.

Muhammad of Ghor (Muhammad Ghorī, Shihāb-ud-dīn). Sultan Alā-ud-dīn Husain, the destroyer of Ghaznī, died about four years after the sack of that city (*ante*, p. 102), and was succeeded in Ghor by his son, who was assassinated a year later. The local nobles then raised to the throne the murdered chief's cousin, elder son of Bahā-ud-dīn Sām, who assumed the title of Sultan Ghiyās-ud-dīn. His younger brother, Muhammad, was known in early life as Shihāb-ud-dīn ('the flame of religion'), but afterwards as Sultan Muizz-ud-dīn. His coins also describe him as Muhammad, son of Sām. The historians of India are accustomed to designate him, with various corruptions, either as Shihāb-ud-dīn or Muhammad Ghorī. We shall call him Muhammad of Ghor.

Occupation of Sind and the Panjāb. Muhammad of Ghor, having reduced Ghaznī to obedience of his brother, turned his attention to the rich plains of India. In A.D. 1175–6 he attacked Multān, and shortly afterwards obtained possession of Ūchh in Sind through the treachery of the Rānī. In 1178–9 Muhammad attempted to penetrate into Gujarāt, but was badly defeated by the Rājā of Anhilwāra. In 1186 or 1187, as already mentioned (*ante*, p. 102), he deposed Khusrū Malik, the last prince of the house of Sabuktigīn, and so made himself master of the Panjāb, as well as of Sind.

First and second battles of Tarāīn. But the ambition of Muhammad was not satisfied by the possession of these frontier provinces. He desired to enjoy the plunder and acquire the sovereignty of the richer kingdoms of the interior. The Hindu Rājās combined against him, as they had done against the Amīr Sabuktigīn and the Sultan Mahmūd, and met the invader on the plain of Tarāīn or Talāwarī, fourteen miles from Thānēsar. The Hindus, under the supreme command of the brave Prithirāj Chauhān, Rājā of Ajmēr and Delhi (*ante*, p. 104), routed the sultan, who was wounded in the arm (A.D. 1191). Next year, A.D. 1192, the sultan returned, fought the Hindu confederacy on the same ground, charged the enemy with twelve thousand picked cavalry, utterly defeated them, and captured the commander-in-chief, Prithirāj, who was executed. Ajmēr was sacked and the inhabitants either killed or sold as slaves.

Reduction of Hindustan. The following year, A.D. 1193

(A.H. 589), Delhi, Kanauj, and Benares all fell before the resistless invader. Three years later Gwalior surrendered. In 1197 Anhilwāra, which had baffled the Muslim arms nearly twenty years before, was taken, and in A.D. 1203 the capitulation of Kālanjar, the strong fortress of the Chandēls, completed the reduction of Upper India. The Gaharwār Rājpūts of Kanauj migrated to Mārwār in Rājputāna, where they became known as Rāthōrs and founded the Jodhpur State. Many similar movements of Rājpūt clans occurred about the same time in order to escape from the armies of Islam.

Death of the sultan. After these momentous events the sultan, who had succeeded his brother early in A.D. 1203, returned to Ghaznī, but in the cold season of A.D. 1205 was recalled to India by the revolt of the Khokhars, a powerful tribe in the Central Panjāb. Having 'set a river of blood of those people flowing', he started for Ghaznī, and was murdered on the road by a fanatic of the Mulāhidah sect in March, A.D. 1206:

The martyrdom of the sovereign of sea and land, Muizz-ud-dīn,
From the beginning of the world the like of whom no monarch arose,
On the third of the month Sha'bān in the year six hundred and two,
Happened on the road to Ghaznī at the halting-place of Damyak.[1] (Dhamiāk in Jihlam (Jhelum) District.)

Kutb-ud-dīn Ībak as general and viceroy. The successes gained in India by the arms of Muhammad of Ghor were largely due to the ability of his general, Malik Kutb-ud-dīn Ibak, a native of Turkestan, who had been bought as a slave by the sultan, and was still legally a slave when he subdued Hindustan. He led the vanguard in the action of Chandwār near Itāwa, when Rājā Jaichand of Kanauj was killed by an

[1] *Tabakāt-i-Nāsirī.* This account by a contemporary should be accepted, not that which appears in Elphinstone and the text-books. The Khokhars usually are miscalled 'Gakkars', who were a totally different tribe in the Salt Range.

arrow which struck him in the eye. He then pushed on to Benares and acquired a vast amount of booty. The sultan having returned to Ghaznī, Kutb-ud-dīn was left in charge of the operations in India. The capture of Kālanjar was his work, and on that occasion 50,000 captives were enslaved. He next occupied Mahoba, the Chandēl capital (*ante*, p. 92), and thence returned to Delhi through Budaon. He received the title of sultan from Sultan Ghiyās-ud-dīn Mahmūd, the successor of Muhammad of Ghor on the throne of Ghor and Ghaznī.

Kutb-ud-dīn Ibak as Sultan of Delhi. From this time (A.D. 1206) Kutb-ud-dīn may be regarded as an independent Indian sovereign, the first of the long line of the sultans of Delhi. He strengthened his position by judicious matrimonial alliances, himself marrying the daughter of Tāj-ud-dīn Yildūz (Eldoz), a rival chief, who, like Kutb-ud-dīn, had been a slave; giving his sister to Nāsir-ud-dīn Kubācha, another slave, who became the lord of Sind; and his daughter to Īltutmish (Altamsh), governor of Bihār, and also a slave. He died in the year A.H. 607 (A.D. 1210–11) from the effects of a fall from his horse. 'His gifts', says the chronicler, 'were bestowed by hundreds of thousands, and his slaughters likewise were by hundreds of thousands.'

The Kutbī Mosque and Mīnār. During the period of his viceroyalty, between the years A.D. 1193 and 1198, Kutb-ud-dīn built the great mosque near Delhi, which was subsequently enlarged by his son-in-law, the Sultan Īltutmish (Altamsh), who also built the celebrated tower known as the Kutb Mīnār. Both mosque and mīnār are called Kutbī, not because they were built by Kutb-ud-dīn Ibak, but because they are consecrated to the memory of the saint Kutb-ud-dīn Ūshī, who lies buried close by.

Conquest of Bihār. Kutb-ud-dīn Ībak was well served by his lieutenant, Ikhtiyār-ud-dīn Muhammad, son of Bakhtyār, a Khalj Turk, who is ordinarily called in the text-books 'Muhammad Bakhtiyār', father and son being rolled into one. In or about A.D. 1197, several years after the fall of Delhi, this officer secured the control of Bihār by a raid of almost incredible audacity, seizing the fort of the town of Bihār with a party of only two hundred horsemen. The Buddhist monasteries, which still flourished under the patronage of the Pāla kings (*ante*, p. 104), were destroyed, and the monks killed or dispersed. The Muhammadan onslaught extinguished the life of Buddhism in its old home and last refuge. After this time the indications of the existence of that religion anywhere in India are very slight.

Conquest of Bengal. Bengal was brought under Muslim domination about two years later (A.D. ? 1199) with even greater ease. The aged Sena king, Rājā Lakhmaniya or Lakshmana-sena, surprised in his capital of Nūdīah (Nuddea, Navadvīpa) by a party of only eighteen horsemen, fled by the back door and took refuge in the Dacca district, leaving Nūdīah to the fury of the conqueror, who sacked the town and made Lakhnautī or Gaur the seat of his government. Muhammad and his officers endowed mosques, colleges, and Muhammadan monasteries in all parts of the kingdom, and sent much booty to their chief, Kutb-ud-dīn.

Death of Muhammad, son of Bakhtyār. Some years later, in A.D. 1204–5 (A.H. 601), Muhammad, the son of Bakhtyār, rashly undertook to invade the mountains. He managed to enter those beyond Darjeeling, but, being unable to secure any safe foothold, was compelled to retreat. During the retirement he lost almost all his force. Next year he was assassinated.

The so-called 'Pathān dynasties' and 'Pathān empire'. The sultans of Delhi, beginning with Kutb-ud-dīn in 1206, ending with Ibrāhīm Lodī in 1526, and including the Sūr claimants up to 1556, are often erroneously called the 'Pathān kings', and their rule is designated the 'Pathān empire'. But, as a matter of fact, only the sultans of the Lodī and Sūr families were Pathāns (properly Paṭāns), that is to say, Afghans. Kutb-ud-dīn and the other so-called Slave Kings were natives of Turkestan, of Turkish blood. The sultans of the Khaljī (Khiljī) dynasty also were Turks. The Tughlak sultans seem to have been of mixed Turkish and Hindu blood, and the so-called Sayyid princes claimed Arab descent from the prophet Muhammad.

Sultan Īltutmish (Altamsh). Ārām, the adopted son of Kutb-ud-dīn, succeeded him, but proved incapable, and was soon replaced (A.D. 1211) by Shams-ud-dīn Īltutmish (Altamsh &c., of the text-books), governor of Bihār. The new sultan had to fight and overcome his brother slaves Tāj-ud-dīn Yildūz (Iyaldūz) and Nāsir-ud-dīn Kubācha. He compelled the successors of Muhammad, the son of Bakhtyār, in Bengal to acknowledge his authority. After some more fighting in various directions Īltutmish died in May 1236, and was buried beside the mosque which he had enlarged and the mīnār which he had built at Delhi.

Sultan Razīyah (Raziyyat-ud-dīn). Rukn-ud-dīn, son of Īltutmish, a worthless fellow, 'whose inclinations were wholly towards buffoonery, sensuality, and diversion', was deposed after seven months of misrule, his place being taken by his sister Raziyyat-ud-dīn, commonly called Razīyah, a capable sovereign, whose chief fault seems to have been her sex. 'Sultan Raziyyat—may she rest in peace!—was a great sovereign, and sagacious, just, beneficent, the patron of the learned, a dispenser of justice, the cherisher of her subjects, and of warlike talent, and was endowed with all the admirable attributes and qualifications necessary for kings; but, as she did not attain the destiny in her creation of being computed among men, of what advantage were all these excellent qualifications unto her?' She tried to secure her throne by submitting to marriage with a turbulent Turkī chief, but other nobles, who would not endure a woman's rule, defeated her in October, A.D. 1240, after a disturbed reign of three and a half years. She and her husband were killed by certain Hindus.

Sultan Nāsir-ud-dīn Mahmūd. She was followed by two

insignificant princes, and in 1246 Nāsir-ud-dīn Mahmūd, one of her brothers, became sultan of Delhi. He was a quiet, studious man, ill fitted for rule in such times, but managed to retain his throne for twenty years by the help of an able slave minister, Ulugh Khān, otherwise called Ghiyās-ud-dīn

KUTB MĪNĀR

Balban, whose daughter was married to the sultan, and who fought hard throughout his master's reign to establish the Muslim supremacy in Hindustan. The *Tabakāt-i-Nāsirī*, a valuable history by Minhāj-i-Sirāj, the chief Kāzī, was written in this reign and derives its name from the sultan. Some quotations from it are made in this work.

Sultan Ghiyās-ud-dīn Balban. 'Balban, being already in possession of all the powers of king, found no difficulty in assuming the title.' He was nearly sixty years of age when he ascended the throne, but age had not quenched his vigour. He proved himself to be a strong ruler, severe and even cruel in his punishments, and utterly regardless of bloodshed. The Mewātīs near Delhi gave him much trouble, and were chastised with merciless ferocity. His principal military operation was the suppression of a revolt in Bengal. His court was adorned by many princely fugitives from various kingdoms of Asia then devastated by the Mongol hordes, and he was a liberal patron of Persian literature, and especially of Amīr Khusrū, the poet.

The Mongols (Mughals of the Syllabus).[1] A young Mongol chief named Temujin, born in 1162, gradually acquired supreme power among the nomads of the steppes, and was elected as their sovereign with the title of Chinghīz Khan, by which (with various corruptions) he is generally known. Having made himself master of Mongolia, Northern China, and Turkestan he fell with his savage hordes upon the kingdom of Khwārizm (Khiva), sacked Bukhāra, Samarkand, Merv, and other cities, destroying the inhabitants by millions. The murderous conqueror and his generals then overran the country now called Afghanistan, sacked what remained of Ghaznī, stormed Herat, and even occupied Peshāwar. Jalāl-ud-dīn, the Shāh of Khwārizm, who had fled before the Khan, attempted to make a stand on the Indus, but was defeated, and fled to Delhi, where he was received by the sultan (1221, 1222). The Khan thought of returning to Mongolia through

[1] Mongol (or, more strictly, Monggol) and Mughal (Mogul, &c.) really are only different forms of the same word, the nasalized *g* being represented in Arabic by *ghain*. But it is convenient and desirable for a historian of India to apply the term Mongol to the 'narrow-eyed' and heathen nomads who formed the bulk of the hordes led by Chinghīz Khan, and to restrict the term Mughal to the section of the Muhammadan Turks represented by Bābur and his successors. The Turks and Mongols often associated and intermarried, and Bābur himself, a Turk on the father's side, was of Mongol descent on the mother's side. The Turks resemble Europeans (Aryans) in physique, and are not 'narrow-eyed'.

India and Assam, and even asked the permission of Sultan Iltutmish to do so, but happily desisted from his purpose, and India was spared the unspeakable horrors which befell Central Asia, and from the effects of which those regions have never recovered. Raids by bodies of Mongol troops long continued, and gave much anxiety to the Sultan Ghiyās-ud-dīn Balban, whose eldest son was killed in battle with them. The death of this son, who became known as the Martyr Prince, deeply affected Balban, then about eighty years of age, and hastened his end. On the west the Mongol hordes penetrated into Europe as far as the Dnieper in Russia.

Sultan Kaikobād; end of Slave Kings. When Balban died in 1287 he was succeeded on the throne of Delhi by his grandson Kaikobād (Muizz-ud-dīn), a good-for-nothing, debauched youth. Some Turkish chiefs of the Khalj or Khiljī tribe put him out of the way, and raised to the throne one of themselves, by name Jalāl-ud-dīn. Thus ended in (A.H. 689) A.D. 1290[1] the dynasty of the Turkish Slave-Sultans of Delhi, which had begun with Kutb-ud-dīn Ībak in 1206.

Muhammadan Conquest of Hindustan.

	A.D.
Sultan Muhammad of Ghor (Ghorī, Shihāb-ud-dīn, Muizz-ud-dīn)	
Occupied Ūchh in Sind	1175–6
Defeated by Rājā of Gujarāt	1178–9
Deposed Khusrū Malik of Lahore	1186 or 1187
First battle of Tarāīn	1191
Second battle of Tarāīn	1192
Reduction of Delhi, Kanauj, Benares, and Bihār	1193–7
Conquest of Bengal	1199 or 1200
Capture of Anhilwārā	1197
Capture of Kālanjar	1203
Death of the sultan	1206

[1] Elphinstone's date, A.D. 1288 = A.H. 687, as given by Firishtah, is erroneous.

The Sultans of Delhi.

The Slave Kings.

Kutb-ud-dīn Ībak . .	acc. 1206 (mosque at Delhi)
Ārām Shah	acc. 1210
Īltutmish (Altamsh) . .	acc. 1211 (Mongol invasion, 1221, 1222)
Rukn-ud-dīn and Raziyah .	acc. 1236
Bahrām, &c. . . .	acc. 1240
Nāsir-ud-dīn Mahmūd . .	acc. 1246 (*Tabakāt-i-Nāsirī*)
Balban (Ghiyās-ud-dīn) . .	acc. 1266
Kaikobād (Muizz-ud-dīn) .	acc. 1286 or 1287 killed 1290

CHAPTER XIII

The Khiljī sultans of Delhi: Alā-ud-dīn; the Tughlak dynasty.

Jalāl-ud-dīn Khiljī. Sultan Jalāl-ud-dīn was an old man seventy years of age when he was called to undertake the rule of Hindustan. A famine occurred in A.D. 1291, of such severity that the historian records that multitudes of Hindus, 'from excess of hunger and want', drowned themselves in the Jumna. Jalāl-ud-dīn conducted an indecisive campaign in Mālwā, and, like his predecessors, had to defend his realm against incursions of the Mongols (Mughals of the Muhammadan writers). His forces repelled them from Lahore, and three thousand of the nomads, who surrendered, became Muhammadans and entered the service of the sultan, who allotted them for residence a suburb of Delhi, thence called Mughalpur. Jalāl-ud-dīn, being far advanced in years, left most of the fighting to be done by his brother's son, Alā-ud-dīn, who was also his son-in-law.

Expedition of Alā-ud-dīn to the Deccan. The first attack by the armies of Islam on the countries to the south of the Narbadā was made in A.D. 1294 by Alā-ud-dīn, who marched seven hundred miles into Berār and Khandesh, and compelled Rājā Rāmachandra-deva, the Yādava ruler of Deogiri and the Western Deccan (*ante*, p. 95), to surrender Elichpur with its dependencies. Immense booty was brought to Delhi.

Murder of Jalāl-ud-dīn. Alā-ud-dīn was on bad terms with his wife, the daughter of the sultan, as well as with her mother, and this domestic feud may have influenced him in his treachery to his uncle, who trusted him blindly, and would listen to no warnings. However that may be, the old man was persuaded to place himself in the power of Alā-ud-dīn at Karā in the Allahabad district during the month of Ramazan, A.H. 695 (July 1296), and was there foully murdered as he clasped his nephew's hand.

Alā-ud-dīn Khiljī. The army, won over 'by the hope of the red gold' which Alā-ud-dīn distributed lavishly, condoned the crime and accepted the murderer as sultan. The sons and various relatives and adherents of the old monarch were massacred, and the usurper's throne thus secured. During his reign the Mongols entered India no less than five times, but were always repulsed. The last repulse in 1303, when they threatened Delhi, was so effectual that 'from that day the Mughals lost their enthusiasm for the conquest of Hindustan, and the teeth of their ambition became blunted'. Alā-ud-dīn found the Mongol converts to Islam troublesome, and had a general massacre of them carried out under secret orders on a fixed day in A.D. 1297. He captured the strong fortresses of Ranthambhor and Chitor in Rājputāna.

Malik Kāfūr's conquest of the south. The most notable events of the reign are the campaigns conducted in the south by Malik Kāfūr, a slave eunuch high in the sultan's favour. During the many ages since the time of Samudragupta no northern army seems to have entered the south, except that led into Khāndesh and Berār by Alā-ud-dīn in 1294, during his uncle's reign. These southern campaigns lasted from A.D. 1302 to 1311, and in the course of his operations Malik Kāfūr overran the Yādava kingdom of Deogiri, the Hoysala kingdom of Mysore (Dorasamudra), and the Tamil states of the Far South (*ante*, p. 96). Musalman governors were established on the Ma'abar, or Coromandel coast. The southern currency was then exclusively in gold, of which metal enormous treasures were brought to the capital.

Buildings at Delhi. The sultan employed the wealth thus gained in extensive building operations at Delhi, where he formed a new city called Sīrī, enlarged the Kutbī mosque, and erected a noble gateway. The savagery of the times is illustrated by the remark of Amīr Khusrū, concerning the new fortress at Delhi: 'It is a condition that in a new building blood should be sprinkled; he therefore sacrificed some thousands of goat-bearded Mughals for the purpose'. He began a huge mīnār intended to outshine the creation of Īltutmish, but the work was soon stopped.

Death and character of Alā-ud-dīn. Towards the close of his reign the sultan's health was impaired, and he became the prey of unjust suspicions of others, while placing implicit confidence in the eunuch Kāfūr, who is suspected of having hastened his end. He died in January, A. D. 1316. Alā-ud-dīn was a fierce despot of the Central Asian type—illiterate, arrogant, fanatical, cruel, and sanguinary. He was an able general, and, in times when sultans were not expected to be merciful, was reputed a capable sovereign. He liked to be considered a 'second Alexander', and used that title in his coin legends. His internal policy was characterized by many arbitrary and vexatious regulations, which died with him. As regards the Hindus, the bulk of his subjects, his policy was to 'grind them down' and reduce them to poverty.

Kutb-ud-dīn Mubārak. Malik Kāfūr tried to retain power by placing on the throne an infant son of the deceased sultan, but the minister was promptly assassinated, and an adult son of Alā-ud-dīn's, by name Kutb-ud-dīn Mubārak, was made sultan. At first he showed some energy, marching into the Deccan and defeating Harapāla, the Yādava Rājā of Deogiri, whom he cruelly flayed alive. On his return he gave himself up to filthy sensuality, and allowed a low-born Hindu convert, Khusrū Khan, to mismanage state affairs. In 1320 this minister murdered his worthless master and seized the throne. He tried to organize a Hindu reaction during his brief tenure of power, but had not the personal qualities deserving of success. Four months later he paid the penalty of his ill deeds, and was himself killed by Fakhr-ud-dīn Jūnā Khan, son of Ghāzī Khan (or Malik or Beg) Tughlak, governor of the Panjāb. Ghāzī Khan was invited by the nobles to assume the royal power, and, in 1320 (A. H. 720), became sultan under the style of Ghiyās-ud-dīn.

The Tughlak dynasty ; Ghiyās-ud-dīn. The new sovereign is said to have been the son of a Turk slave of the Sultan Balban by a Hindu Jat mother. Certainly he was not a 'Pathan'. During his reign of four years he won a good reputation as an administrator, and reduced to a certain amount of obedience the Muhammadan princes who then ruled Bengal and Eastern Bengal in practical independence. In February, A. D. 1325 (A. H. 725), he was killed by the fall of a pavilion erected for his reception by his son Fakhr-ud-dīn Jūnā. There is good reason for believing that the 'accident' was caused intentionally.

Muhammad Ādil, son of Tughlak. No opposition was made to the assumption of power by Jūnā, who is generally known to history as Muhammad, son of (*bin*) Tughlak. He enjoyed a long reign of twenty-six years, and during the earlier part of it controlled twenty-three provinces, a dominion far larger than that of any of his predecessors. But the empire never was at rest ; no sooner was one section brought back to its allegiance than another would seek to assert its independence, and by the end of Muhammad's reign it was falling to pieces.

A vein of insanity ran through the sultan's character, which is rightly described by Badāonī as 'a mixture of opposites'. His natural great abilities were constantly perverted, and he could not resist indulgence in mad schemes, which ruined his people and shook the throne. In spite of all, he died in his bed ; as the historian observes, 'at length disease overcame him, and the sultan was freed from his people, and the people from their sultan.' This deliverance was accomplished in March, A. D. 1351, near Tatta (Thattah) in Sind, where the sultan was engaged, as usual, in the pursuit of rebels.

Transfer of capital to Daulatabad. One of the maddest of his schemes was the transfer of the capital from Delhi to Deogiri in the Deccan, which he renamed Daulatabad. The tyrant's order was carried out with such ruthless completeness that Delhi 'became so deserted that there was not left even a dog or a cat in the city'. Ibn Batuta, the contemporary traveller, found Delhi 'almost a desert', and tells a gruesome story that, the sultan's 'servants finding a blind man in one of the houses and a bedridden man in another, the emperor commanded the bedridden man to be projected from a balista, and the blind one to be dragged by his feet to Daulatabad, which is at the distance of ten days, and he was so dragged; but his limbs dropping off by the way, only one of his legs was brought to the place intended, and was then thrown into it; for the order had been that they should go to this place'. The unhappy people were afterwards forced to return to Delhi.

Other mad schemes; cruelty. The sultan aspired to the fame of a universal conqueror, and accordingly collected a vast army for the subjugation of Persia, which dispersed without effecting anything beyond pillage of his subjects. Again, he thought to subdue China and sent 100,000 men into the Himalayas, where 80,000, mostly cavalry, perished miserably. In order to provide funds for his schemes of world-wide conquest, he tried to force people to take copper or brass money as silver, engraving upon it the legend, 'He who obeys the sultan, truly, he obeys God'. But, of course, the scheme failed in practice, 'till at last copper became copper, and silver, silver', while heaps of the brass coins lay at Tughlakabad (a Delhi fort), 'and had no more value than stones'. His administration, which he believed to be the perfection of justice, was so cruel and sanguinary that 'there was constantly in front of his royal pavilion and his civil court a mound of dead bodies and a heap of corpses, while the sweepers and executioners were weary of dragging the wretched victims and putting them to death in crowds. So that the people were never tired of rebelling, nor the king of punishing'. He also committed frightful massacres on a large scale, and is said to have organized man-hunts, driving men and women like game to the slaughter.

Ruin of the empire. In the earlier days of his reign Muhammad had completed the reduction of the Deccan and brought it into some sort of order like the home provinces. But Bengal secured its independence about 1340, and before the end of the reign the Deccan, conquered with so much difficulty, had shaken off its allegiance.

Character of Muhammad bin Tughlak. Mr. E. Thomas has fairly summed up this 'mixture of opposites' by describing him as 'learned, merciless, religious, and mad'. He was eloquent, accomplished, skilled in Arabic, Persian, logic, mathematics, and Greek philosophy. He abstained from strong drink, the ruin of so many kings of Delhi, led a moral life, and was distinguished for his personal gallantry. But all these fine qualities were more than neutralized by his savage temper and insane ambitions, so that his reign stands out as one of the most calamitous in Indian history.

CHAPTER XIV

Decline of the sultanate of Delhi: Fīrōz and the other successors of Muhammad bin Tughlak; Tīmūr; the Lodī dynasty.

Fīrōz Shah Tughlak. Fīrōz, the first cousin and designated heir of Sultan Muhammad Ādil, was invited by the nobles present at Thattah to accept the crown and rescue the state. Fīrōz accepted his election with great reluctance. As soon as possible, and with much difficulty, he brought back the army to the capital. Three years later he built the new city of Fīrōzabad near Delhi. The sultan's principal interest lay in building and the carrying out of public works. Fīrōz Shah's name is now chiefly remembered for the system of canals which he constructed for the supply of water from both the Jumna and the Sutlaj. Although most of these works have been obliterated by changes in the courses of the rivers and other causes, one of them still exists in a modified form and does good service as the Western Jumna canal.

Events of his reign. In 1356 Fīrōz Shah held the whole of Hindustan, except Bengal, which he twice attempted to subdue; and was, of course, obliged to assert his authority in Hindustan by expeditions in various directions. As he grew old he left affairs of state almost entirely in the hands of his ministers, a father and son, who both took the title of Khan-i-Jahān. As early as 1359 he had associated his own son, Fath Khan, with himself in the royal power, and long after the death of that son he made another son, Muhammad Shah, his colleague in 1387, but in the next year removed him and nominated a grandson in his place. Fīrōz Shah does not seem to have been ever well fitted for his position by reason of strength of will, but he was a man of lofty character and merciful disposition, and has deservedly left a good reputation behind him.

Fīrōz a bigot. The praises lavished by Muhammadan historians on the personal character and comparatively peaceful reign of Fīrōz Shah must be qualified by recognition of the fact that he was a thoroughgoing Sunnī bigot, like Aurangzeb in a later age. A brief tract written by the Sultan himself is extant. In it he relates with pride how he caused a Brahman to be burnt alive for practising Hindu rites in public. He also tells us that he cut off the heads of certain Shīa missionaries, and that he destroyed all new idol temples, executing the builders as a warning that Hindus should not take liberties 'in a Musalman country'. He encouraged his Hindu subjects to embrace the religion of the prophet by promising exemption from the poll-tax (*jizya*), in consequence of which promise 'great numbers of Hindus presented themselves and were admitted to the honour of Islam'. It is thus clear that he regarded himself as the sultan of the Muslim minority, not as the impartial sovereign of all races in his dominions.

Successors of Fīrōz Shah. The death of Fīrōz Shah in September 1388, at the age of 79, was followed by a prolonged struggle for the succession between various sons and grandsons, the details of which have been related by the Muhammadan historians, but are not worthy of remembrance. A series of worthless or puppet sultans pass across the stage, without doing anything deserving of record. The kingdom dwindled almost to nothing, and at one time, for three years, from about 1394 to 1397, things came to such a pass that Sultan Mahmūd was known as king in Old Delhi, while his relative Nasrat Shah enjoyed the same rank and title in Fīrōzābād, a few miles distant. 'Day by day', Badāonī says, 'battles were fought between these two kings, who were like the two kings in the game of chess.' 'And', he adds, 'all over Hindustan there arose parties each with its own Malik' (lord).

Tīmūr. Towards the end of A. D. 1398 this squalid squabbling was stilled by the irruption of another terrible chieftain from Central Asia, Tīmūr the Lame, the Tamerlane of tradition, who entered India by way of Multān, and reached Fīrōzabad near Delhi, 'sweeping the greater part of the country with the bitter whirlwind of rapine and pillage'. At his camp opposite Delhi he butchered 50,000, or, according to some authorities, 100,000, prisoners, not even sparing the Indian-born Musalmans, although himself a Muhammadan, and found little difficulty in occupying Delhi, which he sacked without mercy. Happily he did not stay long. When departing, he made over the charge of the city and its dependencies to Khizr Khan, a reputed Saiyid, and then returned to Samarkand. At that time Mahmūd Tughlak, the last of his line, and always 'a very shadow of a king', was the nominal sultan of Delhi. He lived until February, A. D. 1413. After the departure of Tīmūr 'such a famine and pestilence fell upon the capital that the city was utterly ruined, and those of the inhabitants who were left died, while for two whole months not a bird moved a wing in Delhi'.

Dynasty of the so-called Saiyids. Khizr Khan, whom Tīmūr had left in charge, died in A. D. 1421, after some seven years of constant fighting. He was succeeded on the precarious throne of his limited dominions in the neighbourhood of Delhi by three members of his family, the last of whom, Alā-ud-dīn or Ālam Shah, abdicated in 1451, and retired to Budaon, which he was permitted to rule in peace by virtue of a friendly agreement with Bahlōl Lodī, an Afghan noble, who had made himself the leading man in the state.

The Patān (Pathān), or Afghan, Lodī dynasty; Sultan Bahlōl. Bahlōl Lodī, who assumed the cares of sovereignty in 1451, really was an Afghan or Pathān, and is the first person entitled to be called a 'Pathan king of Delhi'. At that time the kingdom of Jaunpur had been independent for more than fifty years, and at the beginning of his reign Bahlōl had to accept the situation, the king of Jaunpur and he agreeing to retain their respective possessions. Sultan Bahlōl could not endure this rival monarch, and presently engaged in wars, in which he uniformly won, while Sultan Husain 'met with the defeat which had become a second nature to him'. Ultimately Bahlōl annexed the Jaunpur kingdom, known as the Sharkī, or Eastern, and bestowed it on his son Bārbak Shah. In July 1489 (A. H. 894) Bahlōl died in the Doāb. He is described as 'a man of simple habits, pious, brave, and generous'.

Sikandar Lodī. On hearing of the death of Bahlōl, one of his sons named Nizām Khan, hastened to Delhi, and was proclaimed sultan under the title of Sikandar without serious opposition. His elder brother, Bārbak Shah of Jaunpur, after a time came to terms, and tendered his allegiance. Sultan Husain, the ex-king of Jaunpur, also tried to recover his heritage, but was defeated as usual. Sultan Sikandar then annexed Bihār and Tirhūt, which had been held by the king of Jaunpur, and occupied much time in bringing the territories near Gwalior into subjection. He had an intense horror of idolatry, and made a point of destroying all the temples and images which he came across. Muhammadan writers give him a good character, and praise his administration as having been just and vigorous. We have no record of Hindu opinion. After a prosperous reign of twenty-eight years, during which he had extended his dominions considerably, he passed away in November, A.D. 1517.

Earthquake; buildings at Agra. A notable event of his time was the earthquake in A.D. 1505, which shook the whole of Hindustan and Persia, so that 'men supposed that the day of resurrection had arrived', and believed that no such earthquake had been known since the days of Adam. Sikandar was the first of the kings of Delhi to make Agra his occasional residence. The village of Sikandra, where Akbar's mausoleum stands, bears his name, and the building there known as the Bāradarī is a palace built by him in 1495.

Ibrāhīm Lodī. The nobles selected Ibrāhīm, the third son of Sikandar, to succeed his father as sultan of Delhi, bestowing the kingdom of Jaunpur on the second son, Sultan Jalāl. This arrangement naturally led to friction, and a war between Ibrāhīm and his brother of Jaunpur ended in the destruction of Jalāl. Ibrāhīm could not get on well with his nobles, and was troubled continually with revolts, which he punished with arrogant severity. Ultimately Daulat Khan Lodī, a governor in the Panjāb, applied for help against his sovereign to Bābur, king of Kābul, who gladly seized the opportunity for invading India. On the field of Pānīpat, to the north of Delhi, and not very distant from the ancient battlefields of Kurukshetra and Tarāīn, on April 21, 1526, Ibrāhīm met Bābur, and suffered a crushing defeat, which cost him his throne and life.

Interruption of the narrative. The battle will be described in connexion with the reign of Bābur, but before we enter on the history of the Mughal dynasty, it will be well to pause and take note of the principal kingdoms which shaped themselves in various parts of India during the decay of the Sultanate of Delhi following on the death of Muhammad bin Tughlak. We shall also pass briefly in review the state of society, religion, literature, and art during the period of the Delhi sultanate (A. D. 1206–1526), commonly miscalled the 'Pathān empire'.

The Sultans of Delhi.

The Khilji (Khalji) Dynasty

(Omitting some minor names).

Jalāl-ud-dīn (Fīrōz Shah)	acc.	1290
Famine		1291
Annexation of Elichpur		1294
Alā-ud-dīn (Muhammad Shah)	acc.	1296
Massacre of Mongol converts		1297
Southern campaigns of Malik Kāfūr		1302–11
Mongol raid		1303
Kutb-ud-dīn Mubārak	acc.	1316
Destruction of Harapāla Yādava		1318
[Khusrū Khan (Nāsir-ud-dīn), usurper		1320]

Tughlak Dynasty.

Ghiyās-ud-dīn	acc.	1320
Muhammad Ādil (Fakhr-ud-dīn-Jūnā)	acc.	Feb. 1325
Fīrōz Shah	acc.	Mar. 1351
	died	1388
Struggle for the succession		1388–1451
(Including the so-called Saiyid dynasty)		1414–51)
Sack of Delhi by Tīmūr		1398

The Lodī Dynasty.

Bahlōl	acc.	1451
Sikandar (Nizām Khan)	acc.	1489
Earthquake		1505
Ibrāhīm		1517
Battle (first) of Pānīpat		1526

CHAPTER XV

The Muhammadan kingdoms of Bengal, Jaunpur, Gujarāt, Mālwā, and the Deccan: the Hindu kingdoms of Vijayanagar, Mewār, and Orissa; literature and architecture; the Urdu language; spread of Muhammadanism; Hindu religious sects.

The Muhammadan kingdom of Bengal. From the time of the successful raid by Muhammad, the son of Bakhtyār, in A.D. 1199 (*ante*, p. 115), Bengal was considered to be a province of the sultanate of Delhi, and its rulers were regarded officially as the deputies of the sultans. But the control of Delhi was little more than nominal, and the governors of Bengal, twenty-five in number, between 1193 and 1338, usually could do what they liked. The Muhammadan province of Bengal, or Lakhnauti, ordinarily consisted of the territory bounded by the Sundarbans on the south, by the Brahmaputra on the east, by Kūch Bihār and the Tarāi on the north, and by the Kosi river on the west. But at times Tirhūt and South Bihār were added to the kingdom, which did not include either Orissa or Chutia Nagpur. The three ancient capitals, Gaur or Lakhnauti, Pandua or Fīrōzabad, and Tānda were all situated in the Mālda District.

Iliyās Shah and his successors. During the reign of Muhammad bin Tughlak (*ante*, p. 125) Iliyās Shah established himself as independent king, and was formally recognized as such by Sultan Fīrōz in 1355. He was reputed to be a vigorous and successful ruler. His son, Sikandar Shah (1358–89), equally capable, is famous as the builder of the Ādīnah mosque at Pandua, apparently copied from the great mosque at Damascus, and regarded as the finest building in Bengal.

Husain Shah and Nasrat Shah. Husain Shah (1493–1518) is considered to have been the best and greatest of the Muhammadan kings of Bengal. He gave shelter and a residence to Sultan Husain of Jaunpur, when that prince was turned out of his kingdom by Bahlōl Lodī (*ante*, p. 128). The occupation by the Lodī sultan of Bihār, which had been held by the kings of Jaunpur, brought the sultans of Bengal and Delhi into direct touch with one another. Nasrat Shah of Bengal (1518–32) annexed Tirhūt, and consequently was attacked by Bābur, but peace was made.

Sher Shah and his Afghan successors. After Bābur's death in 1530 a long struggle ensued between Sher Shah, the Afghan governor of Bihār, and Bābur's son Humāyun. In the course of this struggle Sher Shah made himself sultan of Bengal, and a little later (1520) became for a time also the king of Delhi. Sher Shah's dynasty soon came to an end, and another line of Afghan chiefs obtained the sultanate of Bengal. The last of this line, Dāūd Shah, was defeated and executed by Akbar's general in 1576, from which time Bengal became a province or Sūba of the Mughal empire. Subsequently Orissa was nominally included in the Sūba of Bengal, but was never thoroughly mastered by the Musalman governments.

The Muhammadan kingdom of Jaunpur. The history of the kingdom of Jaunpur is short, extending over less than a century. The present city was founded by Fīrōz Shah of the Tughlak dynasty in A. D. 1360, on the site of a Hindu town. In 1394 the powerful noble Khwāja Jahān was appointed by Mahmūd Tughlak to be the Lord of the East (*Malik-us-shark*), with his head-quarters at Jaunpur. The troubles ensuing on the sack of Delhi by Tīmūr in A. D. 1398 (*ante*, p. 127) enabled Khwāja Jahān's adopted son to sever the slight bond of allegiance which bound him to Delhi, and to set up as a king with the style of Mubārak Shah Sharkī.

Ibrāhīm and his successors. He was succeeded by his younger brother Ibrāhīm, the most famous of the Jaunpur kings, who reigned prosperously from 1400 to 1440. He is described by Abūl Fazl, from the Muhammadan point of view, as 'an active and good prince, equally beloved in life, as he was regretted by all his subjects'. Perhaps the Hindus may have thought otherwise, for Ibrāhīm is also described as 'a bigoted Musalman, and a steady if not a bloody persecutor'. Unluckily, no Hindu version of the story of the sultanate of Delhi and other kingdoms exists. All our information comes from Muslim writers who believed in the merit of sending Hindus 'to hell'—to use their habitual language. Ibrāhīm's son Mahmūd was equally able, and conducted his wars with success. The last independent king of Jaunpur was the unlucky Sultan Husain, who was driven from his throne by Bahlōl Lodī in 1476, and took refuge with his namesake in Bengal (*ante*, p. 127). Bahlōl appointed his own eldest son Bārbak to be viceroy of the Jaunpur kingdom in 1486. Bahlōl's successor, Sikandar Lodī, completed the reduction of the Jaunpur dominions, including Bihār.

Literature and art under the kings of Jaunpur. All the members of the Sharkī dynasty were patrons of Persian and Arabic literature, and Sultan Husain, although unfortunate in war, was distinguished as a musician and composer. The reputation of Jaunpur stood so high that the city was described as 'the Shirāz of India'. The great mosques of Jaunpur, the Atāla, built by Ibrāhīm, the Lāl or Red, built by his son, and the Jāmi, built by Husain, are among the most notable monuments of the miscalled 'Pathan' architecture. These mosques have no minarets and are characterized by their massive and imposing gateways with walls sloping inwards.

The Muhammadan kingdom of Gujarāt. Gujarāt, the fine province corresponding to the northern parts of the Bombay Presidency, with Baroda and the southern portion of Rājputāna, was annexed by Sultan Muhammad of Ghor in 1196, and thenceforward continued to be more or less subject to the rulers of Delhi until the invasion of Tīmūr in 1398. At that time the governor, like his colleague in Jaunpur, set up as an independent king under the title of Muzaffar Shah. His grandson, Ahmad Shah (1411–43), founded Ahmadabad, which replaced Anhilwāra as the capital, and waged many wars with Mālwā and other neighbouring states.

Mahmūd Shah and Bahādur Shah. The best and most renowned of the kings of Gujarāt was Mahmūd Shah Bīgarha, who came to the throne as a boy of thirteen, and reigned for fifty-two years (1459–1511). He carried on a long war with the Rānā of Mewār, and was victorious in many conflicts with his neighbours. He was less successful in his resistance to the Portuguese, who were now becoming a power in Western India, and lost his fleet in a battle fought with them off Diu in 1509. At about the same time Sikandar Lodī, the sultan of Delhi, recognized the independence of the kingdom of Gujarāt. Bahādur Shah, fourth son and successor of Mahmūd, annexed the kingdom of Mālwā in 1531 and three years later besieged and took the famous fortress of Chitor from the Rānā of Mewār.

The last sultan of Gujarāt was crushed in 1572 by Akbar,

who annexed the kingdom to his empire, completing the conquest in 1592–3.

Architecture in Gujarāt. Many very beautiful Hindu and Jain temples, erected in the time of Siddharāja and Kumārapāla (*ante*, p. 105), served to a large extent as materials and models for the equally beautiful architecture of the Muhammadan kings. Ahmadabad was made the handsomest city in India, and still deserved that epithet at the end of the sixteenth century, its buildings being unsurpassed for elegance, grace, and profuse decoration. Architecture is still a living art in Gujarāt, which is almost the only province where modern architects retain the early traditions of their craft and to a considerable extent the skill of the ancients.

The Muhammadan kingdom of Mālwā. Mālwā, which had been conquered by Alā-ud-dīn Khiljī, and then administered by governors for about a century, became independent shortly after Tīmūr's invasion. The most famous of its kings was Hoshang Shah (1405–35), who made Māndū the capital. The buildings of that city rivalled those of Ahmadabad. For a short time (1531) Mālwā was absorbed by Gujarāt, and in 1564 it was annexed to the empire of Delhi by Akbar.

The Muhammadan kingdom of Khāndesh. The small kingdom of Khāndesh in the valley of the Tāptī became independent, like so many other provinces, in the closing years of the fourteenth century, and continued to exist under the government of a family of Arab descent until A. D. 1610, when Akbar's son, Prince Dāniyāl, took the fortress of Asīrgarh, which commanded the road to the Deccan. The prince was made governor of the conquered province, to which in compliment to him the emperor gave the name of Dāndesh.

The Muhammadan kingdoms of the Deccan: the Bahmanī kingdom. The numerous independent states formed in the Deccan can be noticed only very briefly. An Afghan officer named Hasan, and surnamed Gangū Bahmanī, established during the reign of Muhammad bin Tughlak (1347) an extensive kingdom with its capital first at Gulbarga, in the south-

Gateway, Atāla devī Mosque, Jaunpur

west of the territory now constituting the Nizam's dominions, and afterwards at Bīdar, sixty miles distant.[1] The dynasty became known as the Bahmanī from the surname of its founder. For more than a century (1374–1482) the Bahmanī kingdom stretched right across India from sea to sea, including a large part of what is now the Bombay Presidency, as well as the Nizam's dominions, and the 'Northern Circars' of the Madras Presidency. The kings were mostly engaged in war with the powerful Hindu state of Vijayanagar on the south, which then dominated the whole of the Tamil territory. After 1482 the kingdom was split up, and the later Bahmanī kings had merely nominal rank. A Turkish officer founded a small independent principality, which is known to history as the kingdom of Bīdar, and lasted for more than a century. The rulers of this principality are called the Barīd Shahis.

Other Muhammadan kingdoms: Bijāpur. The Bahmanī dynasty, which saw its best days in the early part of the fifteenth century, was no longer able to control the more distant territories in the time of its decline. In 1490 a Turkish governor of Bijāpur threw off his allegiance, and set up as an independent king. The dynasty so founded, known as the Ādil Shahi from the title of its founder, lasted until 1686, when Aurangzeb put an end to it. The ancient city is said to measure thirty miles round, and impresses all visitors by the grandeur of its ruins. The great mosques and tombs of the Ādil Shahi kings, which differ much in style from those at Agra and Delhi, are pronounced by a good judge to be 'scarcely, if at all, inferior in originality of design and boldness of execution'.

Ahmadnagar. The Nizām Shahi dynasty of Ahmadnagar was founded at about the same time as the Ādil Shahi by another rebellious governor, Ahmad Shahi, son of Nizām-ul-mulk. The details of its history are not of general interest, and it will be sufficient to note that a gallant lady, Chānd Bībī, had the good fortune to repulse Akbar in 1596. Four years

[1] Mr. Sewell spells 'Kulburga', but Gulbarga seems to be correct.

THE COUNCIL HALL, VIJAYANAGAR

later the capital fell temporarily into the hands of the emperor, who formally constituted a Sūba, or province of Ahmadnagar, but an Abyssinian minister named Malik Ambar recovered possession of the city, and the final annexation of the kingdom did not take place until 1637.

Golkonda. The kingdom of Golkonda (more accurately, Gulkandah), another fragment of the Bahmanī dominion, separated in 1512. The dynasty, known as the Kutb Shahi, lasted until 1687, when it was suppressed by Aurangzeb. Golkonda is close to Hyderabad, now the capital of the Nizām's dominions. The ancient fortress, which contains some magnificent tombs, is used by the Nizam as a state prison and treasure-house.

Berār or Elichpur. Yet another revolted governor set up a small kingdom in Berār, with its capital at Elichpur, which lasted for about eighty-four years, until 1574, when it was annexed by Ahmadnagar. The kings are spoken of as the Imād Shahi dynasty.

The five sultans of the Deccan : summary. Thus it appears that on the ruins of the Bahmanī kingdom arose five distinct Muhammadan sultanates, namely :

(1) the Barīd Shahis of Bīdar ;
(2) the Ādil Shahis of Bijāpur ;
(3) the Nizām Shahis of Ahmadnagar ;
(4) the Kutb Shahis of Golkonda ; and
(5) the Imād Shahis of Berār or Elichpur.

The history of Southern India between A. D. 1400 and 1565 may be summed up as that of a conflict between the Hindu kingdom of Vijayanagar and the five sultans of the Deccan, which ended in the decisive victory of the Musalman powers, who in their turn were forced to bow before the might of the Mughal emperors of Delhi.

The Hindu kingdom of Vijayanagar. Shortly after the destruction by Muhammad bin Tughlak of the Hoysala power (*ante*, p. 95) five brothers, feudatories of that state, began to create an independent kingdom to the south of the Krishnā and Tungabhadra rivers. Two of them, Harihara I and Bukka

(A.D. 1336–76) are counted as the first two kings of Vijayanagar. The new kingdom grew so quickly that during the lifetime of the brothers the Muhammadans were driven from Madura, the old Pāndya capital, and the Chola kingdom also was absorbed in the dominions of the new-born state. The learned Brahman Mādhavācharya, and his brother Sāyana, the famous commentator on the Vedas and other sacred literature, were ministers of the first three kings.

The city. The capital was established at Vijayanagar, now represented by the extensive ruins at Hampi and the neighbourhood in the Bellary District of Madras. The kings, who were Kanarese by birth, assumed the Kanarese title of Rāya. Under their care the city progressed with such rapidity that when it was visited in 1443 by a Persian ambassador named Abdur Razzāk, it was one of the most magnificent cities in Asia. Its ruins, which have been surveyed recently in detail, are crowded with fine Hindu buildings, and cover many square miles. The city was protected, like ancient Kanauj and Delhi, by seven distinct lines of fortifications, and its bazaars swarmed with dealers in all the commodities of the eastern world.

A few sentences from Abdur Razzāk's detailed description may be quoted :

'The city is such that the pupil of the eye has never seen a place like it, and the ear of intelligence has never been informed that there existed anything to equal it in the world. It is built in such a manner that seven citadels and the same number of walls enclose each other. Around the first citadel are stones of the height of a man, one half of which is sunk in the ground, while the other half rises above it. These are fixed one beside the other in such a manner that no horse or foot soldier could boldly or with ease approach the citadel. . . .

'Above each bazaar is a lofty arcade with a magnificent gallery, but the audience-hall of the king's palace is elevated above all the rest. The bazaars are extremely long and broad.

'Roses are sold everywhere. These people could not live without roses, and they look upon them as quite as necessary as food. . . . Each class of men belonging to each profession has shops contiguous the one to the other ; the jewellers sell publicly in the bazaars pearls, rubies, emeralds, and diamonds. In this agreeable locality, as well as in the king's palace, one sees numerous running streams and canals formed of chiselled stone, polished and smooth. . . . This empire contains so great a population that it would be impossible to give an idea of it without entering into extensive details. In the king's palace are several cells, like basins, filled with bullion, forming one mass. . . . The throne, which was of extraordinary size, was made of gold, and enriched with precious stones of extreme value.'

Government, &c., of the kingdom. Portuguese authors, especially one named Nuñiz, who wrote about 1535, give a vivid picture of the government, administration, and institutions of the Vijayanagar kingdom or empire in the days of its splendour.

The government was of the most absolute kind possible, the king's power over everybody, great or small, being without check of any kind. All the attendance on the king was done by women, many of whom were armed.

'These kings of Bisnaga eat all sorts of things, but not the flesh of oxen or cows, which they never kill in all the country of the heathen because they worship them. They eat mutton, pork, venison, partridges, hares, doves, quail, and all kinds of birds; even sparrows, and rats, and cats, and lizards, all of which are sold in the city of Bisnaga.'[1]

The empire was divided into about two hundred provinces or districts, each under the control of a governor, who was absolute in his domain, but was himself entirely at the mercy of the king. Each governor had to supply a certain number of equipped soldiers. The army thus raised numbered fully a million of men. A huge revenue was collected. While the king and nobles lived in luxury, the common people were ground down to the dust, and left barely enough to support life.

The punishments for crime were of appalling severity.

[1] Bisnaga is the Portuguese form of the name. 'Heathen' means Hindus, as distinguished from 'Moors', or Muslims.

'For a thief, whatever theft he commits, howsoever little it be, they forthwith cut off a foot and a hand, and if his theft be a great one he is hanged with a hook under his chin.'

It is not surprising to be told that thieves were 'very few'. Impalement and the other horrible penalties then common throughout India were also inflicted.

Duelling was permitted, with the sanction of the minister, and persons who fought duels were held in high honour. The victor was given the estate of the opponent whom he killed.[2] Suttee (*satī*) was widely practised, and when the king died, four or five hundred of his women had to burn with him. Telugu women were buried alive with their husbands.

Such was life under a purely Hindu government in the early part of the sixteenth century.

Later history of Vijayanagar; Krishnarāya Deva. As already observed, the external history of the Vijayanagar kingdom may be summed up in the statement that the Rāyas were engaged continually in fighting their Musalman rivals—at first the Bahmanī kingdom, and then the five sultanates of the Deccan. The most notable of the Rāyas was Krishnarāya Deva (1509–29) who overcame the armies of Orissa, Golkonda, and Bijāpur. He was the last great Hindu sovereign of Southern India. Krishnarāya Deva was famous for his religious zeal and catholicity.

'His kindness to the fallen enemy, his acts of mercy and charity towards the residents of captured cities, his great military prowess, which endeared him alike to his feudatory chiefs and to his subjects, the royal reception and kindness that he invariably bestowed upon foreign embassies, his imposing personal appearance, his genial look and polite conversation which distinguished a pure and dignified life, his love for

[1] Mr. Frederick Fawcett informs me that in the Malabar District the custom of duelling among the Nairs was well remembered less than twenty years ago, and celebrated in popular ballads. The weapons used were swords.

literature and for religion, and his solicitude for the welfare of his people, and above all, the almost fabulous wealth that he conferred as endowments on temples and Brahmans, mark him out indeed as the greatest of the South Indian monarchs who sheds a lustre on the pages of history.' [1]

Battle of Talikota. When Sadāsiva became nominal Rāya, the actual power was wielded by his brother-in-law, Rāmarāja, whose arrogance so incensed his neighbours that the five sultans laid aside their private quarrels to combine against the common Hindu enemy. Enormous armies on both sides met in battle in January 1565, at a spot to the north of the Tungabhadra not far from the capital. The battle is known in history by the name of Talikota, although that village is distant from the scene of the conflict. The Hindu host was utterly defeated, and Rāmarāja was captured and killed. His splendid city was mercilessly sacked, and ever since has lain desolate.

Grant of the site of Madras. The history of the kingdom of Vijayanagar as an important dominant state ends with the disaster of Talikota, but the successors of Sadāsiva long ruled a considerable principality in the south, with their capital at first at Penukonda, and afterwards at Chandragiri. In 1640 (N.S.) the Rājā of Chandragiri, in consideration of a yearly rent, executed a conveyance of a strip of sandbank, situated on the bank of the Couum river to the north of the decayed Portuguese settlement of San Thomé, in favour of Mr. Francis Day, a British merchant, Member of Council in the East India Company's Agency at Masulipatam. On the site so granted the city of Madras was founded. The gold plate on which the conveyance is said to have been recorded is alleged to have been lost during the French occupation of Madras, 1746–9.

The Hindu state of Mewār (Udaipur). The Rānā of Mewār, who belongs to the Sīsodia or Çahlot clan of Rājpūts, is admittedly the premier Rājpūt prince. His ancestors never

[1] Krishna Sastri, 'The Second Vijayanagara Dynasty', in *Ann. Rep. A. S., India*, 1908-9, p. 186.

permitted the purity of their blood to be defiled by marriage of their daughters with the Mughal emperors, and their state never submitted to Musalman power, except to Jahāngīr on honourable terms. The ancient capital, the famous fortress of Chitor, is supposed to have been occupied in the eighth century. Its three sieges, by Alā-ud-dīn Khiljī in 1303, by Bahādur Shah of Gujarāt in 1534, and by Akbar in 1567, gave occasion for the display of prodigies of valour by the Rājpūt defenders, and for ghastly tragedies in the sacrifice of the women by fire (*johar*) to save them from capture. After the last siege the Rānā changed his residence to Udaipur, which has been the capital ever since. The two towers at Chitor known as the Kīrti Stambh and Jai Stambh are notable works of Hindu art. The conflict between Rānā Sanga and Bābur will be noticed in the next chapter.

The Hindu kingdom of Orissa. Orissa, including the modern Division of that name in the province of Bihār and Orissa, as well as the Ganjām and Vizagapatam Districts of Madras, always lay by reason of its situation outside the main stream of Indian history. During the greater part of the period of the sultanate of Delhi the country was governed by the Eastern Ganga dynasty. The first of this line in Orissa, Anantavarman Cholaganga, reigned for seventy-one years (A. D. 1076–1147), and established his power over the whole territory between the Ganges and Godāvarī. The temple of Jagannāth at Puri was built under his orders towards the close of the eleventh century.

Muhammadan attacks on Orissa. The Muhammadan historians apply the name of Jājnagar to Orissa. The first Muhammadan inroad into the province was made by an officer of Muhammad-i-Bakhtyār in 1205. Later incursions were led by Fīrōz Shah and others, tempted by the facilities for obtaining elephants in the country. Akbar subdued the kingdom more or less completely, and attached it to the Sūba of Bengal. The way had been prepared for this measure by the invasion of Kāla Pāhār, a general of the sultan of Bengal, a few years earlier.

Orissan architecture. The province offers a long series of fine examples of the 'Indo-Aryan' style of temples with heavy steeples and few pillars. The noble temple of the Sun (Konārka, Kanaruc) at Konakona is proved by inscriptions to have been built or rebuilt by Rājā Nrisimha in the thirteenth century (1238–64), but looks, and probably is in part, much older. The magnificent group of temples at Bhuvanesvar appears to extend over a considerable period.

Government of the sultans of Delhi. The government of the sultans of Delhi was an absolute despotism, tempered by rebellion and assassination. The control over distant provinces was lax and slight, and the bonds which connected them with Delhi were easily broken in the disturbed times which followed the tyranny of Muhammad bin Tughlak. The subordinate governments were equally despotic, and when the rulers were Musalmans the Hindus generally seem to have had a bad time. Fīrōz Shah Tughlak was the only sultan who cared to execute public works for the general benefit.

Literature and architecture. Many of the Muhammadan princes had a nice taste in Persian literature, which they liberally patronized, and, as we have seen (*ante*, p. 105), the Hindu Rājās often maintained brilliant courts and encouraged Sanskrit letters. The numerous splendid architectural works in the various provinces have been noticed, as well as some of the buildings with which Delhi was adorned. The name of Delhi is applied for convenience to a series of cities beginning with the Old Delhi (Dillī) of Ānanga Pāla in the eleventh century and extending to the New Delhi (Shahjahānabad) of Shahjahān in the seventeenth. Yet another Delhi is now being built to serve as the official capital of India from 1912, in pursuance of the command of H.M. the King-Emperor. The architecture of the sultanate—that is to say, of the Muhammadan buildings—was designed in various foreign styles, executed and modified by Hindu architects, whom the conquerors were obliged to employ. The term 'Pathan architecture' is as erroneous and misleading as the corresponding terms 'Pathan kings' and 'Pathan empire'. The architects imitated various Muslim buildings in Damascus, Mecca, and other places.

The Urdu language. The Urdu, or Persianized Hindustani, language grew up gradually as a means of communication between the foreign conquerors, who generally spoke either Turkī or Persian, and their Hindu subjects. The Western Hindī dialect of Delhi and the upper Doāb is the basis of the language now called Hindustani. When Persian and Arabic words and phrases are freely admitted, that language takes the name of Urdu. The word Urdu is the Turkī for 'camp', and is the origin of the English word 'horde'. It was specially applied to the encampment of the warrior Musalman kings, whose camp was their court, and in the Mughal period coins are often marked as struck in the *urdū*, or royal camp. The Urdu language, therefore, means the form of Hindustani, or polished Western Hindī, spoken about the court, and thus diffused, in several varieties, over the greater part of India. The earliest Urdu literature, written in verse, in the *Rekhta* dialect, was composed in the Deccan towards the close of the sixteenth century. Urdu prose is a recent development under English influence.

Spread of Muhammadanism. We have seen something of the ferocity displayed by the early Muhammadan conquerors against Hindus, Jains, and Buddhists, all equally hated because of their use of images in worship. Occasionally a Hindu Rājā and his followers were tempted to save their lives by professing the creed of Islam, and many of the Indian Musalman families of the present day are descended from converts made at the point of the sword in the period of the sultanate. Desire to escape payment of the *jizya* or poll-tax imposed on all non-Muhammadans was a powerful motive which influenced many conversions, especially among the lower classes. Constant immigration of Musalmans also went on, and the natural increase of the offspring of such settlers soon formed a large Muhammadan element in many parts of India, most numerous at and near the capital cities.

Guru Nānak

Causes of Muslim victories. The student may ask for an explanation of the fact that the Muslim armies were almost always victorious over much more numerous Hindu hosts. The combatants on both sides were equally brave and ready to sacrifice life for the sake of a cause, and the Hindu failure was not due to cowardice. But the Muhammadans were in practice the better fighting men, because they were better equipped, animated by a fierce fanatical spirit which welcomed death, and bound together by a sentiment of equality and unity. They were free, too, from the excessive respect for the traditions of antiquity which fettered the freedom of Hindu action. The invaders, coming from colder climates and using a meat diet, were personally more hardy and vigorous on the whole than their opponents. They were better provided with armour, and from the time of Bābur utilized the European invention of big guns. Islam regards all Muslims as equal and as brethren. The Muhammadans, rich and poor, freemen and slaves, fought with one mind, and so had an enormous advantage over the Hindus, broken up by endless caste divisions and sectional jealousies. Union was strength, as it always is. The comparatively small numbers of the invaders forced them to fight for victory or death. They had no fear of death, but rather longed for it as the gate to the paradise reserved for the *ghāzī*, the slayer of the idolatrous infidel, whom it was a pleasure 'to send to hell'. The Hindu could not look forward to any such special reward for slaying a Musalman. The Indian generals thought too much of antiquated rules of their *shāstras*, and relied too confidently on their elephants. They had quite forgotten the lesson taught them ages earlier by Alexander of Macedon, who proved the uselessness of elephants against horsemen and archers well led by bold commanders. Ingenuity might, perhaps, suggest other reasons, but so many may suffice.

Influence of Islam on Hinduism. The religion of the strangers, with its insistence on the great doctrine that 'there is one God', undoubtedly influenced the spirit of Hindu teaching and had much to do with the appearance of a number of religious reformers who preached to the effect that all religions are essentially the same, and all honour the one God under different names.

Rāmānuja, Rāmānand, Kabīr, Nānak, Chaitanya. Rāmānuja, who lived at Srīrangam in the south at the close of the eleventh and in the first half of the twelfth century, is recognized as one of the greatest of the teachers who gave special devotion to the Deity in the form of Vishnu. 'It was the school of Rāmānuja', Professor Barnett observes, 'that first blended into a full harmony the voices of reason and of devotion by worshipping a Supreme of infinitely blessed qualities both in His heaven and as revealed to the soul of man in incarnate experience'—a doctrine hardly to be distinguished in substance from the Christian idea of the Incarnation. The teaching of Rāmānuja, which even in his lifetime was not confined to the south, was propagated in the north during the fourteenth century by Rāmānand, who sought especially to save the souls of the poorer and more despised classes. He preferred to honour God under the name of Rāma. The most renowned of his twelve disciples was Kabīr (A. D. 1380–1420), whose terse sayings are on everybody's lips in Upper India. His teaching appealed equally to Musalmans and Hindus. In the fifteenth century, Nānak, the founder of the Sikh sect, taught his disciples on Kābīr's lines, and had followers among the Musalmans as well as the Hindus. Bengal especially venerates the memory of Chaitanya of Nuddea (Navadvīpa, 1486–1534), who denounced the use of animal food, the practice of bloody sacrifice, and the use of stimulants. He, in common with many other teachers, rejected the old Brahman doctrine of salvation by knowledge, and pleaded that men and women could be saved only by fervent living faith (*bhakti*) in a personal, loving God.

The doctrine of faith (*bhakti*). This doctrine of *bhakti*, which has much in common with some forms of Christianity, may be traced back to the *Bhagavad-gītā* (*ante*, p. 39), and lies at

CHAITANYA

(From a photo of a contemporary wooden statue preserved at Pratâpapur, Orissa, supplied by Bābū N. N. Vasu.)

the base of a great part of mediaeval and modern Hindu literature in the various vernaculars. The writers may be divided into three classes according as the object of their worship is Rāma, Krishna, or some form of Siva or his consort. Tulsī Dās (*ante*, p. 40) (1532–1623) has done much to teach the masses of the people in Upper India the beauty of faith in Rāma, the Saviour. Chaitanya found the objects of his devotion in Krishna and his divine queen, Rādhā, and by the addition of the feminine element produced a highly emotional form of religion, congenial to the Bengali temperament.

BOOK IV

THE MUGHAL EMPIRE FROM A.D. 1526 TO 1761

CHAPTER XVI

Bābur[1]; Humāyun; Sher Shah and the Sūr dynasty.

Early life of Bābur. Bābur (Zahīr-ud-dīn Muhammad), king of Kābul, whom Daulat Khan called in as his ally against Sultan Ibrāhīm Lodī of Delhi (*ante*, p. 129), was the most remarkable prince of his age. Descended in the male line from Tīmūr, in the female from the stock of Chinghīz Khan, he succeeded his father, Omar Shaikh, on the throne of the little Central Asian kingdom of Ferghana or Khokand at the age of eleven. In the course of a stormy youth he passed through countless adventures, and by the time he was twenty-eight years of age (A. D. 1511) had been driven out of his ancestral realm and had twice won and lost the kingdom of Samarkand. Seven years earlier he had seized Kābul, and from that time, being disappointed in his ambition to restore the empire of Tīmūr in Central Asia, directed his thoughts and hopes towards the rich plains of India.

Raids on India, A. D. 1505–25. In 1505 Bābur occupied Ghaznī and raided the Indian frontier as far as the Indus, but he did not cross that river until 1519, when he effected a temporary occupation of part of the Panjāb. That campaign was notable for Bābur's effective use of European artillery, then a novelty in the East. In 1524, in response to the appeal of Daulat Khan and of Ālam Khan, the uncle and rival of Sultan Ibrāhīm, he reached Lahore and Debālpur, sacking both. But in consequence of Daulat Khan's desertion, Bābur was obliged

[1] Bābur or Bābūr, not Bābar (*J. and Proc. A. S. B.*, 1910, vol. vi, N.S., extra number, p. iv).

BĀBUR

to return to Kābul for reinforcements, and his final invasion of India did not begin until November, 1525.

First battle of Pānīpat, 1526. Bābur's little force of less than 12,000 men met the host of Sultan Ibrāhīm, estimated to number about 100,000 men, on the plain of Pānīpat, some fifty miles to the north of Delhi, on April 21, 1526. The invader had the advantage of possessing seven hundred field-guns ; the sultan, after the Indian manner, relied on his elephants and, like Porus, found them useless to protect his infantry against cavalry well handled. Bābur executed the manœuvre which Alexander had found so successful against Porus, and wheeling his horsemen round with resistless speed, attacked the enemy's rear. In the course of the forenoon the army of Delhi was completely routed, and Sultan Ibrāhīm lay dead on the field with fifteen thousand of his men. 'By the grace and mercy of Almighty God', Bābur wrote, 'this difficult affair was made easy to me, and that mighty army, in the space of half a day, was laid in the dust.'

Bābur proclaimed as Padshah. The victor, who used the title of Padshah in preference to that of Sultan, quickly occupied Delhi and Agra, being proclaimed sovereign at both cities on Friday, April 27. Vast booty having been distributed, Bābur's troops, disgusted with the intense heat, longed to return to the cool hills of Kābul, and were appeased with difficulty by a speech from their commander.

Battle of Kanwāha or Sikrī, 1527. During the short remainder of his life Bābur was employed in trying to secure the foothold which he had obtained in the country, and had no leisure to think of the problems of civil government. His most formidable foe was the gallant Rānā Sanga, lord of the fortress of Chitor, chieftain of Mewār, head of the Rājpūt clans, and leader of a confederacy comprising more than a hundred Hindu princes. The Rānā, the 'fragment of a man', a 'collection of casualties', whose valour in countless fights was proved by the eighty wounds on his body, brought into the field a huge army supposed to number 200,000. Bābur's force, which was much inferior in numbers but superior in artillery and generalship, met the Hindu host at Kanwāha (Kanwa, Khānua, or Khanwah) near Sikrī, about twenty miles from Agra, on March 16, 1527. From morning until evening the battle was fiercely contested, but was decided against the Hindus by the tactics which had succeeded at Pānīpat. The victory was complete, and the Rājpūt power was broken. The storming of Chanderi, a strong fortress in the south-east of Mālwā, crowned the victory, and left Bābur free to deal with other enemies.

Battle of the Ghāghra (Gogra). Bābur's third great Indian battle was fought in May, 1529, near the confluence of the Ghāghra with the Ganges, against the Afghan chiefs of Bihār and Bengal, who had taken up the cause of Mahmūd, the brother of Sultan Ibrāhīm, who fell at Pānīpat. This conflict too resulted in victory for the Padshah, who made a treaty with Nasrat Shah, the independent king of Bengal, and became the sovereign of Bihār. But Bābur's sovereignty was of a very precarious kind, and depended solely on the power of his sword ; the task of converting a mere military occupation into a well-ordered government was reserved for his grandson.

Death of Bābur. Bābur's stormy life ended in 1530, when he was only forty-eight years of age. A pathetic story related in an appendix to his *Memoirs* tells how his beloved son Humāyun was desperately ill with fever, and was believed to have been saved by his father's taking the malady on himself. 'He entered his son's chamber, and going to the head of the bed, walked gravely three times round the sick man, saying the while: "On me be all that thou art suffering."' The prayer was answered. The son regained health and the father died. This touching incident happened at Sambhal in Rohilkhand. On December 26, 1530, Bābur passed away in his palace at Agra. His dust lies in the garden below the hill at Kābul, 'the sweetest spot in the neighbourhood', which he had chosen to be his last resting-place.

Character of Bābur. Few warrior princes have left behind them a memory as pleasing as that of Bābur. Like all the kings of his family he loved literature and the society of polished and learned men. In his inimitable *Memoirs* he has drawn a living picture of himself, his virtues and vices, his wisdom and his folly, which stands almost alone in literature. Valiant, strong, and fearless beyond the common, he was no mere soldier, but is justly entitled to the higher praise due to a capable general. At times, no doubt, he allowed himself to display something of the bloodthirsty ferocity of his ancestors, but in general his conduct was marked by chivalrous generosity. He was a man of strong affections, and inspired by a tender, passionate admiration for the beauties of nature which is rare among the 'men of blood and iron'. For some years he, like many of his ancestors and descendants, allowed his noble qualities to be obscured by intemperance. His will, however, was strong enough to subdue his vice, and when he found himself committed to a life-and-death struggle with Rānā Sanga he broke his cups and never tasted wine again. But he missed his liquor sorely, and lamented in verse:

> 'Distraught I am since that I gave up wine;
> Confused, to nothing doth my soul incline.'

Humāyun. Humāyun, the eldest of his four sons, and designated by Bābur as his successor, was nominally master of an empire extending from the Karamnāsa on the frontier of Bengal to the Oxus, and from the Himalayas to the Narbadā. But he was obliged immediately to relinquish the Kābul and Panjāb territories to his next brother, Kāmrān, in practical independence, and had no firm hold of any part of his wide dominions. The Mughal Padshah at this time was merely the leader of a horde of foreign adventurers compelled continually to battle for existence against the leaders of earlier settled Muslim hordes and innumerable Hindu Rājās.

Expulsion of Humāyun, 1540. Cut off from the north-western territories by Kāmrān's kingdom, Humāyun was placed between two strong powers—Gujarāt, under Bahādur, on the west, and Bihār, under Sher Khan, on the east. Early in his reign Humāyun defeated Bahādur and marched across his country to Cambay on the coast, but was recalled to meet the eastern danger, and Bahādur quickly recovered his kingdom. Sher Khan, the Afghan, who had made himself master of Bihār and the strong fortress of Rohtās inflicted two crushing defeats on Humāyun, at Chausa on the Ganges near the mouth of the Karamnāsa (1539), and again in the following year at Kanauj. The last battle cost Humāyun his throne, which was occupied by his opponent under the title of Sher Shāh (1540). As Sher Shāh belonged to the Sūr tribe of Afghans or Pathans his dynasty is known by the name of Sūr. It is the fashion to regard him as an usurper, because in the end his rival won, but, as a matter of fact, Sher Shāh had as good a right to the throne as Humāyun had. Neither had any right save that of the sword.

Exile of Humāyun. Humāyun now became a homeless wanderer. He tried in vain to obtain help from his brother Kāmrān, but that prince withdrew to Kābul, and left the Panjāb to Sher Shāh. The exile then sought aid from the chiefs of Sind and the Hindu Rājā, Maldeo of Marwār, without success. In the course of painful wanderings with a few followers through waterless desert Humāyun reached Umarkot in Sind, where, on November 23, 1542, his son Akbar (Muhammad Jalāl-ud-dīn) was born.[1] Thence the ex-king moved to Kandahar, then held by his brother Askarī under Kāmrān, and ultimately was obliged to throw himself on the mercy of Shah Tahmāsp of Persia. During these times the child Akbar underwent many dangers and was long separated from his father.

Sher Shāh's government. Sher Shāh, the new ruler, controlled Bihār and Bengal as well as North-western India, and

[1] 14th Shaban, 949 A. H. = Thurs., Nov. 23, 1542, as recorded by Jauhar, who was with Humāyun at the time. The official date, Sunday, October 15 (Old Style), given by Abūl Fazl and other historians, probably was adopted in order to conceal the true time of the nativity, and so protect Akbar against witchcraft, as well as for other reasons. (*J. A. S. B.*, part i, 1886, p. 88.)

TOMB OF HUMĀYUN

waged successful war with Mālwā, but did not live long enough to establish a settled form of government, being killed in May, 1545, by an explosion while besieging the fortress of Kālanjar in Bundelkhand. Sher Shāh was something more than the successful leader of a swarm of plundering Afghans, and had some notion of civil government. He followed the example of the old Hindu sovereigns by laying out high roads, planting them with trees, and providing the stages with accommodation for travellers. He repressed crime by enforcing strictly the liability of the villagers for all offences committed within their borders. The punishments he inflicted were savage and terrifying. No man could expect favour by reason of his rank, and the king's rough justice was equal to all. No injury to the lands of cultivators was permitted. An elaborate system of revenue 'settlement', based on the measurement of lands, was devised, which served as the basis for the better-known measures of Rājā Todar Mall, Akbar's finance minister. The coinage, which had been in much disorder, was reformed, and silver rupees, excellent alike in purity and execution, were abundantly issued. Sher Shāh erected many notable buildings. The tomb at Sahsarām, where he lies, is one of the finest monuments in India.

Islām (Salīm) Shah Sūr, 1545–54. Sher Shāh was succeeded by his second son, Islām or Salīm, who managed to retain the throne for more than seven years, although not without continual dispute. He is reputed to have been an able man, but the times were too unsettled to permit him to make his mark. When he died his infant son, who was proclaimed king, was promptly murdered by his maternal uncle, Mubāriz Khan.

Muhammad Shah Ādil and other Sūr claimants. The murderer ascended the throne under the title of Muhammad Shah Ādil, the last word meaning 'just', being singularly inapplicable to a man who was a good-for-nothing sensualist. He can hardly be said to have reigned, because all power was in the hands of his minister Hēmū, a clever Hindu baniya of Mewāt, and Muhammad Ādil's right to the royal seat was contested by two relatives—Ibrāhīm, at Agra and Delhi, and Ahmad Khan, who took the title of Sikandar Shah, in the Panjāb.[1] Muhammad Shah Ādil withdrew to Chunar in the east. It is unnecessary to recount the details of the contests between these claimants.

Return of Humāyun. Early in 1555, Humāyun, who had secured Persian help by conforming to the Shiah creed, crossed the Indus, his forces being commanded by Bairām Khan, a competent officer. The exiled king reoccupied Delhi in July, 1555, but enjoyed his recovered throne for a few months only, losing his life in January, 1556, by a fall from the stairs of his library.

Character of Humāyun. As a private gentleman Humāyun deserved nothing but praise. Like most members of his family, he was highly educated and deeply interested in literature and science, his special hobbies being mathematics and astronomy. As a king in troublous times he was not a success, and there is reason to believe that the weakness and instability of character which he displayed in the conduct of public affairs were largely due to his addiction to the vice of opium-taking, which benumbed his will and energies. He was generous and merciful in disposition, and seems to have been almost free from the Mongol ferocity, flashes of which sometimes broke out even in Akbar.

CHAPTER XVII

European voyages to India: discovery of the Cape route; the Portuguese, Dutch, Danish, French, and English Companies; early settlements.

Survey of early European settlements. Before entering on the story of the Mughal empire as established by Akbar it will be convenient to take a brief survey of the early European intercourse with and settlements in India, which began at the close of the fifteenth century and steadily developed during

[1] Hēmū evidently is the short colloquial form of some name like Hēmchand or Hēmrāj. Such short forms of names are commonly used in Northern India.

the sixteenth and seventeenth centuries, the time of the glory of the 'Great Moguls'. Reference has been made to the victory gained by the Portuguese in 1509 over the combined fleets of Egypt and Gujarāt (*ante*, p. 133); and the frequent mention of the foreign settlers on the coasts in the following pages will be made more easily intelligible by the help of a connected account of their proceedings.

Discovery of the Cape route. Although in the early centuries of the Christian era the Roman merchants had been familiar with the navigation between the Red Sea and the Malabar coast, the Muhammadan occupation of Egypt in the seventh century completely closed all intercourse between Europe and the East through Egypt, and the trade by sea passed exclusively into Muhammadan hands. In the fifteenth century the European explorers, then very active, and having no hope of reopening the old Egyptian route, busied themselves with trying to discover a long sea route by sailing round Africa, a process commonly called 'doubling the Cape', that is to say, sailing round the Cape of Good Hope. That process, now so easy, was difficult in the fifteenth century for tiny sailing ships, commonly of less than one hundred tons burden. But in 1487 a Portuguese captain, Bartholomeu Diaz de Novaes, showed how the thing could be done.

Vasco da Gama at Calicut, 1498. Eleven years later, in the summer of 1498, another Portuguese officer, Vasco da Gama, following the track of Diaz, arrived at Calicut on the Malabar coast with three little ships, and having done some trade with friendly Hindu princes, made his way back to Lisbon, the capital of Portugal. The king of Portugal, delighted at the prospect of acquiring the riches of the Indies, was arrogant enough to assume the title of 'Lord of the conquest, navigation, and commerce of Ethiopia, Arabia, Persia, and India'.

Conquest of Goa, &c.; Albuquerque. Many other Portuguese expeditions followed, and gradually the foreigners succeeded in establishing either factories—that is to say, trading

ALBUQUERQUE

stations—or fortresses at Calicut, Cannanore, Goa, and other places on the western coast. They also occupied Ceylon, the island of Socotra near the entrance to the Red Sea, Ormuz in the Persian Gulf, and Malacca in the Far East. The basis of the Portuguese power was Goa, captured in 1510 by Albuquerque, the greatest of the Portuguese governors. The strangers assumed full sovereign powers within the limits of the island of Goa, where they built a magnificent city, now desolate and in ruins, but still under the Portuguese flag. Albuquerque, who, like all his countrymen, hated Muhammadans with a bitter hatred, begotten of the long struggle in Europe between the Portuguese and the Musalman kingdom of Southern Spain, disgraced his victory at Goa by the massacre of the whole Muhammadan population, men, women, and children.

Albuquerque's administration of Goa. Albuquerque's cruelty was reserved for the followers of Islam, for, as an old Muhammadan writer puts it, 'he evinced no dislike towards the Nairs and other Pagans of similar descriptions'. In the administration of the Goa district he made free use of Hindu officials and clerks, and established schools for the education of the latter. He also employed a force of sepoys, or native soldiers, and had the courage to prohibit absolutely the burning of widows as *satīs*, which continued to be lawful in British India until 1829.

The Portuguese empire and its decline. Although during almost the whole of the sixteenth century, up to 1595, the Portuguese were masters of the Eastern seas, and held the monopoly or sole control of the Indian sea-borne foreign trade, their power declined as quickly as it had risen, and before the date named had been much reduced. The destruction in 1565 of the Hindu kingdom of Vijayanagar, with which Goa did much business, was a serious blow to the prosperity of that city. The union of the crowns of Spain and Portugal in the person of Philip II in 1580 dragged the lesser kingdom into the Spanish wars with Holland and England, and the strain of keeping up a maritime empire in the East proved to be too great for the resources of so small a country as Portugal. Grave mistakes in policy also were made, of which the most fatal was the mad attempt to force all natives in the Portuguese possessions to become Christians. Of course the attempt failed, but while it lasted was attended by much cruelty and oppression. This blunder was the work of Albuquerque's successors, not of the 'Great Captain' himself. The small settlements at Goa, Damān, and Diu on the western coast are now all that is left of the Portuguese dominions in India.

Dutch command of the Eastern seas. In the first half of the seventeenth century the command of the Eastern seas gradually passed to the Dutch, with whom it was disputed by the English. In 1602 all the Dutch private trading companies were combined under state patronage into 'The United East India Company of the Netherlands', which quickly became a rich and powerful corporation. At various dates the Portuguese settlements on the coast of India were attacked or occupied, and in 1658 the Dutch drove the Portuguese from Ceylon. But the centre of the Dutch power in the East always was in the Malay Archipelago rather than in India, and Holland, in spite of many ups and downs of fortune, still retains Java and other valuable possessions in the Far East.

Danish settlements. Denmark made an effort to share in the profits of the Indian trade, and in 1620 founded a settlement at Tranquebar in the Tanjore district, where a mint was established. Later, Serampore near Calcutta was occupied. The Danes never made any deep impression on India, and in 1845 were content to sell their small settlements to the British Government.

Struggle between the Dutch and English. The struggle during the seventeenth century between the Dutch and the English for command of the Eastern seas and control of the sea-borne trade was long and severe. The general result was that the Dutch retained their leading position in the Malay

Archipelago and Ceylon, but failed to attain considerable power in India. Their principal settlements on the mainland were at Pulicat and Tuticorin on the Coromandel coast and at Chinsurah near Calcutta. Clive forced Chinsurah to capitulate in 1759, and now nothing remains of the Dutch settlements except many tombs with quaint armorial bearings, and a few old houses and small canals. During the Napoleonic wars Holland lost Ceylon, and even Java, but that valuable possession was restored to her in 1816. Ceylon was retained by England, and ever since has been administered as a Crown colony.

The Company's first charter ; Portuguese opposition. The first serious effort made by Englishmen to claim a share in the Eastern trade was marked on the last day of the year 1600 by the incorporation under charter from Queen Elizabeth of the East India Company in its first form as 'The Governor and Company of Merchants *of London* trading into the East Indies'. The Portuguese and Dutch did their best to hinder the progress of their new rivals, but the Portuguese opposition was crushed by naval defeats inflicted on them in 1612 and 1615 off Swally (Suvāli) near Surat, and by the temporary occupation in 1622 of Ormuz in the Persian Gulf. Cromwell, in 1654, forced the Portuguese to acknowledge by treaty England's right to trade in the Eastern seas.

Factory at Surat ; Sir Thomas Roe. The first English factory or trading station was established at Surat in 1608 and confirmed by Imperial grant after the naval victory over the Portuguese in 1612. Three years later King James I of England sent out Sir Thomas Roe as his ambassador to the Padshah Jahāngīr. Sir Thomas spent more than three years in India, and, although he failed to obtain the treaty which he asked for, was able to do a good deal to help his countrymen. He wrote a book giving a very interesting account of the character, court, and administration of Jahāngīr as they appeared to an intelligent foreigner. Sir Thomas Roe's chaplain, the Rev. Edward Terry, also recorded his experience and observations in a quaint book.

English stations on western coast; Bombay. From time to time during the seventeenth century English trading stations, or factories, were established at various points on the Indian coasts, including one set up in 1644 at a place called Vizhingam in Travancore. The cession by the Portuguese in 1661 of the island of Bombay as part of the dowry of Princess Catharine of Braganza, who married King Charles II of England, was intended to check the Dutch power, and marks an important stage in the development of the Anglo-Indian Empire. But so little was the future grandeur of

COIN OF CHARLES II: BOMBAY RUPEE

Bombay foreseen that the king granted the island to the East India Company for £10 a year, equivalent in purchasing power to about a thousand rupees at the present time.

The English settlement at Bombay made little progress during the eighteenth century. Most of the territory now governed from Bombay was acquired as the result of the Marāthā wars waged under the direction of the Marquess Wellesley and the Marquess of Hastings during the early years of the nineteenth century. Aden was taken in 1839, and Sind was added in 1843.

Growth of the Presidency of Madras. The purchase of the site of Madras in 1640 has been already mentioned (*ante*, p. 142). The area so bought comprised only six square miles of 'a dreary waste of sand'. The next considerable piece of territory acquired by the Madras settlers was the Jāgīr, now the Chingleput District, granted in perpetuity by the

Nawāb of the Carnatic in 1763. The northernmost districts of the Madras Presidency, formerly known as the 'Northern Circars' (Sarkārs), were taken over in 1765, 1766, and 1788. Lord Wellesley annexed the dominions of the Nawāb of the Carnatic in 1801. The rest of the territory now controlled by the Government of Madras was mostly acquired as the result of the third and fourth Mysore wars, which ended respectively in 1792 and 1799.

English stations on eastern coast; Calcutta. The earliest English trading stations on the eastern coast were established about 1625 at Armagaon in the Nellore District and at Masulipatam in the Kistna (Krishnā) District. A few years later, about 1633, factories were founded at Balasore and an obscure place called Hariharpur in Orissa. In 1651 a settlement was made at Hūglī (Hooghly), official favour being won through the professional services rendered by a surgeon named Gabriel Boughton to the family of the Muhammadan governor of Bengal. Job Charnock, the chief of the station at Hūglī, tried to set up a branch establishment on the site of Calcutta in 1686, but was driven out by the hostility of Nawāb Shāyista Khan, Aurangzeb's uncle, and obliged to take refuge at Madras.[1] In 1690 he came back, under authority given by Aurangzeb, and definitely founded the small settlement which has grown into Calcutta, now the second largest city in the British Empire.

Early history of Calcutta. The settlement founded by Job Charnock, who died in 1692 and lies buried in the cemetery of St. John's Church, was at the village of Sūtānutī. Fortifications were erected by permission of the Nawāb of Bengal in 1696, and the fort built a few years later was named Fort William, in honour of King William III, the reigning sovereign of England. During the eighteenth century the original fort was replaced by the present structure. About 1700 the Company purchased Sūtānutī with two other

[1] Shāyista Khan was transferred in 1663 from the Deccan to Bengal. He died in 1694, aged 91 or 93 lunar years, at Agra.

villages, Kalikāta and Govindpur, from Azīm-ush-shān, governor of Bengal, grandson of Aurangzeb, and father of the Emperor Farrukhsīyar. The city which began to grow up on the sites of the three villages became known as Calcutta. Important privileges are said to have been again secured to the settlers by means of services rendered by another surgeon, named Hamilton, to Farrukhsīyar. In 1742 the Marāthās under Bālājī Rāo Peshwā were at the height of their power, and their attitude was so threatening that the English obtained permission from Nawāb Allahvardi Khan to protect their settlement by an outer line of imperfect fortification, which remained for a long time famous as 'the Mahratta ditch'. It corresponds with the line of the modern Circular Road.

After the tragedy of the Black Hole in 1756 and the battle of Plassey in the following year, the history of Calcutta merges in that of British India. Its rank as the capital of the Indian Empire dates from 1774, when Warren Hastings was appointed the first Governor-General, and lasted until 1912, when the seat of the Government of India was moved to Delhi. In the seventeenth century the Bengal settlements had been subordinate to Madras, which was itself supposed to be dependent on Surat.

Early history of the East India Company. The Company, notwithstanding Queen Elizabeth's charter, had serious rivals in other associations of English merchants, and did not become really prosperous until 1661, when it obtained a fresh Charter from Charles II, and was granted the rights of coinage and jurisdiction over English subjects in the East. But some thirty years later the Company again became involved in great difficulties, which lasted until 1702, when it was reconstructed as 'The United Company of Merchants *of England* trading to the East Indies'. The union of the rival Companies was confirmed by Parliament in 1708.

The subsequent dealings of the Crown and Parliament with the Company will be noticed from time to time in the course of the historical narrative.

French settlements. The French were late in making their appearance on the Indian coasts, and never acquired direct control of any considerable territory. Various early adventures having proved to be failures, a strong association, entitled *La Compagnie des Indes*, was formed in 1664 under the patronage of King Louis XIV. But the French Government failed to keep up a lively interest in the Company's affairs, and French enterprise in India always suffered for want of adequate support from home. However, Pondicherry on the Madras coast, founded in 1674, became a flourishing settlement, and still is a fairly prosperous town. After the Napoleonic wars the French were permitted to retain or recover Pondicherry and Karikal on the Madras coast, Mahé on the west coast, Yanaon at the mouth of the Godāvarī, and Chandernagore near Calcutta, over all of which the flag of the French Republic still waves. These settlements are of no political importance. The events of the contest between the French and English for supremacy in Southern India will be dealt with as incidents in the general history.

CHAPTER XVIII

The reign of Akbar: Todar Mall; Abūl Fazl.

Accession of Akbar. When Humāyun died (*ante*, p. 159), his eldest son Akbar, a boy of thirteen, was in the Panjāb with his guardian Bairām Khan, an officer much trusted by Humāyun, and then in command of an army engaged in the pursuit of Sikandar Sūr, one of the claimants to the throne. Humāyun's death was concealed for a few days in order to allow of arrangements being made for Akbar's accession. The proper moment having come, the young prince was enthroned, with such ceremony as was possible, at Kalānaur, a town then of some importance, situated to the west of Gurdāspur.[1]

[1] The throne still exists. It is a plain brick structure, built on a masonry platform. At a later date it was surrounded by a garden and ornamental

At the time of his enthronement Akbar had no kingdom. News came in that Hēmū had succeeded in taking both Delhi and Agra. Hēmū renounced his allegiance to Muhammad Ādil Sūr, the other claimant to the throne, then far away to the east at Chunar near Mirzāpur, and set up as an independent king, under the title of Rājā Bikramajit (Vikramāditya), borne so often by famous Hindu monarchs of the olden time. Timid counsellors advised retreat to Kābul, but Bairām Khan resolved that the empire of Hindustan was worth fighting for, and prepared to meet the foe. We may feel assured that Akbar agreed to the decision.

Second battle of Pānīpat, November 5, 1556. The Hindu claimant, 'with 1,500 elephants of war, and treasure without end or measure, and an immense army, came to offer battle at Pānīpat', on the field where Ibrāhīm Lodī and so many gallant men had met their death thirty years before (*ante*, p. 153). Hēmū began badly by losing his artillery, but relied chiefly, in the old Hindu fashion, on his elephants, which delivered a terrifying charge. They were received with a shower of arrows, one of which struck Hēmū in the eye, rendering him unconscious. His army then fled, and Hēmū, who still breathed, was captured. The boy Akbar refusing to flesh his sword on a dying prisoner, Bairām Khan and some of his officers dispatched him. 'Nearly 1,500 elephants, and treasure and stores to such an amount that even fancy is powerless to imagine it, were taken as spoil.' A minaret was built of the heads of the slain, and Delhi and Agra were promptly occupied by the victors.[1]

buildings, which were destroyed by railway contractors in search of ballast. Recently, measures have been taken to preserve reverently what is left, and an inscribed tablet has been put up.

[1] The account of Hēmū's death in the text follows Badāonī (Lowe's transl., vol. ii, p. 9). Abūl Fazl, Faizī and the *Tārīkh-i-Dāūdi* agree that Akbar refused to strike. But Jahāngīr, in his authentic *Memoirs* (Rogers & Beveridge, vol. i, p. 40), states that Akbar 'told one of his servants to cut off his head'. Ahmad Yādgār (Elliot, v, 66) asserts that 'the Prince, accordingly, struck him, and divided his head from his unclean body'.

AKBAR

Occupation of Ajmēr, Gwalior, and Jaunpur. Akbar was now firmly seated on the throne of the sultans of Delhi, which had been occupied for a few years by his father and grandfather, but he had yet many fights to wage before he could feel himself emperor of Hindustan. During the next three years the claimants belonging to the Sūr dynasty were defeated, and Ajmēr, Gwalior, and Jaunpur were occupied. Bairām Khan, with the title of Khān-i-Khānān, governed on behalf of Akbar as Regent or Protector.

Dismissal and death of the regent. In March, 1560, young Akbar, conscious of the powers of budding manhood, and spurred on by the ladies of the court, determined to free himself from the control of his too-masterful regent, and sent a message to Bairām Khan, requiring him to proceed on pilgrimage to Mecca, in these terms: 'As I was fully assured of your honesty and fidelity, I left all important affairs of State in your hands and thought only of my own pleasures. I have now determined to take the reins of government into my own hands, and it is desirable that you should make the pilgrimage to Mecca upon which you have been so long intent. A suitable *jāgīr* out of the *parganas* of Hindustan will be assigned for your maintenance, the revenues of which shall be transmitted to your agent.' The regent yielded to this imperious command and surrendered the insignia of office, but, on second thoughts, attempted rebellion. He was defeated, pardoned, and sent off to Mecca. He arrived at Pātan in Gujarāt, and was there stabbed to death by an Afghan, whose father had been executed by his orders. Thus was Akbar freed from his Bismarck, and left at liberty for forty-five years to carry out his policy of converting a military occupation into an ordered empire.

Akbar's wars. But when we speak of an 'ordered empire' we must not think of a country as peaceful as the India of the

De Laët agrees that 'the unworthy deed' was done by Akbar's hand (*De Imperio Magni Mogolis*, 1631, 2nd issue, p. 174). It is difficult to decide which of the stories is true. I am disposed to believe Ahmad Yādgār.

present day. Throughout Akbar's long reign the sword was never sheathed, and the great nobles were never at rest. The detailed chronicles of the time are full of stories of intrigues, murders, rebellions, and wars. Akbar himself, although terrible in his hot wrath, was of a merciful and forgiving disposition, and rarely allowed himself to be tempted to the commission of deeds of cruelty. His generals often displayed the old Mongol ferocity, and even Badāonī, who was not easily shocked, was horrified at the bloodthirsty proceedings of Pīr Muhammad Khan during the reduction of Mālwā in the early years of the reign. The main interest of Akbar's notable rule lies, not in his numerous wars, which were like other wars, but in his personal character and his unique policy.

Siege of Chitor, 1567–8. Among the most famous military feats of the reign was the storming of the Rājpūt fortress of Chitor (*ante*, p. 133), the siege of which lasted for four months, from October, 1567, to February, 1568. The operations of the besiegers were under the personal direction of Akbar, who himself shot the Rājpūt commander, Jaimall, through the head. That shot decided the fate of the fortress. The defenders quitted the walls, and saved the honour of their wives and daughters by the awful rite of *johar*, or sacrifice by fire. Then they devoted themselves to death, fighting in every house and for every foot of ground, until they were all slain. The Rānā was not in the fortress during the siege, but remained in hiding, and subsequently transferred his capital to Udaipur. Within the following two years Akbar compelled the surrender of Ranthambhor in Rājputāna and Kālanjar in Bundelkhand, then considered two of the strongest forts in India.

Reduction of Gujarāt. The next great military operation undertaken was the conquest of Gujarāt, which had long been independent (*ante*, p. 133), and was occupied only temporarily by Humāyun in 1535. But that transitory conquest effected by his father was enough to give Akbar a pretext for an effort to re-annex the kingdom, and so to make himself master of Western India to the sea-coast. The imperial designs were furthered by dissensions among the local nobles. The annexation was carried out without very much fighting, and the unheroic king, Muzaffar Shah, was found hiding in a cornfield. He was treated with contemptuous lenity and given a pension of thirty or forty rupees a month. After some years he escaped and gave much trouble until he committed suicide.

Surat; suppression of revolt, 1573. The important fortress of Surat was taken in the early part of 1573, after investment for a month and a half. On this occasion the emperor for the first time came into contact with the Portuguese, who sent an embassy from Goa to meet him. At Cambay he had his first look on the sea. In June Akbar returned to Sikrī near Agra, and was hardly back when reports were received of a revolt in the newly conquered kingdom. He made all necessary military arrangements with the utmost quickness, and starting himself from Sikrī in August, mounted on a swift dromedary, covered the 800 miles between that place and the outskirts of Ahmadābād in nine days. The rebels, who could hardly believe the news of his arrival, were defeated after a hard fight, and Akbar returned to Sikrī on October 6, after an absence of forty-three days. It would be difficult to find in history an example of equally rapid and decisive action by the sovereign of a great monarchy. Sikrī was given the name of Fathpur, 'the city of victory,' and became the usual residence of the court until 1584.

Dāūd, king of Bengal. Bengal, as we have seen (*ante*, p. 131), had been independent, usually under Muhammadan kings, since the fourteenth century. Sulaiman, an able monarch, whose general, Rājū, surnamed Kālā Pahār, had plundered the temple of Jagannāth and overrun Orissa, acknowledged a nominal dependence on Akbar. When he died in 1572 he was succeeded, after an interval of dispute, by his son Dāūd, who was not disposed to submit to the Mughal power. He is described as 'a dissolute scamp, who knew nothing of the business of governing'. Akbar, while engaged in Gujarāt, kept his eye on the affairs of Bengal, and as soon as he had arranged the business in the west, commissioned Todar Mall to undertake the subjugation of the east.

Defeat and death of Dāūd, 1576. In 1574, during the height of the rainy season, Akbar in person appeared on the scene near Patna, defeated Dāūd, and occupied Patna, where immense booty was taken. Dāūd escaped into Orissa, and at the beginning of 1575 Akbar returned to Fathpur-Sikrī. Soon afterwards the king of Bengal was forced to consent to do homage and pay tribute, but quickly broke his engagements. Next year (July, 1576) he was captured by the imperial officers and put to death. Thus ended the independent kingdom of Bengal. But when historians speak of independent Bengal, the phrase must be understood as referring only to the independence of the kingdom from the control of the rulers of Delhi and Agra. In those days the Hindu population of the province was of little account, and possessed no authority, the kings and chiefs who fought the sultans and Padshahs of the north-west being usually foreign chiefs of Afghan origin.

Rājpūt rising; battle of Gogūnda, 1576. During the progress of the operations in Bengal the emperor's forces had to contend with a formidable uprising in Rājputāna, under the leadership of Rānā Partāb Singh of Udaipur. He was defeated in June 1576 by Mān Singh at Gogūnda (also known as Haldighāt), north of Udaipur, in a hotly contested battle, vividly described by the historian Badāonī, who took an active part in it. Arrangements were made to curb the Rājpūts by building fifty blockhouses (*thānas*) in the hills, but the Udaipur country was never really subdued. In fact, Partāb Singh gradually recovered possession of most of his country before Akbar's death.

Result of twenty years' war. In 1576, twenty years after the second battle of Pānīpat, Akbar had succeeded in making himself the lord paramount of all India proper to the north of the Vindhyas, exacting a more or less complete and willing obedience from innumerable turbulent feudatories. But fighting never ceased, and the imperial generals had much to do in Bengal and Bihār until 1586. Those provinces were not wholly quieted until 1592.

Revolt of Bengal and Bihār in 1579. A serious rebellion in Bengal, which began in 1579, was caused partly by the anger of the Muhammadan nobles at the harsh measures of the imperial officials, who cut down their revenue-free grants, and partly by resentment against Akbar's growing hostility to Islam. That hostility, which had its root in his early studies of Sūfism, may be said to have become marked from 1574 when Abūl Fazl came to court, and to have come to a head in 1579 when Akbar compelled the leading theologians to admit the right of the emperor to pass rulings on matters of religion. That remarkable decree will be cited in full presently. It is mentioned here because it was closely connected with the revolt of Bengal and other disturbances. The rebels in Bengal desired to replace Akbar by his more orthodox half-brother, Muhammad Hakīm of Kābul. Ultimately the Bengal rebellion was suppressed.

Annexation of Kābul, 1585. Muhammad Hakīm Mīrzā, who was born at Kābul in 1554, and so was twelve years junior to Akbar, had been recognized from infancy as the nominal ruler of the Kābul province, which was actually administered by various nobles in succession, apparently in practical independence. In 1582 Muhammad Hakīm, who had hopes of winning his brother's Indian throne, invaded the Panjāb, but was repulsed and obliged to accept Akbar's suzerainty. His death, due to drink, in July 1585, enabled Akbar to include Kābul in his dominions as a Sūba or province.

Lahore, Akbar's capital for fourteen years. The death of his brother and other pressing affairs made it necessary for the emperor to move towards the north-west. Starting from Fathpur-Sikrī in August 1584, he reached Attock (Atak-Banāras) towards the end of December. He remained in the north until November 1598, making Lahore his capital for nearly fourteen years. At the end of 1585 four imperial armies were in motion, directed severally against the tribesmen in the Khyber Pass on the road to Kābul, the Yūsufzī of the Peshāwar country, the Balōchis, and Kashmīr, which kingdom Akbar was resolved to annex. Early in 1586 the force operating against the Yūsufzī suffered a severe defeat, the slain including Rājā Bīrbal, the Brahman, one of Akbar's dearest and most intimate friends. The tribesmen were sternly chastised, but not subdued.

Conquest of Kashmīr, 1586–7 ; and Sind. From the time of Bābur, the Mughal sovereigns of India had felt a desire to possess the delightful valley of Kashmīr, but neither Bābur nor Humāyun had leisure to undertake the conquest of the country. A cousin of Bābur's, Haidar Mīrzā Doghlat, the celebrated author of the history entitled *Tārīkh-i-Rashīdī*, made himself master of it, and ruled well and wisely for eleven years, until 1551. In 1572 the reigning king, also a Musalman, made a formal recognition of the supremacy of Akbar, by consenting that his name should be recited as that of the sovereign in the public prayers. But then, and for many years afterwards, Akbar was far too busy in Gujarāt, Bengal, and elsewhere to be able to attend to Kashmīr. He could not attempt the conquest of the mountain kingdom until he had made his position in the plains fairly safe. When he was free to make the attempt, a pretext for interference was easily found. The occupation was effected by Akbar's generals without excessive difficulty in 1586–7, and from that time Kashmīr became an integral part of the Mughal empire, attached to the Sūba of Kābul. A little later, after a tedious campaign, the province of Sind, partially subdued in 1588, was finally conquered, and united with the Sūba of Multān. Kandahar was taken from the Persians in 1594.

Result of forty years' wars. By 1596 Akbar was master of the whole of Northern India, from the Bay of Bengal on the east of the Arabian Sea on the west, as well as of the Indus valley, and the greater part of the present kingdom of Afghanistan. The conquest of the south remained. But that great design was not destined to be accomplished, except to a small extent.

Preparations for invasion of the Deccan. Akbar's long-cherished designs on the Deccan were much aided by the dissensions of the local princes and nobles, who were unable to form a firm league among themselves to withstand the common foe. The ordinary political strife was made more bitter by sectarian quarrels of the Shīah with the Sunnī Muhammadans. In 1591 Akbar sent embassies to the four kingdoms of the Deccan, Khāndesh, Bijāpur, Golkonda or Hyderabad, and Ahmadnagar, to demand recognition of his authority. The sultan of the small state of Khāndēsh submitted readily, and thus secured for the emperor free passage by the Burhānpur and Asīrgarh road, but the other kingdoms refused to do homage.

Siege of Ahmadnagar, 1595. Traitorous invitations smoothed the path of the Mughals, and in December 1595 the emperor's second son, Prince Murād, invested Ahmadnagar. The imperialist operations were weakened by discord between the prince and his colleague, Abdurrahīm Khan-i-Khānān, the son of Bairām Khan, regent in Akbar's youth. The defence was heartened by the gallantry of a woman, Chānd Bībī, a lady of the royal house, rightly called Chānd Sultan, who donned armour, and sword in hand held the breach made by the besiegers' mines. The attempt to storm failed, and Murād withdrew when Chānd Bībī agreed to cede Berār.

Fall of Ahmadnagar, 1600. In the autumn of 1600, Chānd Bībī meantime having been murdered, Ahmadnagar was again besieged and taken by Prince Dāniyāl, Akbar's youngest son. The emperor formally constituted a new Sūba, or government, under the name of Ahmadnagar, but, as a matter of fact, the greater part of the kingdom remained under the rule of members of the local royal family, and was not really annexed until 1637, in the reign of Shahjahān.

Siege and capture of Asīrgarh, January 1601. Meantime, the little state of Khāndēsh, which had been friendly to Akbar in 1591, had become hostile in consequence of local revolutions. The ruler of this kingdom possessed the stronghold of Asīrgarh, situated north-east of Burhānpur on a spur of the Sātpura range, and thus commanded the main road to the Deccan. The capture of this fortress, the strongest in India, was necessary for the progress and safety of the imperial army. The siege accordingly was begun early in 1600 and lasted for more than eleven months, until January 1601 (Ilāhī year 45), when an outbreak of pestilence within the walls rendered the place untenable. In 1820 the same fortress surrendered to Sir John Malcolm after a bombardment of eleven days.

The last of Akbar's conquests. The taking of Ahmadnagar and Asīrgarh closes the long roll of the victories of Akbar, who was unable to make further progress in the subjugation of the south. His force was now spent, and the record of the last four years of his strenuous life leaves on the mind a painful impression of disillusion, disappointment, sorrow, and failure. Akbar returned to Agra during the year which witnessed the fall of Asīrgarh, leaving his youngest son Dāniyāl as viceroy of the southern and western provinces. Khāndēsh was renamed Dāndēsh in compliment to the prince.

Akbar's unworthy sons. Prince Dāniyāl, a good-for-nothing, drunken sot, was undeserving of the paternal favour, and died from the effects of drink a few months before his father passed away. The same vice had destroyed Prince Murād six years earlier. The eldest son, Prince Salīm, although equally intemperate, had a stronger constitution than his brothers, and survived to become the successor of Akbar.

Rebellion of Prince Salīm. Salim, in accordance with many evil precedents, was eager to anticipate the course of nature and usurp his father's place. Akbar, well informed concerning his traitorous designs, endeavoured to keep him employed by commissions to hunt down rebels in Rājputāna and Bengal, but the prince would neither come to court nor proceed to execute the imperial orders. He continued to sulk and play the tyrant at Allahabad, and at last, in 1601, there assumed the imperial titles and took possession of the treasures of Bihār.

Murder of Abūl Fazl by order of Salīm. A little later, in August 1602, Salīm inflicted a deadly wound on his father's feelings by causing a Bundela robber-chieftain to waylay and murder Shaikh Abūl Fazl, the guide, philosopher, and friend of the emperor. 'If Salīm', said Akbar, 'wished to be emperor, he might have killed me and spared Abūl Fazl.' Ultimately, through the mediation of Sultan Salīmah Begam, widow of the regent Bairām Khan, who long before had become one of Akbar's many consorts, a peace was patched up, and Salīm was induced to come to court.

Salīm nominated as successor. By this time, Akbar, much affected by the death of his youngest, and the ingratitude of his first-born son, and further weakened by indulgence in the dangerous consolations of opium, was failing visibly. Rājā Mān Singh and several other influential nobles, who dreaded the assumption of absolute power by Salīm, sought to set him aside and substitute his son Khusrū. But these schemes came to naught. No absolutely trustworthy account of the last days of Akbar exists. The long story usually quoted is that told in the so-called *Memoirs of Jahāngīr* as translated by Price, a document largely falsified and wholly without authority. The best evidence is that of the Dutch writer van den Broecke (in De Läet, 1628 or 1629), who based his work on an official chronicle. He states that

> 'the King, while hopes of his recovery still existed, was visited by Prince Salīm, on whose head he placed his own turban, girding him at the same time with the sword of his own father Humāyun.'

That simple statement may be accepted as probably true. Assuming its truth, the failure of the plot in favour of Khusrū is explained by the natural unwillingness of the nobles to defy the expressed will of the great monarch whom they had obeyed for so long.

Death of Akbar. Akbar, then almost sixty-three solar years of age, died at Agra on October 15, 1605, in the presence of a crowd of anxious nobles. Salīm does not seem to have been present. The partisans of Khusrū made a feeble attempt to put their candidate forward, but Rājā Rāmdās declared for Salīm and settled the question by posting a strong guard of Rājpūt cavalry over the immense treasure in the fort, which included nearly two hundred millions of rupees' worth of coin, in addition to great sums stored in six other fortresses. Salīm's succession was thus secured. On the third day Rājā Mān Singh and the Khan-i-Azam effected an outward, though insincere, reconciliation between Khusrū and his father. It is interesting to note that the fulfilment of Akbar's will was due to the trusty Rājpūts on whose devotion he had relied for so many years.[1] Before attempting to estimate the character of India's greatest sovereign since the time of Asoka, we must devote a few pages to a consideration of his policy and innovations, and to the enumeration of the leading men among his chosen advisers and friends.

Principle of Akbar's conquests. The summary chronicle recorded in the foregoing narrative, if it stood alone without comment, would naturally lead the reader to regard Akbar merely as a specially able king of the ordinary aggressive type. But, although no doubt he accepted the current opinion that a respectable monarch is bound to enlarge his dominions, Akbar the victorious kept before his mind a pur

[1] Authorities differ concerning the exact date of Akbar's death. Mr. W. Irvine, who kindly examined them for me, found that the weight of evidence is in favour of October 15, Old Style = October 25, New Style. The Dutch authority is followed for the facts relating to Salīm's succession. The exact amount of the treasure left by Akbar is recorded by Manrique, Mandelslo, and De Läet. The cash may be taken as equal to twenty-two millions of pounds sterling. Manrique describes in detail how he obtained the figures from an official document.

pose higher than that of mere ambition. It is clearly apparent that at an early stage in his career he formed a plan for bringing all India under his sole government in such a way that all races, native and foreign, Hindus as well as Musalmans, might be brought to work together for the common good. He believed himself to be the vicegerent of the Most High, and as such empowered to give India a better government than her own sons could provide.

Abolition of the jizya. As early as the ninth year of his reign, when he was a young man twenty-two years of age, and long before he came under the influence of the freethinkers, Faizī and Abūl Fazl, Akbar had abolished the *jizya*, or special poll-tax imposed on non-Muhammadans, which was intensely galling to the Hindus forming the great majority of the population. That measure alone, which was supplemented later by the abolition of the tax on pilgrimages, is enough to prove that Akbar in early youth realized that he, a foreigner, could not build up a stable empire without the aid of the indigenous civilization.

Marriages with Rājpūt princesses; Hindu friends. The royal marriages with Rājpūt princesses, following the example set by Humāyun, who had one Hindu consort, were arranged in pursuance of the same principle, and all the leading states, except Mewār, sent daughters to court. The Emperor Jahāngīr was the son of a princess of Jaipur. Several of Akbar's most trusted officers and intimate friends were Hindus. Rājā Bhagwān Dās of Jaipur and Rājā Mān Singh of the same state fought valiantly by his side even against Rājpūts and were raised to the highest dignities. Mān Singh governed in succession the great provinces of Kābul and Bengal. Another dear Hindu friend of the emperor was a Brahman of Kālpī named Gadāī Brahmandās,[2] known to history as Rājā Bīrbal, the reputed author of many wise and witty sayings still current, whom even Badāonī admits to

[1] This is the name given by Badāonī. Count von Noer calls him Mahesh Dās, following another authority.

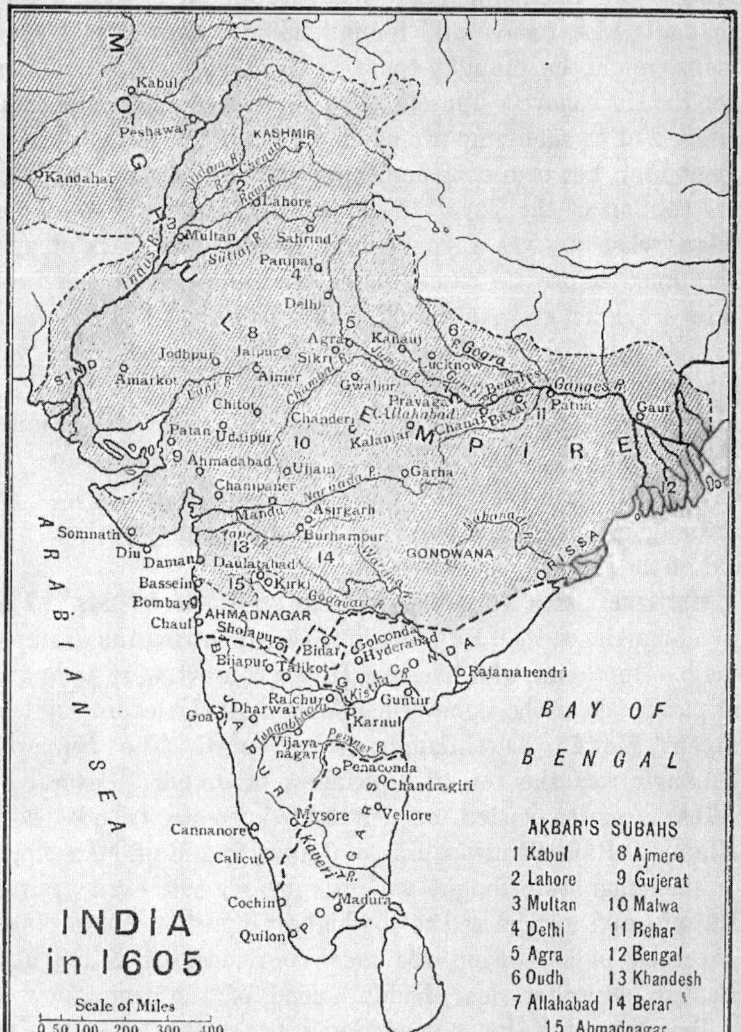

WAXTYPE GEORGE PHILIP & SON, LTD.

have been 'possessed of a considerable amount of capacity and genius'. He lost his life in battle with the Yūsufzī tribesmen (*ante*, p. 176).

Rājā Todar Mall and land 'settlement'. Rājā Todar Mall, a Khatri from Oudh and a devout Hindu, who rendered good service as a general in the Khyber and Peshāwar country, is chiefly remembered for his revenue administration and system of land settlement, based on foundations laid by Sher Shah (*ante*, p. 158), and serving in its turn as the basis of the existing system in Upper India. He caused a detailed survey of the land and elaborate calculations of the average produce and the Government's share of the same to be made. The collections were ordinarily made in cash. The 'settlements', or contracts with the landholders, at first annual, were subsequently extended for an indefinite period.

Sūbas, sarkārs, &c. For administrative purposes the empire was divided into fifteen Sūbas, or local governments, namely, Agra, Ahmadabad, Ajmēr, Allahabad, Bengal (including Orissa), Bihār, Delhi, Kābul (including Kashmīr), Lahore, Mālwā, Multān (including Sind), and Oudh, with the addition of Ahmadnagar (*ante*, p. 177), Berār, and Khāndesh or Dāndesh, in the Deccan, late in the reign. The Sūbas were divided into more than a hundred Sarkārs, or districts, subdivided into Parganas or Mahāls, which were grouped into Dastūrs for certain fiscal purposes. For example, the Sūba of Agra included 13 Sarkārs and 203 Parganas; the Sarkār of Agra, 1,864 square miles in area, comprising 31 Parganas, grouped in 4 Dastūrs. The Sūbadār, or Sipāh-sālār, the governor of a Sūba, was either a prince of the blood or other great noble, vested with practically unlimited powers, subject to the obligation of providing men and money for the needs of the empire.

Mansabdārs, &c. The executive officials, who all ranked as military officers, however employed, were called Mansabdārs, classified in thirty-three grades, regulated nominally by the number of horsemen supposed to be supplied by the officers.

grades ranged from commands of 10,000 to those of 10. The Mansabdārs drew pay in proportion to their rank, and in practice had not to furnish the number of men indicated by their grade. The highest grades were reserved for members of the imperial family. The Mansabdār system appears to have been devised by Akbar. It is not mentioned before his reign. Many officials held grants of land or fiefs (*jāgīr*), subject to conditions of service. Free grants to men of reputed sanctity or learning were called Sayūrghāls.

Finance and army. The mainstay of the imperial treasury, as always in India, was the land revenue, or Crown rent, the state's share of the produce, paid in either kind or cash. The land revenue in 1600 is estimated to have amounted to about nineteen millions of pounds sterling, and the customs and miscellaneous revenue to about as much again, but the figures are open to doubt. Many taxes were remitted by Todar Mall.

The army was chiefly a cavalry militia raised by the Mansabdārs and Jāgīrdārs, who were much addicted to making false returns. Akbar tried to correct such abuses, but with only partial success. The standing, or permanently enrolled, army was small, 25,000 men in the latter part of the reign, of whom about half were troopers, the rest being gunners and infantry. The practice of enslaving prisoners of war was forbidden in 1573.

Āīn-i-Akbari and Abūl Fazl. The imperial regulations concerning the court and every department of the administration are recorded in detail in the unique work of Abūl Fazl entitled *Āīn-i-Akbari*, or 'Institutes of Akbar', which forms part of the *Akbarnāma* or 'History of the Reign of Akbar'. Shaikh Abūl Fazl, who was introduced to Akbar in 1574, was one of the most learned men of his age, and is still remembered as 'the great munshī'. He was the most influential of Akbar's councillors, and the emperor's gradual estrangement from Islam was largely due to his intimacy with Abūl Fazl and his equally learned and freethinking brother, Shaikh Faizī, who had come to court six years earlier. The nature of Abūl

Fazl's philosophy may be gathered from the following lines composed by him:

> 'O God, in every temple I see people that seek Thee, and in every language I hear spoken, people praise Thee! . . .
> If it be a mosque, people murmur the holy prayer, and if it be a Christian church, people ring the bell from love of Thee,
> Sometimes I frequent the Christian cloister, and sometimes the mosque,
> But it is Thou whom I search for from temple to temple'.

Akbar's loss of faith. The teaching of Abūl Fazl and his brother was only one of the influences which shook the faith of Akbar. As a boy he had been attracted by the heretical mysticism of the Sūfī poet Hāfiz, closely akin to certain Hindu doctrines, and from an early age he had been much in company with Hindus. His marriages with Hindu princesses, who practised their religious rites within the palace, gave ample opportunities for filling him with Hindu notions. Akbar, while extremely curious about religious problems, found it hard to accept any definite creed. He delighted in hearing the arguments of rival Christian, Hindu, Muslim, Jain and Zoroastrian teachers, but would never declare himself the disciple of any one guide.

Akbar and Christianity. The arrival of two Jesuits from Bengal in 1576 first drew the attention of the emperor to Christianity. He became much interested, and asked the Portuguese at Goa to send him learned theologians. They complied gladly and dispatched three separate missions which stayed at court respectively from 1580 to 1583, from 1590 to 1591, and from 1595 to the end of the reign, and later. The Jesuits at one time had good hopes of converting Akbar, but he only played with them, and was never in real earnest. The story, when read in detail, is of fascinating interest.

Akbar's supremacy in religious matters. Although Akbar could not make up his mind which, if any, of the rival religions was true, he decided quite clearly that Islam was false. That conviction may be dated from about 1579. In that year he forced the leading *maulavis*, or Muhammadan theologians, to sign a decree declaring the binding force of an imperial ruling on any religious question. The enacting part of the decree runs as follows :

'Further, we declare that the king of Islam, Amīr of the Faithful, Shadow of God in the world—Abū-l-fath Jalāl-ud-dīn Muhammad Akbar Padshah Ghāzī—whose kingdom God perpetuate! is a most just, a most wise, and a most God-fearing king. Should, therefore, in future a religious question come up, regarding which the opinions of the *mujtahids* [theologians] are at variance, and His Majesty, in his penetrating understanding and clear wisdom, be inclined to adopt, for the benefit of the nation, and as a political expedient, any of the conflicting opinions existing on that point, and issue a decree to that effect, we do hereby agree that such decree shall be binding on us and on the whole nation.

'Further, we declare that should His Majesty think fit to issue a new order, we and the nation shall likewise be bound by it, provided that such order be not only in accordance with some verse of the Koran, but also of real benefit to the nation; and further, that any opposition on the part of his subjects to such an order passed by His Majesty shall involve damnation in the world to come, and loss of property and religious privileges in this.'

Akbar thus assumed a position similar to that taken up by Henry VIII of England when he established the royal supremacy over the English Church, in virtue of which he ventured to deal with matters of faith, as defined in the Ten Articles of 1536.

Hostility to Islam. From the date of the decree onwards Akbar showed open hostility to Islam, and issued a multitude of orders which violated his declared principle of toleration for all forms of belief.

For instance, the public prayers and call to prayers were stopped, the Ramazān fast and the Mecca pilgrimage were forbidden. In short, as Badāoni puts it, 'every command and direction of Islam, whether special or general . . . all were doubted and ridiculed.' Wanton insults to Muhammadan feeling were offered, as, for example, mosques were turned into stables the name of Muhammad was proscribed, and so forth.

It is a wonder that Akbar did not lose his throne. The fact that he did not is the best proof possible of the immense personal power which he exercised over the minds of men. If the British Government should try to do any one of such things, it would not last a week.

The Dīn Ilāhī, or Divine Faith. Akbar, not finding any religion to suit him, fancied that he could devise a new one made to order out of the best bits of the old ones. He was foolish enough to believe that such an invention could be set up by the imperial authority as a substitute for the existing religions, and that it might be accepted as a bond of union throughout the empire. That was a mad dream. His new creed laid stress on the doctrine of the unity of God and half deified the Padshah as the representative of God on earth. He called it 'Tauhīd Ilāhī', the Divine Unity, or 'Dīn Ilāhī', the Divine Faith.

Certain time-serving courtiers accepted it, and took the required four vows to sacrifice in Akbar's service life, property, honour, and religion, but, outside the court, the scheme was a failure.

It died with its author, or perhaps earlier.

Akbar almost a Hindu. Towards the close of his life, Akbar became practically a Hindu in most respects, adopting many Hindu usages, such as shaving his beard and whiskers, abstaining from beef, and to a large extent from meat of any kind. He issued many regulations framed on Hindu models, and sanctioned suttee (*satī*), provided that the woman's consent was ascertained.

But notwithstanding those facts, there is fairly good evidence that on his death-bed he made formal profession of the Muhammadan faith.

Literature and art. Akbar resembled most of the members

of his family in enjoying and patronizing literature and art. As a boy he had steadily refused to learn his lessons, and to the end of his days was absolutely ignorant of reading and writing. He could not even read or sign his own name. But he kept other people busy reading to him continually, and so learned by the ear more than most men can learn by the eye. He had a marvellously strong memory and an extremely keen understanding.

He collected an enormous library, comprising 24,000 manuscripts, valued at nearly six and a half millions of rupees. The high valuation, working out at about 270 rupees, then equal to thirty pounds sterling, a volume, was due to the employment of the most famous scribes to write the texts, and the most skilled artists to illustrate the contents and bind the books. A few volumes have escaped destruction, and many works by the artists employed are extant.

In the seventh year of his reign Akbar compelled the Rājā of Rīwā (Bhath) to send to court Tānsēn, the poet and musician. Abūl Fazl says that such a singer had not been known in India for a thousand years.

The excellent imperial taste in architecture is best attested by the numerous beautiful buildings still standing at Fathpur-Sīkrī. Akbar wasted huge sums on building that city, which was occupied for a few years only.

Character of Akbar. Although Akbar cannot be described as 'a mixture of opposites', like Muhammad bin Tughlak or Jahāngīr, his nature was complex, and not easy to understand. He was a very human man, not a saint, and was not free from serious faults and frailties. The portrait drawn by most historians—all light with no shadow—is false. In the early years of his reign, after the fall of Bairām Khan, he was in the hands of bad advisers, including the scoundrel Pīr Muhammad, who was allowed to commit appalling cruelties in Mālvā without censure, so far as appears. Towards the close of the reign, when Akbar had exercised uncontrolled power for some forty years, and his generous nature had become to a certain extent corrupted, he committed various foolish and unworthy acts, especially the deliberate insults to Islam above mentioned. He had then acquired the evil opium habit, which probably shortened his life. In earlier days he sometimes drank more than was good for him.

The Jesuits, who give by far the best personal descriptions, rightly praise Akbar's zeal and care in the administration of justice. It must be understood that the justice was of the bloody, ferocious kind then in fashion, and that men were commonly impaled, torn to pieces by elephants, and mutilated. Akbar, however, does not seem to have taken pleasure in witnessing such scenes, as Jahāngīr and Shahjahān did.

Akbar's vanity was, perhaps, his weakest point, as may be learnt from the critical pages of Badāonī. His insatiable curiosity led him into absurd positions from time to time.

Nevertheless, when all that can be said against him has been said, it remains true that Akbar was one of the greatest of kings, comparable in India with Asoka alone, and fully worthy to stand as an equal beside his European contemporaries Elizabeth of England (1558–1603) and Henry IV of France (1593–1610).

He possessed exceptional bodily strength, and courage as undaunted as that of Alexander of Macedon. His fights in Gujarāt and his nine days' ride to Ahmadābād were heroic performances.

The Jesuit accounts. Space does not permit me to quote in full the vivid Jesuit accounts of Akbar as he was in 1582, when forty years of age, but a few of their phrases must be cited. In eating he was ordinary and simple to a notable degree. He was a man of excellent parts with much judgement, prudence, and intelligence, and exceedingly sagacious. He was also very magnanimous and generous, pleasant-mannered and kindly, while still preserving his gravity and sternness. There was nothing that he knew not how to do, whether matters of war, or administration, or the mechanical arts. He rarely lost his temper, but his occasional outbursts of wrath were terrible. He was ready to forgive, being naturally gentle, humane, and kind. 'In truth', we are told, 'he was great with the great, and lowly with the lowly.' It was not easy to find the clue to his thoughts, because, although apparently free from mystery and guile, he was in reality close and self-contained.[1]

That picture, even when thus drawn in bare outline, is a noble one.

Akbar's deeds as a conqueror and administrator stand out clearly on the page of history. He was the real founder of the Mughal empire, and succeeded in establishing an authority which nothing could shake during his lifetime. He took the broad views of a true statesman. He knew how to choose, use, and keep loyal servants. His policy of toleration for all religions was wholly his own, unknown in Europe or Muhammadan Asia in his days.

The stately eulogy bestowed by Wordsworth on a hero now obscure may be applied fitly to Akbar the Great:

> 'Yet shall thy name, conspicuous and sublime,
> Stand in the spacious firmament of time,
> Fixed as a star; such glory is thy right.'

Chronology of Akbar's reign.

Death of Humāyun, accession of Akbar	Jan., 1556
Second battle of Pānīpat; defeat and death of Hēmū	Nov., 1556
Occupation of the Panjāb	1556
Assumption of full authority by Akbar	March, 1560
Abolition of the *jizya* tax	1565
Siege of Chitor	1567–8
Foundation of Fathpur Sikrī	1569
Reduction of Gujarāt	1572
Capture of Surat; suppression of revolt in Gujarāt; completion of fort at Agra	1573
Introduction of Abūl Fazl at court; abolition of tax on pilgrimages	1574
Conquest of Bengal and Bihār; death of Dāūd	1574–6
Rājpūt rising; battle of Gogūnda	1576

[1] Translated from various passages in the Italian of Peruschi and Bartoli.

Decree making Akbar head of the Church	1579
Death of Muhammad Hakīm; annexation of Kābul	1585
Akbar's capital at Lahore	1585-98
Defeat of Rājā Bīrbal by the Yūsufzī	1586
Conquest of Kashmīr	1586-7
Conquest of Sind	1588-90
Embassies to the kingdoms of the Deccan	1591
Annexation of Kandahar	1594
Defence of Ahmadnagar by Chānd Bībī	1595
Death of Prince Murād	1599
Fall of Ahmadnagar	1600
Capture of Asīrgarh	1601
Rebellion of Prince Salīm; murder of Abūl Fazl	1602
Death of Akbar	Oct., 1605

CHAPTER XIX

The reigns of Jahāngīr and Shahjahān: Sir Thomas Roe; Bernier; Mughal architecture.

Accession of Jahāngīr; rebellion of Khusrū. Prince Salīm, then in the thirty-seventh year of his age, ascended the throne without open opposition, taking the style of Jahāngīr, 'World-seizer'. Four months after his accession the intrigues begun during the preceding reign produced a rebellion in favour of his eldest son Khusrū, who occupied Lahore. Jahāngīr, acting on his doctrine that 'kingship regards neither son nor son-in-law: no one is a relation to a king'—pursued the rebel with untiring diligence and crushed the revolt in a month. Khusrū was captured while trying to cross the Chināb, and was brought in chains before his father, who inflicted a terrible penalty on his son's followers. Under the date Thursday, April 23, 1606, the emperor writes in his authentic *Memoirs*:

'For the sake of good government I ordered posts to be set up on both sides of the road from the garden [where I lodged] to the city [Lahore], and ordered them to hang up and impale the seditious Aimāqs and others who had taken part in the rebellion. Thus each one of them received an extraordinary punishment.'

The men impaled are said to have numbered 300. The Dutch author De Laët (1631) adds that Jahāngīr mounted his unhappy son on an elephant and led him between the lines of his writhing followers, while Mahābat Khan (Zamāna Beg) recited the names of the sufferers.

Khusrū was partially blinded and kept in confinement, more or less strict, until 1622, when he was reported officially to have died of colic. But there is sound reason for believing that he was strangled by order of his half-brother, Prince Khurram (Shahjahān), who was resolved to clear away every relative who might possibly claim succession to the throne. The remains of Khusrū lie in the well-known garden at Allahabad which bears his name.

Wars. Jahāngīr, although mentally and morally inferior to his father, was no fool, and was able to preserve intact without much exertion the empire which he had inherited. Early in his reign he visited Kābul, and some years later suppressed a rebellion in that province. The central Sūbas gave him little trouble, but from time to time armies had to be sent into Rājputāna, Bengal, and the Deccan, as well as to Kābul and Kāngrā.

Jahāngīr's ambitions ; Kandahār. Jahāngīr inherited from his father and personally cherished two great objects of ambition—one, to recover the ancestral dominions of his house beyond the Oxus, the other to bring all Southern India under his sway. He did not succeed in effecting either purpose. His armies never got near the Oxus. Their most distant achievement was the recovery of Kandahār from the Persians early in the reign. Later, towards the close of 1621, the Persians retook the city.

The Deccan. In the Deccan, Ahmadnagar, taken by Akbar's forces in 1600 (*ante*, p. 177), had been recovered for the local dynasty by an Abyssinian minister named Malik Ambar, who forced the imperial troops to retire to Burhānpur, and harassed them by attacks of light cavalry, worked in that Marāthā fashion which, at a later date, proved too much for all the resources of Aurangzeb. Jahāngīr was never able to make much progress in the conquest of the Deccan, although the city of Ahmadnagar was regained for a time.

Bengal. A rebellion in Bengal, headed by Usmān Khan, an Afghan chief, which had begun in the preceding reign, was ended in 1612 by the killing of the rebel leader.

Mewār. Amar Singh, the proud Rānā of Mewār (Udaipur), and head of the Rājpūt clans, whose ancestors had defied Bābur and Akbar, was reduced to submission in the ninth year of the reign (1614) by Prince Khurram (Shahjahān). The Rājpūt prince was pursued so unceasingly that he could hold out no longer. He and his son Karan, who were received with marked honour and courtesy by the prince, acknowledged the Padshah as their superior lord. Jahāngīr caused life-sized marble statues of the Rānā and his son to be carved and set up in the garden under the audience-window at Agra. Unfortunately, those interesting works of art have disappeared.

Conquest of Kāngrā. Another important military success was gained later in the reign (1620) by the reduction of the famous fortress of Kāngrā in the Panjāb, which Akbar had failed to subdue. Jahāngīr was extremely proud of this victory. Afterwards, he visited the stronghold and destroyed its sanctity in Hindu eyes by slaughtering a bullock and erecting a mosque within the precincts.

Plague. In the tenth year of the reign a deadly outbreak of plague occurred in the Panjāb. The disease, which Jahāngīr believed to have been previously unknown in India, spread to Delhi, Kashmīr, and most parts of Hindustan. Rats were affected, just as they have been by the plague which began in 1896.

The Empress Nūrjahān. Perhaps the marriage of Jahāngīr, in May 1611, with the Persian lady named Mihr-un-nisā may be regarded as the most important event of his reign, because she became the real sovereign, the power behind the throne. That lady, on whom Jahāngīr conferred at first the title of Nūrmahall (' Light of the Palace '), and later that of

Nūrjahān ('Light of the World'), by which she is usually known, had attracted his admiration during his father's lifetime. Akbar discouraged the prince's suit, and married Mihr-un-nisā to an officer named Ali Kulī, better known by his title of Sher Afgan Khan ('the tiger-thrower'). After the accession of Prince Salīm to the throne Sher Afgan was appointed Governor of Bardwān in Bengal. He incurred the displeasure of Jahāngīr, who sent his own foster-brother Kutb-ud-dīn Khan with orders to dispatch Sher Afgan to court, and if he should resist to punish him. When Kutb-ud-dīn attempted to enforce his orders Sher Afgan killed him and was himself slain by the followers of the imperial official, who, to quote Jahāngīr's words, fell upon Sher Afgan, 'cut him in pieces, and sent him to hell'. The emperor adds the comment that 'it is to be hoped that the place of that black-faced scoundrel will ever be there'. Although there is no positive evidence that Jahāngīr ordered the destruction of Sher Afgan in order that he might gain possession of the widow, the ferocity of the remark quoted permits of little doubt on the subject. Mihr-un-nisā was brought to court, but allowed fully four years to pass before she consented to accept the position of principal consort to Jahāngīr. Once she was installed as empress, her husband submitted to her guidance without reserve, and granted her privileges beyond all precedent. She sat at the audience-window to hear petitions, and her name appeared on the coinage along with that of Jahāngīr. In fact, she governed the empire. The Muhammadan chroniclers affirm that Jahāngīr used to say that 'Nūrjahān was wise enough to conduct the business of State, while he wanted only a bottle of wine and a piece of meat wherewith to make merry'. Nūrjahān certainly exercised a good influence on her husband, whose intemperance and cruelty she checked to some extent. She is said to have been 'an asylum to all sufferers' and a generous patron of many needy suppliants, especially of dowerless girls. Her power came to an end after the accession of Shahjahān, but she was well treated and allowed a liberal income. She lived until

1645, when she died at Lahore, where she was buried by the side of Jahāngīr. Her father, Itīmād-ud-daula, her able brother, Āṣaf Khan, and numerous other relatives had shared her wealth and power while they lasted.

Intrigues; rebellion of Prince Khurram. The empress sought to secure her position at court by marrying to Prince Khurram, third son of the emperor, her brother's daughter, the famous Mumtāz Mahall, 'the Lady of the Tāj', and by uniting her own daughter by her first husband to Shahryār, the youngest son of Jahāngīr. At first she favoured Prince Khurram, but when the Deccan wars enhanced his reputation, she grew jealous and transferred her support to Prince Shahryār. Her intrigues on his behalf drove the elder brother into rebellion. He was defeated by Mahābat Khan, his father's general, and compelled to flee, first to Masulipatam on the east coast, and thence to Bengal. In 1625 he was partially reconciled with his father, who conferred on him the title of Shahjahān, 'King of the World'.

Rebellion of Mahābat Khan. In course of time, Mahābat Khan in his turn became the object of the jealousy of the empress, and was forced to rebel in self-defence. In the year 1626, when Jahāngīr was on his way to Kābul, the insurgent general cleverly secured the trump card in the game of intrigue by seizing the emperor's person, and in the next year Nūrjahān, with equal cleverness, enabled him to regain his freedom.

Sir Thomas Roe. Sir Thomas Roe, the dignified ambassador of James I of England (*ante*, p. 164), was admitted to close intimacy with the drunken monarch to whom he was accredited, and had to do his best to take his share in the frequent midnight orgies. He has left on record a lively description of Jahāngīr and his court. Another Englishman, William Hawkins, who had visited Agra a few years earlier, and joined more willingly in the royal potations, was much disgusted by the bloodthirsty cruelty of the emperor.

Death of Jahāngīr, 1627. Jahāngīr habitually spent the

hot season in Kashmīr, which he called 'a garden of eternal spring, a delightful flower-bed, and a heart-expanding heritage for dervishes'. In October 1627, when returning thence, he was taken ill and died suddenly after a reign of twenty-two years. His remains lie in a fine mausoleum at Lahore, which city was usually treated as his capital.

Character of Jahāngīr. Jahāngīr has been described as 'a talented drunkard'. In his youth he had been spoiled, and he grew up to be a wilful, cruel man, easy-going and good-natured when not thwarted, but a ferocious savage when angered. Like Muhammad bin Tughlak, he was 'a mixture of opposites'. We know all about him, because we have his own account of nineteen years of his reign recorded in his authentic *Memoirs*, in addition to many narratives by Indian and European writers, not to speak of numerous life-like portraits, the work of skilled artists. We can thus see the man as he was—the typical Asiatic despot, a strange compound of tenderness and cruelty, justice and caprice, refinement and brutality, good sense and childishness. Jahāngīr prided himself especially on his love of justice. When recording the execution of a notable personage for the crime of murder, he observes: 'God forbid that in such affairs I should consider princes, and far less that I should consider Amīrs.' But his justice was bloody and cruel, rarely tempered with mercy. For instance, he had no hesitation in sentencing hundreds of men at a time to be impaled on sharp stakes. He could feel the most acute grief for the loss of a wife or child, and yet hamstring and kill certain wretched beaters who had accidentally spoiled his shot at an antelope. He loved both nature and art. He was an expert judge of painting and delighted in fine scenery or lovely flowers. The blossom of the *dhāk* tree, he remarks, 'is so beautiful that one cannot take one's eyes off it'. The Rev. Edward Terry, Sir Thomas Roe's chaplain, while admitting that the emperor did not always abide by his promises, records the fact that Englishmen 'found a free trade, a peaceable residence, and a very good esteem with that king and people'. The life and reign of Jahāngīr deserve treatment better than they have yet received from historians.

Shahryār and Dāwar Baksh ; accession of Shahjahān. When Jahāngīr died two of his sons still lived. Prince Khurram or Shahjahān, the elder of the two and the ablest member of the family, was then far away in the Deccan. Shahryār, the younger, was at Lahore.[1] Āsaf Khan, whose daughter, Mumtāz Mahall, was married to Shahjahān, naturally desired his son-in-law to succeed. In order to gain time until he should arrive, Āsaf Khan set up as Pādshāh, Khusrū's son, Dāwar Baksh, nicknamed Bulākī, who, according to some authorities, had been nominated as heir-apparent by Jahāngīr. Shahryār, who was known as Nā-shudanī or 'Good for nothing', was easily defeated by Āsaf Khan and blinded. Shahjahān, summoned by an express messenger, hurried to the north and gave orders for the killing of all his male relations who might possibly claim the throne. His orders were carried out so secretly that the exact truth could not be known, and authors consequently differ concerning both the names of the princes who perished and the manner of their deaths. It is certain that Shahryār and several young cousins of Shahjahān were put to death. Dāwar Baksh escaped to Persia, where two European travellers, Olearius and Tavernier, met him.

Shahjahān, having thus cleared away all rivals, ascended the throne in February 1628.

Wars in the Deccan. Shahjahān, like his father and grandfather, aimed at the recovery of the lost provinces near the Oxus and the conquest of Southern India. He was more successful in both projects than Jahāngīr had been. His early wars in the Deccan lasted for about seven years (1630–7). At the beginning of them he had to suppress a troublesome revolt by a noble named Khan Jahān Lodī, who was hunted down and killed. Six years later the king of Bijāpur promised to pay

[1] The fate of Khusrū, the eldest son, has been narrated. Parvīz, the second son, died a year before his father. A son named Jahāndār had died in childhood.

tribute, and in 1637 the kingdom of Ahmadnagar was finally annexed to the empire. Towards the close of the reign (1657) both Bijāpur and Golkonda were again attacked and seemed to be on the point of submission, when operations were suspended owing to the war of succession between Shahjahān's four sons.

Kandahār, Balkh, and Badakshān. In the year which saw the fall of Ahmadnagar (1637) Ali Mardān Khan, an officer of the king of Persia, was persuaded to sell Kandahār for a lakh of rupees, and to take service under Shahjahān, who promoted him to high honour. In 1644 Ali Mardān Khan took possession of the province of Balkh, the ancient Bactria, situated between the Hindū Kush mountains and the Oxus. Prince Murād Baksh, the emperor's youngest son, then occupied Badakshān, the mountainous region to the east of Balkh, but left his government without leave, and was superseded by his younger brother, Prince Aurangzeb, who was driven out of Balkh with heavy loss (1647). Kandahār was recovered by the Persians in the following year (1648), and so passed for ever from the control of the Mughals.

Famine in Gujarāt, 1630–2. During the early years of the Deccan wars, the province of Gujarāt (including Khāndēsh) suffered from a fearful famine (1630–2), described in the *Badshah-nāma*, and also in the *Travels* of Peter Mundy, an English merchant, who journeyed on business from Surat to Agra and Patna and back again while the famine and consequent pestilence were raging. People were afraid to travel for fear of being eaten, and 'the flesh of a son was preferred to his love'. The ground was strewn with corpses so thickly that Mundy could hardly find room to pitch a small tent. In towns the dead were dragged 'out by the heels, stark naked, of all ages and sexes, and there are left, so that the way is half barred up. Thus it was for the most part hitherto', that is to say, midway between Surat and Burhānpur. The sickness was so deadly that at Surat seventeen out of twenty-one English traders died. Meantime, the camp of Shahjahān at

Burhānpur was overflowing with provisions. So far as Mundy saw, the Government did nothing to help the people, but the author of the *Badshah-nāma* asserts that Shahjahān opened a few soup-kitchens, gave a lakh and a half of rupees in charity spread over twenty weeks, and remitted one-eleventh of the revenue. The relief thus granted was too trifling to be of any use. Of course it would have been impossible to collect the full assessment. Sir Richard Temple justly observes that 'it is worth while to read Mundy's unimpassioned, matter-of-fact observations on this famine, if only to grasp the difference of the conditions of native life under the Mogul and the British Governments'.

Destruction of Hindu temples. Shahjahān, who wished to be considered an orthodox Musalman, unlike Akbar and Jahāngīr, issued orders in 1632 for the destruction throughout his dominions of all Hindu temples recently built. In the Benares District alone seventy-six temples were destroyed in compliance with that order. Figures for other localities are not recorded.

The Portuguese of Hūglī. Both Akbar and Jāhangīr had shown favour to Christians and Christianity, one motive which influenced Jahāngīr being his desire to benefit from European trade. The Portuguese, who had been allowed to settle and build a fort at Hūglī (Hooghly), thirty miles above the site of Calcutta, abused the privileges granted and broke the peace of the empire by shameless piracy and a cruel slave-trade. They were rash enough to give special offence to Mumtāz Mahall, who used her all-powerful influence to compass their destruction. In 1631, the year of her death, an officer of Shahjahān stormed the Portuguese stronghold, killing about 10,000 of the defenders, who were 'either blown up with powder, drowned in water, or burnt by fire'. Between 4,000 and 5,000 prisoners were brought to Agra and treated with great cruelty. Their misery, Bernier tells us, was 'unparalleled in the history of modern times'. Unfortunately, it cannot be said that their sufferings were wholly undeserved.

Shahjahān pulled down the belfry of the church at Agra, but did not completely destroy the building, which still exists.

Character and administration of Shahjahān. Most modern historians, dazzled by the beauty of the imperial buildings, and misled by a phrase of Tavernier to the effect that Shahjahān governed his people 'like a father' with exceptional mildness, as well as by the authority of Elphinstone, have been inclined to give Shahjahān undeserved praise for the supposed excellence of his personal character and the alleged efficiency of his administration. Aurangzeb has been held up to universal reproach because he made his way to the throne through the blood of his brothers, while Shahjahān, who did exactly the same thing, is allowed to escape without censure. He was even credited by Elphinstone with 'a life not sullied' by crime. Older writers knew better. Tavernier, notwithstanding his use of the phrase cited above, states plainly that Shahjahān 'by degrees murdered all those who from having shown affection for his nephew had made themselves suspects, and the early years of his reign were marked by cruelties which have much tarnished his memory'. The Dutch author van den Broecke (in De Läet), writing in 1629 or 1630, while admitting that the character of the new monarch had not yet become fully known, was convinced that a kingdom won by so many crimes and the slaughter of so many innocent victims, could not prosper. In reality, the personal character of the much-censured Aurangzeb was superior to that of the much-praised Shahjahān, who was treacherous, cruel, sensual, and avaricious. The 'justice' with which he has been credited was usually nothing better than the savage ferocity practised by his father.

Peter Mundy, who has been already quoted, gives a glimpse into the actual state of the empire early in the reign (1630–3). When staying at Patna, he found that travelling whether by river or road was unsafe, because 'this country, as all the rest of India, swarms with rebels and thieves'. Provincial governors sought to repress disorder by wholesale massacres, which they were allowed to commit without check by the imperial Government. At a place in the Cawnpore District Mundy saw more than 200 small masonry pillars (*mīnārs*) each three or four yards high, and each containing, set in plaster, thirty or forty heads of persons supposed to be thieves. When he came back a few months later to the same camping-ground, sixty more such pillars had been added. Thus in that one locality a single governor had slaughtered about 8,000 people in a short time.[1] That state of affairs was not exceptional. '*Mīnārs*', we are told, 'are commonly near to great cities.' Much other contemporary evidence might be cited to prove the misgovernment of Shahjahān's dominions, especially in the earlier years of his reign. Some improvement probably took place between 1644 and 1656, when the office of prime minister was held by Sādullah Khan Allāmī, who is reputed to have been the best minister ever known in India. Whatever good administration really existed during the reign should be attributed to him rather than to his unscrupulous master. Murshīd Kulī Khan did good work by introducing into the Deccan the revenue system of Todar Mall, with certain necessary local variations.

Wealth of Shahjahān. The wealth amassed by Shahjahān far exceeded the vast treasure left by Akbar and was of almost incredible amount. The German traveller Mandelslo (1638) states that he was 'credibly informed' that the Mogul's treasure (no doubt including jewels and bullion) exceeded 1,500 millions of crowns, or 3,000 millions of rupees, equivalent to 337½ millions of pounds sterling at the then current rate of exchange (2*s*. 3*d*. to the rupee). Whatever the exact figures should be, the total undoubtedly was stupendous.

Shahjahān thus possessed practically unlimited funds to spend on the costly buildings which were his hobby. The Tāj and connected structures probably cost something like four million pounds sterling, and the expenditure on Delhi was

[1] 260 pillars × 30, the minimum number of heads in each = 7,800.

Dīwān-ī-khās of Delhi Palace

equally extravagant. The splendour of the court was unexampled, millions being lavished on the famous peacock throne. All this reckless display was paid for by the people, who were ground down by hundreds of official oppressors. A learned Hindu historian describes the Mughal empire as 'a system of organized brigandage'. The phrase has an element of truth in it.

The four sons of Shahjahān. Shahjahān had four sons, Dārā Shikoh,[1] Shujā, Aurangzeb, and Murād Baksh. In 1657, when the emperor became seriously ill, these four sons, all men of mature age, prepared to contest the succession to the throne. Their father had attempted to secure the succession for the eldest by keeping him at Agra and appointing his brothers to distant governments, but the device failed, and each claimant, ignoring the sovereign's will, gathered his forces and made ready for battle. Each had, as Bernier, the French traveller, observed, 'no choice between a kingdom and death.'

The contest for the crown. Shujā in Bengal and Murād Baksh in Gujarāt each assumed imperial titles and struck coin in his own name, of which specimens exist. The cautious and wily Aurangzeb did nothing of the kind. The army of Dārā Shikoh, which had speedily put Shujā to flight, now had a more serious task to face in confronting Aurangzeb. He moved northwards in the spring of 1658, dexterously representing himself as being merely desirous to help Murād Baksh, with whose levies he united his own. A fiercely contested battle between Aurangzeb and Murād Baksh on one side and Dārā Shikoh on the other, fought at Samūgarh, nine miles from Agra, ended in the decisive victory of the younger princes.

Shahjahān confined; Murād Baksh captured. In June, 1658, Aurangzeb, who had a friend at court in the person of his sister Roshan Rāi, made his father prisoner, confining him

[1] The title means 'equal in splendour to Darius'. The common practice of citing the prince's name as Dārā (Darius), although convenient, is inaccurate. His personal name was Muhammad. The forms Shikoh and Shukoh are both in use.

to the precincts of the palace, where he had the society of his other daughter, Jahānāra. Next month the hapless Murād Baksh learned the true value of his brother's professions of unselfish support. No difficulty was found in making the foolish young prince hopelessly drunk, and throwing him into chains to await execution at a more convenient time, which came in 1660.

Fate of Dārā Shikoh and Shujā. The pursuit of Dārā Shikoh was continued with unceasing vigour, and at last he was run down in Cutch (Kacchh), brought to Delhi, and paraded through the streets, dressed in the meanest clothes, and mounted on a scarecrow elephant. In September, 1659, he was beheaded, on the pretext that he had become an apostate from Islam and the ally of infidels. It is true that Dārā Shikoh shared his great-grandfather's scepticism, but, of course, his execution was due to his position as claimant of the throne. Shujā made one more effort in Bengal, and was even able to occupy Benares, Allahabad, and Jaunpur. He was overcome by Aurangzeb's able lieutenant, Mīr Jumla, and ultimately driven into Arakan, where, according to some accounts, he was last seen fleeing over the mountains, accompanied by three faithful men and one woman. He certainly perished, one way or another, and was never heard of again.

Accession of Aurangzeb ; death of his father. Aurangzeb, who had been informally proclaimed emperor in July 1658, was now able to assume the imperial position with full ceremony in May, 1659. His old father, although never permitted to quit the palace enclosure, and subjected to many indignities, was allowed plenty of dancing-girls, and lived a voluptuous life until February 1, 1666, when he died at the age of seventy-four. He was buried in the Tāj, the superb monument which he had erected to the memory of his favourite consort.

Mumtāz Mahall ; sensuality of Shahjahān. That lady, known by the title of Mumtāz Mahall (of which 'Tāj' is a corruption), was the niece of Nūrjahān, the able empress of Jahāngīr. She was the mother of fourteen of Shahjahān's children, in all sixteen in number, and during her lifetime was the object of his devoted affection. But after she was gone he allowed himself in his old age to indulge in unseemly pleasures, and lost all capacity for serious business.

Mughal architecture. The masterpieces of Mughal architecture belong by universal consent to the reign of Shahjahān, in connexion with whom the subject is best considered. The beautiful domed architecture of the Mughal period is not a product of India. It is essentially foreign, that is to say, Persian in style. But the earlier specimens were considerably affected in details by the employment of Hindu artisans, and the later examples are much enriched by the use of the Florentine style of inlay (*pietra dura*) apparently imported from Italy by European artists in the service of Shahjahān.

Early Mughal buildings. Bābur and Humāyun, who both possessed excellent taste, are recorded to have erected many splendid edifices, but nearly all these have perished. Akbar loved building, and one of the finest examples of the early Mughal style is the massive mausoleum or tomb of his father near Delhi, finished in the fifteenth year of his reign, and erected at the expense of Hājī Begam, the senior widow of Humāyun. While the general design suggests that of the Tāj, the earlier building is far more simple and severe than the great edifice of Shahjahān. The buildings of Fathpur-Sikrī, begun in 1569, are universally admired. The mausoleum of Akbar, at Sikandra near Agra, planned and erected under the orders of Jahāngīr, is unique in design. The other works of Jahāngīr's time are chiefly at Lahore.

Works of Shahjahān. Everybody is agreed that the crowning glory of Mughal architecture is the mausoleum of Mumtāz Mahall at Agra, commonly known as the Tāj, which occupied a multitude of workmen incessantly for twenty-two years. New Delhi, or Shahjahānabad, was built under the direction of Shahjahān, whose palace there, when perfect, probably was the most magnificent edifice of its kind in the world. During recent years, especially under Lord Curzon's orders, much has

The Tāj Mahal

been done to preserve and restore the numerous Mughal buildings at Agra, Delhi, and elsewhere. The Indo-Persian paintings of Shahjahān's time are very fine, and include a long series of charming portraits.

CHAPTER XX

The reign of Aurangzeb: his treatment of the Hindus; the Rājpūt revolt; Sivājī and the rise of the Marāthās.

Aurangzeb at the time of his accession. In May, 1659, when Aurangzeb assumed the full honours of the imperial dignity under the title of Ālamgīr, conferred by his father, he was forty years of age, mature in body and mind, well skilled in affairs, both civil and military, and firmly convinced that it was his duty to uphold his religion at any cost. The history of his long reign, extending like Akbar's over a period of fifty years save one, may be condensed as being that of the failure of an attempt to govern a vast empire, inhabited chiefly by Hindus, on the principles of an ascetic Muslim saint.

Aurangzeb's principles of government. Aurangzeb never flinched from the practical action logically resulting from his theory, that it was his duty as a faithful Muslim king to foster the interests of orthodox Sunnī Islam, to suppress idolatry, and, as far as possible, to discourage and disown all idolaters, heretics (including Shīah Muhammadans), and infidels. He could not do all he would, but he did all he could to carry his principles into effect. No fear of unpopularity, no consideration of political expediency, no dread of resistance, was suffered to turn him for a moment from his religious duty as he conceived it. The Emperor Aurangzeb was a man of high intellectual powers, a brilliant writer, as his letters prove, an astute diplomatist, a soldier of undaunted courage, a skilled administrator, a just and merciful judge, a pious ascetic in his personal habits, and yet a failure.

Palliation of his fight for the throne. He crossed a river

AURANGZEB

of blood to gain the throne. The best defence that can be offered for the crimes by which he won it, is that indicated in his letter reproaching his old tutor :

> 'Ought you not', he writes, 'to have foreseen that I might at some future period be compelled to contend with my brothers, sword in hand, for the crown, and for my very existence? Such, as you must well know, has been the fate of the children of almost every king of Hindustan.'

That defence, as far as it goes, is sound. If any one of his brothers had gained the prize, Aurangzeb would have suffered death, and he can hardly be blamed because he preferred to inflict, rather than suffer, death. The deposition of his father was a necessary consequence of the defeat of Dārā Shikoh, who had already assumed the imperial authority with the assent of the aged emperor, who was then no longer fit to rule. Once the deposition had been effected, Aurangzeb spared his father's life though sternly refusing him liberty. The brutal treatment of Dārā Shikoh, which cannot be justified, is explained by Aurangzeb's intense hatred for all forms of religious heresy. His eldest brother, an avowed freethinker, was to him a thing accursed, and a fit object for extremest insult. Aurangzeb regarded the world from the point of view of a Muslim ascetic, and as against the rights of orthodoxy the claims of kindred or of justice to Hindu unbelievers were nothing in his eyes. He took up the position of Philip II of Spain in relation to the people of the Netherlands. Like that monarch he was intensely suspicious, trusting neither man nor woman. His love, although perhaps sometimes given, was seldom sought and never returned, except by one grandson, Prince Bedār Bakht.

Mīr Jumla's attack on Assam. In the earlier part of the reign the only wars, other than that of the succession, which claim notice are those with Assam and Arakan. Mīr Jumla, the able general, who had done such good service for Aurangzeb when he was viceroy of the Deccan, and again in hunting down Shujā, was rash enough to follow in the footsteps of Muhammad the son of Bakhtyār (*ante*, p. 115) and to invade

Assam. Mīr Jumla failed like his early predecessor, and, like him, died soon after his return (1663).

Annexation of part of Arakan by Shāyista Khan. In the course of the same year, Aurangzeb's uncle, Shāyista Khan, who had allowed himself to be surprised by the Marāthās in the Deccan, was transferred to Bengal as the successor of Mīr Jumla. He governed the eastern province for about thirty years. His expulsion of the English merchants from his territory in 1686 has been mentioned (*ante*, p. 166). At an earlier date (1666) he had cleared out the Portuguese and other pirates who infested the rivers in the neighbourhood of Chittagong, and sent an expedition against the king of Arakan, who had abetted the evil-doers, and was compelled to cede the Chittagong territory.

Twenty years' peace. 'The expeditions into Assam and Arakan did not disturb the general peace of Hindustan. A profound tranquillity, broken by no rebellion of any political importance, reigned throughout Northern India for the first twenty years of Aurangzeb's rule.' It is true that for nearly three years (1673–5) the Afghan clans beyond the Indus gave trouble, and during part of that time Aurangzeb in person superintended the operations of his generals, but the peace of India, as a whole, was not disturbed by skirmishing on the north-western frontier.

Attack on Hinduism. Much more important than frontier fighting was the change in the emperor's internal policy which began in 1672. Before that date he had not felt himself at liberty to carry out fully his theory of government, but now he deemed his position sufficiently assured to justify an attack on his idolatrous subjects. He went so far as to order 'the governors of provinces to destroy with a willing hand the schools and temples of the infidels; and they were strictly enjoined to put an entire stop to the teaching and practising of idolatrous forms of worship'. Of course such orders could not be carried out completely, but the lofty minarets of the mosque on the bank of the Ganges at Benares, occupying

Nawāb Shāyista Khan

the site of a famous temple, bear witness to their partial execution.

The jizya reimposed. Aurangzeb never became a sanguinary persecutor. No massacres stain the annals of his reign. He was content to worry the Hindus, insult their religion, and make compulsory converts. In pursuance of this perverse policy he made an attempt to seize the children of the deceased Rājā Jaswant Singh of Mārwār, apparently with the intention of bringing them up as Muslims (? 1678), and, in 1679, against all advice, reimposed the *jizya*, or poll-tax on Hindus, which Akbar had wisely abolished (*ante*, p. 181).

Rājpūt rebellion. The outrage on the children kindled a flame in Rājputāna, and produced a serious rebellion in which both Mārwār and Mewār joined, although Jaipur (Ambēr) still remained loyal. Prince Akbar, the emperor's fourth son, who had been sent against the rebels, allowed himself to dream a dream of empire supported by Rājpūt swords, and went over to the enemy. But his father's diplomacy was too much for him—the levies melted away, and the young prince was ultimately driven into exile in Persia (1681), from which he never returned. He lived there until 1706.

Alienation of the Rājpūts. After some time the Rānā of Mewār (Udaipur) made an honourable peace, by a treaty which contained no allusion to the odious *jizya*, and Rājā Jaswant Singh's son was recognized as chieftain of Mārwār. The mischief, however, had been done, and Aurangzeb had wantonly thrown away his most trusty weapon, the devotion of the Rājpūt chivalry. During the following struggle in the Deccan he learned the extent of his loss, but never repented of his action or swerved a hair's breadth from his principles. Notwithstanding the treaty, Rājputāna was not pacified, and the greater part of the country continued in revolt until the end of the reign.

Prohibition of histories. A curious decree of the eleventh year of the reign abolished the office of imperial chronicler and forbade the publication of histories by private persons. This prohibition has caused a certain amount of indistinctness in the details and obscurity in the chronology of the greater part of Aurangzeb's long reign. Such histories as were written secretly had to wait for publication until the emperor's death.

Aurangzeb and the Deccan. In 1657, when called away to take his part in the fight for the throne, Prince Aurangzeb, then viceroy of the Deccan, that is to say of Khāndēsh, Berār, Telingāna, and Ahmadnagar, seemed to be on the point of annexing the kingdoms of Golkonda and Bijāpur and bringing the whole of the Deccan under the rule of his father. Many years elapsed before Aurangzeb as emperor was able to return to the scene of his early labours. Meantime a new power had arisen, which, rashly despised at first, became strong enough to baffle all the efforts of the imperial grand army, and to condemn the aged emperor to long-drawn years of fruitless toil, ending in lonely death, 'without heart or help'.

The new-born Marāthā power. Before taking up the story of Aurangzeb's campaigns in the Deccan during the twenty-six years from the close of 1681 to 1707, we must go back to trace the origin of the new-born Marāthā power and sketch the life of Sivājī, who gave it birth. The Marāthās are the Hindu population of Mahārāshtra, the country of the Western Ghāts, lying to the south of the Sātpura hills, to the west of the Warda river, and extending southwards as far as Goa. In the thirteenth century this region had been the centre of the Yādava power (*ante*, p. 94). Its best known towns are Poona, Sātārā, Kolhapur, and Nāsik.

Description of the Marāthās. The Marāthā people are well described by Elphinstone, who knew them intimately.

'They are', he writes, 'small, sturdy men, well made though not handsome. They are all active, laborious, hardy, and persevering. If they have none of the pride and dignity of the Rājpūts, they have none of their indolence or their want of worldly wisdom. A Rājpūt warrior, as long as he does not dishonour his race, seems almost indifferent to the result of any contest he is engaged in. A Marāthā thinks of nothing but the result, and cares little for the means, if he can attain his object. For this purpose he will strain his wits, renounce his pleasures, and hazard his person; but he has not a conception of sacrificing his life, or even his interest, for a point of honour.'

To this description of the ordinary low-caste Marāthā may be added the remark that the Brahmans of Mahārāshtra are characterized by extreme subtlety and intellectual power, qualities not always devoted in these latter times to the service of the British Government.

Early life of Sivājī. Sivājī, 'the mountain rat', who frustrated the imperial plans for the subjugation of the south, was the son of Shāhjī, who in early life had served the king of Ahmadnagar, and afterwards became governor of Poona, under the king of Bijāpur. While still a lad of nineteen (1646) Sivājī began a career as a brigand chieftain, and seized several hill forts in succession. Between 1649 and 1659 he made himself master of a large tract of country to the south of Poona.

Murder of Afzal Khan. In the year 1659 the king of Bijāpur sent an army against him under the command of Afzal Khan. The Marāthā chief, feigning submission, managed to approach the general and to kill him by a treacherous blow with a concealed weapon, known as a 'tiger's claw'. Three years later Bijāpur made peace, leaving Sivājī in possession of the territory which he had acquired.

Shāyista Khan. The Marāthā now ventured to ravage the Mughal territories, and thus provoked Aurangzeb to send his uncle, Shāyista Khan, to suppress him. But the Mughal commander, having allowed himself to be surprised, was transferred to Bengal, as already narrated (*ante*, p. 210).

Auzangzeb's mistake. Other generals, including Prince Muazzam, were now sent against the rebel, and ultimately (1665) Rājā Jaswant Singh of Jaipur forced Sivājī to submit and even to come to Delhi to do homage. Aurangzeb made the mistake of treating his opponent with disrespect, and so incurring his undying enmity. Sivājī escaped secretly from the court, returned to the Deccan, and in 1667 compelled the Mughal commanders in practice to recognize him as Rājā.

Renewed war; death of Sivājī, 1680. The war was soon renewed, and the Marāthā freely plundered the imperial territories, including the rich town of Surat, but excepting the English factory there. In 1674 Sivājī proclaimed himself sovereign of his territories with royal pomp at his capital of Rāigarh. He then crossed the Narbadā, and levied the *chauth*, or fourth part of the land revenue, a species of blackmail, payment of which was supposed to protect a district from plunder. In the south, where his father and brother had held *jāgīrs*, he occupied the fortresses of Vellore and Jinjī (Gingee), and was granted additional territory by the king of Bijāpur, in payment for help against the Mughals. In 1680 he died at the age of fifty-three leaving behind him a great reputation as the champion of Hinduism, the creator of a nation, and the founder of a powerful kingdom.

Civil administration. Sivājī, who had begun life as a mere robber chieftain, showed, as his power grew, that he knew how to govern his unruly subjects. He was a devout Hindu, and, although illiterate and unable to sign his name, was well versed in the sacred stories dear to all Hindus. His government, accordingly, was organized on a Hindu pattern. The supreme authority under the Rājā was a council of eight ministers who followed the principles of Brahman law. The chief minister was called the Peshwā. Other members of the council severally looked after various departments—finance, the army, and so forth. The Marāthā territory was divided into districts, each with a staff of officials, and each village had its headman (*patēl*). Higher local officers were known as Desādhikārs, Talukdārs, and Sūbadārs. The ministers usually held military commands, and left their civil duties to deputies (*Kārbāris*). The revenue settlements were made annually. Justice was in the hands of *panchāyats*.

Army and navy. The army was controlled by a commander-in-chief, below whom was a regular gradation of officers.

The men were paid. At first Sivājī relied on his infantry recruited from the Western Ghāts and the Konkan—men who could climb like monkeys and capture the hill forts which were the seat of his power. Gradually the light cavalry became the most important Marāthā arm. The horsemen preferred the lance to any other weapon. Discipline was strict. No soldier was allowed to bring a woman into the field, on pain of death. In this respect Sivājī's force differed widely from the armies of the Mughals, and even from those of the East India Company, which were always clogged by a train of female followers. Plunder, the chief object of Marāthā operations, all belonged to the Rājā, and had to be accounted for strictly. Cows, cultivators, and women were not to be injured. A fleet capable of carrying four thousand soldiers helped the operations of the army on the coast.

Character of Sivājī. Sivājī was a born leader of men—born in a time when fraud had to be met by fraud and force by force. None of his enemies surpassed him in guile, nor was any of them his match in decision and vigour when he resolved to employ force. Other things being equal, he preferred fraud to force. It was not a time for men of nice scruples, and Sivājī was as unscrupulous as any of his rivals. The Marāthās, honouring him as the champion of Hinduism, the protector of cows and Brahmans, recognize in him an *avatār* or incarnation of the Deity. Less partial critics are willing to give him full credit for many personal merits and to palliate his crimes as being the result of his evil surroundings.[1]

Aurangzeb assumes command in the Deccan. At the close of 1681, a year after Sivājī's death, Aurangzeb in person took command of the army of the Deccan, resolved to extinguish the kingdoms of Golkonda and Bijāpur, to curb the insolence

[1] Portraits of Sivājī have been published from time to time, but it is doubtful if they really represent him. Grant Duff notes that no description of his person is on record and that no portrait was preserved at either Kolhāpur or Sātārā.

of the Marāthās, and, if possible, to bring the whole south under Mughal rule.

His treatment of the Hindus. The emperor's obstinate adherence to his wrong-headed policy of annoying his Hindu subjects added immensely to the inherent difficulties of his task. The first thing he did was to issue stringent orders for the collection of the arrears of the *jizya* tax in the southern provinces, and in three months he compelled his officers to squeeze 26,000 rupees out of Burhānpur. Insult was added to pecuniary injury by a proclamation that no Hindu should ride in a palankin or on an Arab horse without special licence. Such measures, of course, made the entire Hindu population the friends of his foes; but no consideration of prudence sufficed to turn Aurangzeb from his fixed policy.

The affairs of Golkonda. When he returned to the Deccan he found the government of Golkonda in confusion. The king, Abūl Hasan, had abandoned himself to pleasure and ceased to take any part in public affairs, which were controlled by the representative of the emperor at his court and by two Hindu officials. Aurangzeb, who could not endure Hindu influence, sent his son, Prince Muazzam, to restore order. The prince dallied over his task, but at last attacked the cityof Hyderabad, which he permitted his soldiers to plunder. The king took refuge in the adjoining fortress of Golkonda. In 1685 the prince, having made peace on terms displeasing to his father, was recalled.

Annexation of Bijāpur, 1686. The emperor, leaving Golkonda alone for the moment, deputed another son, Prince Azam, to reduce Bijāpur. He had little success, and was superseded by his father, who took the capital in 1686 after an investment lasting more than a year. The kingdom ceased to exist, and the splendid city became the abode of desolation, as it is for the most part to this day.

Siege and annexation of Golkonda. Aurangzeb then resolved to make an end of the sister state of Golkonda, and to depose the king, who was accused of sending money to the Marāthās, and allying himself with infidels. When Abūl Hasan perceived that his destruction was decided on, he is said to have become a changed man, to have cast aside his evil habits and played the part of a hero. Certainly the city was put in a good state of defence, and when the siege began early in 1687, the imperial troops found that they had been set a hard task. The Marāthās cut off the supplies of the besiegers, who were reduced to extremities by famine and plague. An assault ordered by the emperor failed utterly, and it seemed as if the siege must be raised. But a traitor admitted the Mughal army, and Golkonda fell (Sept. 1687). By these conquests and later operations the imperial commanders were able to levy tribute from Tanjore and Trichinopoly in 1691, which date may be taken as marking the furthest southern extension of Mughal power.

Struggle with the Marāthās. The two Muhammadan kingdoms had been destroyed, but the Marāthās remained unsubdued, and the remaining twenty years of Aurangzeb's life were spent in the vain attempt to subdue them. The emperor never returned to the north, and wasted those weary years gaining 'a long series of petty victories followed by larger losses'. His armies seemed to be getting the upper hand between 1698 and 1701, but in the succeeding years the enemy recovered the lost ground.

Marāthā method of warfare. The Marāthās never, or hardly ever, risked a general engagement, expending all their energies, like the Boers in the South African War, in cutting off supplies, intercepting convoys, and incessantly harassing the enemy. Mounted on hardy ponies, they were able to move with a quickness which completely baffled the imperial armies; and, as each man carried with him his simple food and belongings, they needed no transport trains.

Inefficiency of the Mughal army. The Mughal forces, on the other hand, were unwieldy and almost immovable. The royal tents alone occupied a space three miles in circuit, and a contemporary traveller describes the whole camp as being 'a moving city containing five million souls'. The officers were corrupted by luxury and incapable of active effort. Grant Duff sums up the situation in these words: 'These apparently vigorous efforts of the government were unsubstantial; there was motion and bustle, without zeal or efficacy; the empire was unwieldy, its system relaxed, and its officers corrupt beyond all example.' Success was impossible for such a government.

Execution of Sambhājī; Rājā Shāhu. For a time the emperor's arms had a promise of success, and Aurangzeb had the poor satisfaction of putting to death with torture Sambhājī, a son of Sivājī, in 1689. He spared the life of Sivājī junior, nicknamed Shāhu (Sāhu), the infant son of Sambhājī, and kept him in custody until his own death, when the young man was released and returned to his own dominions. He became Rājā in 1708 after a contest.

Tārā Bāī. A few years after Sambhājī's execution, Tārā Bāī, widow of Rājā Rāma, another son of Sivājī, had retrieved the Marāthā losses, and directed the policy of devastating the imperial territories with such energy that the emperor was shut up in his camp, and his treasure was plundered almost under his eyes.

Retreat and death of Aurangzeb. The Mughal army crumbled to pieces, general famines and pestilences occurred more than once, and ultimately (1706) Aurangzeb was forced to retire on Ahmadnagar, where he died at the beginning of March, 1707 (New Style), in the fiftieth year of his reign and the eighty-eighth of his life. His dust lies under a plain tomb in the village of Rauza or Khuldabad near Daulatabad. His viscera were buried separately at Ahmadnagar.

Aurangzeb's farewell words. However severely the policy and conduct of Aurangzeb may be judged, it is impossible to refuse pity to the old man on his death-bed when he addressed his sons in these sad words:

'I know not who I am, where I shall go, or what will happen to this sinner, full of sins. Now I will say good-bye to every one in this world and entrust every one to the care of God.

INDIAN COINS

1. COIN OF SHER SHĀH 2. COIN OF AKBAR
3. COIN OF JAHĀNGĪR 4. COIN OF AURANGZEB

My famous and auspicious sons should not quarrel among themselves and allow a general massacre of the people who are the servants of God. . . . My years have gone by profitless. God has been in my heart, yet my darkened eyes have not recognized His light. . . . There is no hope for me in the future. The fever is gone, but only the skin is left. . . . The army is confounded, and without heart or help, even as I am ; apart from God, with no rest for the heart. . . . When I have lost hope in myself, how can I hope in others ? . . . You should accept my last will. It should not happen that Musalmans be killed and the blame for their death rest upon this useless creature. . . . I have greatly sinned and know not what torment awaits me. . . . I commit you and your sons to the care of God, and bid you farewell. . . . May the peace of God be upon you.'

Aurangzeb had lived too long.

Causes of Aurangzeb's failure. The causes of Aurangzeb's failure are obvious enough, and have been indicated in the course of the narrative, but it may be well to sum them up briefly. Aurangzeb acted as if he were merely the head of the Sunnī sect of Muhammadans, and not the protector of all the races and creeds of India. Akbar had realized the truth that the authority of the monarch of an empire inhabited chiefly by Hindus could not be lasting unless it rested on the support of all his people. During the greater part of his reign he treated all religions with impartial justice. Only in his latter days he forgot himself so far as to violate his avowed principles by heaping insults upon Islam. Jahāngīr accepted and put in practice the tolerant maxims of his father, encouraging the building of Hindu temples as well as of Christian churches. Shahjahān revived the old evil policy of persecution, harrying the Christians and razing temples to the ground. Aurangzeb went farther, especially after 1678, when the death of Rājā Jaswant Singh deprived his countrymen of their most powerful support. The emperor, then, in 1679, reimposed the hateful *jizya* or poll-tax on non-Muslims which Akbar had wisely abolished. He carried to monstrous lengths the policy of destroying the holy places of Hinduism, and may be reasonably charged with the overthrow of thousands of temples.[1]

His measures forced all Hindus to regard him as their enemy and deprived him of the willing service of the Rājpūt clans. Sivājī, whom the emperor despised as a mere robber chief, was honoured by the Marāthās as a god, the champion and protector of Hinduism against the imperial bigot. Aurangzeb's Sunnī bigotry made him as hostile to the Shīa states of Bījāpur and Golkonda as he was to the Hindu powers. He thus shattered the forces of Islam in the Deccan, by which the Hindu revolt of the Marāthās might have been held in check. The emperor's suspicious disposition, which prevented him from trusting anybody, deprived him likewise of all chance of finding trustworthy agents. He was, consequently, ill served. His life was so prolonged that he continued to grasp the sceptre after he had lost the strength to use it with effect. His officers, corrupted by luxury, lacked the vigour of their ancestors and were incapable of honest exertion. The long-drawn-out Deccan wars exhausted a large part of the huge treasure of Shahjahān, and ruined the finances of the empire. Financial ruin involved the collapse of the whole administration. The subject might be treated from many other points of view, but what has been said may suffice.

Chronology of Aurangzeb's reign.

Deposition of Shahjahān and informal accession . .	July 1658
Formal installation of Aurangzeb	May 1659
Charter granted by Charles II to the E. I. Company; Bombay ceded by the Portuguese to the English	1661
Mīr Jumla's attack on Assam	1662-3
Shāyista Khan surprised by the Marāthās	1663
Foundation of the French *Compagnie des Indes* . . .	1664

[1] In 1679–80 the ruin effected in Rājputāna was enormous. At or near Udaipur 123, at Chitōr 63, and in Ambēr (Jaipur) 66 temples were overthrown, that is to say 252 temples in two states in the course of a year. How many buildings were ruined in the course of forty-one years throughout the empire no man can tell. (*Maāsir-i-Ālamgīrī* in Elliot and Dowson, vii. 88.)

Death of Shahjahān; annexation of part of Arakan by Shāyista Khan	1666
Prohibition of public idolatrous worship	1672
Sivājī formally proclaimed as sovereign	1674
Revival of the *jizya*	1679
Death of Sivājī	1680
Rebellion of the Rājpūts and Prince Akbar	1680-1
Assumption of command in the Deccan by Aurangzeb	1681-2
Annexation of Bijāpur; expulsion of the English from Bengal by Shāyista Khan	1686
Annexation of Golkonda; greatest extension of the Mughal empire	1687-91
Execution of Sambhājī, son of Sivājī	1689
Foundation of Calcutta by Job Charnock	1690
United East India Company	1702-8
Retreat of Aurangzeb to Ahmadnagar	1706
Death of Aurangzeb	1707

GENEALOGY OF THE 'GREAT MOGULS' (PRINCIPAL NAMES).

- Amir Tīmūr
  - Four generations
    - BĀBUR (Zahīr-ud-dīn Muhammad, descended from the stock of Chinghīz Khan through females)
      - HUMĀYUN (Nasīr-ud-dīn Muhammad)
        - AKBAR (Jalāl-ud-dīn)
          - JAHĀNGĪR (Nūr Muhammad)
            - Sultan Khusrū or Khusrau
              - Dāwar Baksh or Bulākī, and two others
            - Sultan Parvīz
            - SHAHJAHĀN (Shihāb-ud-dīn Muhammad)
              - Dārā Shikoh (Muhammad)
                - Four sons
              - Sultan Shujā
                - Three sons
              - AURANGZEB ĀLAMGĪR (Muhammad Muhī-ud-dīn)
              - Murād Baksh
              - Several other children, including two daughters, Jahānārā and Roshanārā, or Roshan Rāe
            - Jahāndār
            - Shahryār
          - Sultan Murād
            - A son
          - Sultan Dāniyāl
            - Threo sons (two Christians)
        - Mirzā Muhammad Hakīm (King of Kābul)
      - Kāmrān and two others

CHAPTER XXI

The successors of Aurangzeb: Bahādur Shah, &c., Muhammad Shah; invasion of Nādir Shah; growth of Marāthā power; Ahmad Shah Durrāni; the third battle of Pānīpat.

War of succession. Aurangzeb left behind him four sons, the princes Muazzam, Azam, Akbar (*ante*, p. 212), and Kāmbaksh. Akbar, the rebel exile, no longer counted; the three others were all equally eligible candidates for the vacant throne. A document in the nature of a will found under the pillow of the dead emperor suggested a division of the empire between these three sons, but none of them had the slightest intention of being content with anything less than the whole. The eldest, Prince Muazzam, had himself proclaimed at Kābul, while his brother, Prince Azam, assumed the imperial dignity in the Deccan camp. Both of these claimants assembled large armies, which met at Jājau, to the south of Agra, in June 1707. The battle ended in the total defeat of Prince Azam, who was killed, along with two adult sons. Shah Ālam or Muazzam thus secured possession of Agra, the treasure city of the empire, and the command of abundant cash, which he distributed freely among his followers. In February 1708 Prince Kāmbaksh was defeated in the Deccan, and died from his wounds. Thus Prince Muazzam became undisputed Padshah. He is known to history as either Bahādur Shah (I) or Shah Ālam (I).

Reign of Bahādur Shah (I). He conciliated the Marāthās by the release of their Rājā, Shāhu (*ante*, p. 219), and patched up a peace with the Rājpūts. The most important event of his short reign was a severe conflict with the Sikh sectaries of the Panjāb, and it will be convenient to notice briefly in this place the origin and early stages in the development of the Sikh power.

Origin and rise of the Sikhs. The Sikhs, or 'disciples', are one of the many reformed sects of Hinduism which have arisen from time to time. The teaching of Nānak, the first *guru* of the sect, late in the fifteenth century, which was based on that of Kabīr (*ante*, p. 148), did not attract much official attention until the beginning of the seventeenth century in Jahāngīr's reign, when the *guru* of the day was put to death. That act of persecution roused the zeal of the martyr's adherents, who took up arms under the leadership of his son Har Gobind and became the declared enemies of the government.

Sikh organization. Guru Gobind Singh (1675–1708), grandson of Har Gobind, converted the sect into a political power by means of an organization (known as the Khālsā) and rule of life which sharply separated the Sikhs from the rest of the population and united them closely among themselves. The disciples, who were forbidden to use tobacco in any form, were required to wear their hair long, and to practise sundry other special observances. The fact that most of the Sikhs were Jats by caste supplied another bond of union, and the result was that during the eighteenth century the sect gradually became a ruling power. But, although the Jats have furnished the majority of Sikh converts, it must be clearly understood that people of all castes may be initiated as Sikhs, and that within the sect no distinction of caste is recognized.

Ravages of Banda, the Sikh leader. When Bahādur Shah died at Lahore, in February, 1712, he was engaged in endeavours to check the barbarous ravages committed by the Sikhs at Sahrind and other places in the Panjāb, under the leadership of Banda, the successor of Guru Gobind Singh. Bahādur Shah was a good-natured, generous man, but lacking in the strength needed by a ruler in troublous times. He was nicknamed the 'Heedless King' (*Shāh-i-bēkhabar*).

War of succession; Jahāndār Shah; Farrukhsīyar. The death of the emperor was followed by the usual war between his four sons. The most competent claimant, Azīm-ush-shan, governor of Bengal, had the ill luck to be the first killed in battle. Two others perished in further fighting. The survivor, Jahāndār Shah, a worthless debauchee of low tastes, was proclaimed emperor by Zulfikār Khan, a powerful noble, who became Vazīr (1712). After a few months Jahāndār Shah was put out of the way, and Farrukhsīyar, son of Azīm-ush-shān, was placed on the throne (January, 1713) by the influence of two Sayyids of Bārha. For some years this clan of Sayyids enjoyed the position of king-makers, and appointed whom they chose to occupy the seat of Aurangzeb. The imperial dignity was quickly becoming an empty although dangerous honour.

Defeat of the Sikhs. The principal event in Farrukhsīyar's reign was the crushing defeat of the Sikhs, whose leader Banda was captured and executed with the most inhuman tortures. About a thousand of his followers also were slain. This severity kept the Sikhs quiet for a generation. Allusion has been made above (*ante*, p. 167) to the important trading privileges gained for the English merchants by the surgeon Hamilton, who attended Farrukhsīyar. The emperor, a timid, helpless creature, not personally of any importance, was murdered early in 1719.

Accession of Muhammad Shah ; break-up of the empire. Several nonentities having been sent up, who lasted only a few months,[1] the Sayyids selected another insignificant prince, who ascended the throne as Muhammad Shah, in October, 1719. During his reign, which was long, and continued until 1748, the empire began to break to pieces. The emperor of Delhi was gradually reduced to a position like that of the later members of the Tughlak dynasty (*ante*, p. 127), while the outlying powers, Hindu, Muhammadan, and foreign, came to the front, with the ultimate result that the sceptre passed into English hands.

Independence of the Deccan ; the Nizām.—A Turki noble, named Chīn Kilich Khan, generally known by his title of

[1] Rafī-ud-darajāt, Rafī-ud-daulat (Shahjahān II), Nikūsiyar, Ibrāhīm. The 'reigns' of the first three fall between February 18 and August 27, 1719. Ibrāhīm claimed the throne in 1720, from October 1 to November 8, and struck coins, now very rare.

Āsaf Jāh, the son of a favourite officer of Aurangzeb, had become viceroy of the Deccan. For a time he held the office of vazīr at Delhi, but in 1723 he retired from court, and after that date may be regarded as an independent sovereign. He was the ancestor of the present Nizām of Hyderabad. Before the withdrawal of Āsaf Jāh to the south, the king-making clan of Sayyids had lost their power through the murder of Husain Ali and the imprisonment of his brother Abdullah, who had been their leaders.

Practical independence of Oudh ; Saādat Khan. About this time, Saādat Khan, governor of Oudh, likewise made himself practically independent and founded the line of the Nawāb-Vazīrs, who were recognized later as kings of Oudh.

Bengal ; Alivardi Khan. The Sūba of Bengal, including Bihār and Orissa, although nominally under the control of the emperor, was really as little subject to his authority as the Afghan kings of Bengal had been before the time of Akbar. Allahvardi (Alivardi) Khan, the Sūbadār from 1740 to 1756, an able despot, ceased to pay tribute to the imperial court.

The Rohillas ; general revolt of provinces. To the north of the Ganges, the Rohillas, a clan of Afghan immigrants, made themselves masters of the rich tract now called Rohilkhand. In short, everywhere a general revolt of the provinces began in the reign of Muhammad Shah, and was completed in the time of his successors.

Shāhū and Bālājī Visvanāth, Peshwā. Tārā Bāī was the last notable member of Sivājī's line. Shāhu, who became Rājā early in 1708 (*ante*, p. 219), had been brought up at the Mughal court, and was more Muhammadan than Hindu in his habits. He preferred pleasure to business, and was glad to leave affairs of state in the hands of ministers, especially in those of a Brahman named Bālājī Visvanāth, who was appointed his Peshwā in 1714, and tried to introduce some order into the confused Marāthā government.

Bājī Rāo I, Peshwā. When Bālājī Visvanāth died, in 1720, he was succeeded by his elder son, Bājī Rāo [I], after an interval of some months. The dignity of Peshwā thus became hereditary. Owing to Shāhu's easy-going disposition, the minister overshadowed his nominal master, and from 1727, when the Peshwā was granted full powers, the Rājā ceased to count. Shāhu survived until 1748, but Bājī Rāo was the real head of the government, and was able to pass on his authority to his son. Bājī Rāo was an able soldier as a leader of plundering bands, but with no taste for civil administration. He largely extended Marāthā influence in the dominions still under the nominal authority of the emperor of Delhi.

Bālājī ; the Peshwā dynasty. On the death of Bājī Rao I, in 1740, his place as Peshwā was taken, after a struggle, by son son Bālājī, who became practically the sovereign of the Marāthās. Nobody asks who succeeded Shāhu as Rājā of Sātārā. All readers of history rightly think of the government of the Marāthās in the eighteenth century as that of the Peshwās. Their position was the same as that of the ministers in modern Nepāl, who have thrust their nominal sovereigns into the background. The name of the Mahārājādhirāj in that country has no interest for anybody. Thus the line of the Peshwās became substantially a ruling dynasty, which may be taken to date from 1727, when Shāhu bestowed full powers on Bājī Rāo I. The dynasty lasted until the general settlement of India effected by the Marquess of Hastings in 1818, but retained little power after the treaty of Bassein, in 1802.

Change in Marāthā government. During the rule of the first three Peshwās the character of the Marāthā government changed. The hereditary dominions in the Ghāts and Konkan left by Sivājī became of comparatively small importance. The main efforts of the Marāthā rulers were directed to securing their power over the dominions of the Mughal emperor and the Nizam, by compelling the sovereigns of those countries to submit to Marāthā blackmail or extortion. Countries which consented to pay the *chauth*, or one-fourth of the land revenue, plus the *sardesmukhī*, or one-tenth, were supposed to be protected from plunder. The emperor Muhammad Shah, in 1719, during the lifetime of Bālājī Visvanāth Peshwā, had been forced not only to acknowledge the Marāthā title to the hereditary dominions of Sivājī (*svarāj*), but to recognize formally the Marāthā right to levy *chauth* and *sardesmukhī* from the six Sūbas of the Deccan.

Complex accounts. The assessment and collection of the claims were purposely made extremely complex, so that the accounts should not be intelligible to any one except the Brahmans in the Peshwā's employ, and an excuse for demanding arrears might thus always be at hand. The curious details of the system are explained at length in Grant Duff's *History of the Mahrattas*. The institutions of Sivājī were neglected, and his rules of discipline were disregarded.

Origin of existing Marāthā states. About this time the chiefs who founded the still existing Marāthā dynasties of the Gaikwār, of Baroda, of Holkar at Indore, and of Sindia at Gwalior, come into notice. The ancestor of the Gaikwār was an adherent of a defeated opponent whom Bājī Rāo I thought it prudent to conciliate. The chiefs of Indore and Gwalior are descended from men of humble origin who became officers of Bājī Rāo and gradually rose to distinction in his service. At the great settlement of 1818 those three dynasties were lucky enough to be confirmed in their possessions. But the Bhonslā Rāj of Nāgpur or Berār lost its independence at the same date, and was finally extinguished by Lord Dalhousie in 1853. The Rāj had been founded in 1743 by a Marāthā leader named Raghujī, who acquired Cuttack (Katak) in 1751, and claimed from Bengal twelve lakhs of rupees as *chauth*. Raghujī is not to be confounded with Raghoba or Raghunāth Rāo, the younger son of Bājī Rāo I, who became prominent in the first Marāthā war.

Foreign invasion ; Nādir Shah. Unhappy India, already bleeding to death from internal disorders, had yet a calamity still greater to suffer. For more than two centuries she had been spared the misery caused by serious invasions from beyond the passes of the north-western frontier, but was now to undergo experiences which recalled the days of Mahmūd and Tīmūr. Early in 1736, the throne of Persia was seized by Nādir Shah, an adventurer who had earned a right to the highest place by the display of extraordinary abilities as a general. Being dissatisfied at the delay of the Delhi government in redressing certain grievances of which he complained, he occupied Ghaznī and Kābul, and, advancing without meeting serious resistance, was within a hundred miles of Delhi before Muhammad Shah could do anything to stop him.

Battle of Karnāl ; massacre at Delhi. Early in 1739, at Karnāl, not far from the historic field of Pānīpat, the imperial forces ventured to bar the invader's path, and were easily routed. Muhammad Shah submitted, and, being courteously received, entered Delhi with the victor. Nādir Shah at first held his troops in check and protected the city, but when the populace attacked him and his men, he let loose 20,000 soldiers to burn, plunder, and kill. Not less than 30,000 people perished in the massacre, which lasted for half a day.

Return home of Nādir Shah, 1739. Nādir Shah wanted something more than blood. The seizure of the crown jewels and the peacock throne (*ante*, p. 203) alone was sufficient to enrich the robber beyond the dreams of avarice, but he was not content until he had extorted from the surviving citizens, great and small, the larger part of their possessions, every form of cruelty being used to compel payment. He then made a treaty with Muhammad Shah, providing for the cession of the provinces beyond the Indus, reseated him on the throne, and after a stay of fifty-eight days returned to his own country, laden with coin, plate, jewels, and precious things of every kind to the value of many millions sterling. Like the early invaders, he also brought away with him hundreds of skilled artisans.

The court of Delhi. The impotent court of Delhi continued to be the scene of endless intrigues and assassinations. The most prominent personages there were the vazīr Kamar-ud-dīn

Khan and Ghāzī-ud-dīn, son of Āsaf Jāh, viceroy of the Deccan.

Ahmad Shah Durrānī. In 1747 Nādir Shah, king of Persia, who had become an insane tyrant, was murdered, and succeeded in his eastern territories by a chieftain named Ahmad Khan, head of the Abdālī or Durrānī clan of the Afghans, who took the title of Ahmad Shah. Next year the Durrānī invaded the Panjāb, and was driven back, after a hard fight at Sahrind, by the imperial forces under the command of the heir-apparent, Prince Ahmad, and the vazīr, who was killed in action.

Ahmad Shah of Delhi, 1748. In April of the same year, Muhammad Shah died and was succeeded by his son, Ahmad Shah, who must not be confounded with his Durrānī namesake and contemporary.

Annexation of the Panjāb by the Durrānī. During the reign of Ahmad Shah, Ghāzī-ud-dīn and other nobles were engaged in constant fighting with one another, and Ahmad Shah Durrānī annexed the Panjāb. In 1754 Ghāzī-ud-dīn blinded his nominal sovereign, and selected as his successor a son of Jahāndār Shah.

Sack of Delhi by Ahmad Shah Durrānī. This prince was enthroned under the title of Ālamgīr II, but had nothing beyond the title in common with Aurangzeb. In 1756 Ahmad Shah Durrānī sacked Delhi and repeated the horrors of Nādir Shah's massacres seventeen years before. He also disgraced himself by a cruel slaughter of unarmed Hindus at Mathurā. Next year the heat caused sickness among his troops and obliged him to retire to his own country.

Marāthā conquest of the Panjāb. The son of Ghāzī-ud-dīn, who bore the same name as his father, called in the Marāthās to help him against his rivals, and the imperial city and the Panjāb were occupied by a Marāthā chief named Raghuba (1758), the younger son of Bājī Rāo I.

Marāthā empire at its greatest extent, 1760. This bold advance of the upstart Hindu power alarmed the Muhammadan princes, and induced them to combine for the expulsion of the intruders, by whom almost the whole of India, from the Himalaya and the Indus to Tanjore, was dominated for the moment. The Marāthā army now included a large park of artillery and 10,000 disciplined infantry, modelled on European principles, as well as Jat and Rājpūt contingents.

The Bhāo at Delhi. Sadasheo Rāo Bhāo, commonly called 'the Bhāo', nephew of the Peshwā Bājī Rāo, took Delhi, and completed the ruin of the palace and city, stripping the silver plating from the ceiling of the hall of audience (*dīwān khāss*), which produced seventeen lakhs of rupees.

Third battle of Pānīpat, Jan. 1761. Ultimately, on Jan. 13, 1761, the Marāthā host, with little or no support from the Jats and Rājpūts, confronted the army of Ahmad Shah Durrānī, who was supported by the troops of Oudh and other Muhammadan principalities, on the plain of Pānīpat, where the fate of India has been so often decided. Delay in bringing on a battle reduced the Marāthā army to a state of famine, and at last the Bhāo was compelled either to fight or to starve. He was utterly routed with enormous slaughter, in which most of the Marāthā chiefs fell. The Peshwā soon after died. The third battle of Pānīpat was the death-blow to the power of the Peshwā, as the sovereign of the Marāthās, the temporary revival of Marāthā influence a few years later being chiefly the work of Sindia, Holkar, and other independent princes.[1]

Withdrawal of the Durrānī. Ahmad Shah Durrānī made no use of his victory, and was content to go home with his plunder. In April, 1767, after inflicting several defeats on the Sikhs, he reappeared once more for a moment near Pānīpat with 50,000 Afghan cavalry, and then retired, troubling himself no more with the affairs of Hindustan.

[1] The three battles of Pānīpat:

(1) Defeat of Ibrāhīm Lodi by Bābur, 1526;
(2) Defeat of Hēmū by Bairām Khan and Akbar, 1556;
(3) Defeat of Marāthās by Ahmad Shah Durrānī, 1761.

Causes of decline of Mughal empire. Akbar, Jahāngir, Shahjahān, and Aurangzeb were all strong, hardy men of dauntless personal courage, able and willing to meet man or beast in deadly combat, as many anecdotes prove. But the sons of Aurangzeb seemed to be of a different breed. All the spirit was crushed out of them by their father. Their sons and grandsons grew up as nerveless weaklings in the society of women, eunuchs, and the riff-raff of the palace. The nobles became as debased as the members of the royal family, and were better fitted to buy over a commandant than to storm his fort. They went to war riding in palankins, attended by a swarm of worthless followers of both sexes, and were served in camp with all the pomp and luxury of the Delhi court. Such people could not be successful. The rule of a despotic monarch cannot be maintained except by a man who knows how to rule. The successors of Aurangzeb had not such knowledge. It is not surprising that in the course of a century and a half the Mughal dynasty should have lost its vigour; the wonder rather is that the Padshahs for four successive generations possessed character and ability sufficient to hold together a vast empire and to govern it in such a fashion that it made at least a show of strength. The Deccan wars exposed the internal rottenness of the imperial organization. In the whole of India there was not a man capable of effecting the necessary reforms. The weakness of the empire was plainly seen by European observers. Manucci, the Italian physician, writes, late in Aurangzeb's reign:

> 'Having set forth all the grandeur and power of the Moguls, I will, with the reader's permission, assert from what I have seen and tested, that to sweep it entirely away and occupy the whole empire, nothing is required beyond a corps of thirty thousand trusty European soldiers, led by competent commanders, who would thereby easily acquire the glory of great conquerors.'

That opinion probably was quite sound. It was held a little later by Clive, although he did not care to act upon it.

Condition of India under Aurangzeb's successors. The condition of India during the half-century following the death of Aurangzeb may be summed up in one word—misery. Even before his death, the French physician Bernier, not an unfriendly critic, declared that 'no adequate idea can be conveyed of the sufferings of the people'. He writes of

> 'a tyranny so excessive as to deprive the peasant and artisan of the necessaries of life, and leave them to die of misery and exhaustion—a tyranny, owing to which these wretched people either have no children at all, or have them only to endure the agonies of starvation, and die at a tender age—a tyranny, in fine, that drives the cultivator from his wretched home. . . . . As the ground is seldom tilled otherwise than by compulsion, and no person is found willing and able to repair the ditches and canals for the conveyance of water, it happens that the whole country is badly cultivated and a great part rendered unproductive from the want of irrigation. The houses, too, are left in a dilapidated condition.'

After the old emperor had passed away, hell was let loose, and the people were ground to the dust by selfish nobles, greedy officials, and plundering armies. Hardly any one appears on the stage of history who is worthy of remembrance for his own sake, and there is little to be said about literature or art.[1] In most parts of the country the 'great anarchy' continued for another half-century, until the advance of the English power, in the early years of the nineteenth century, brought some measure of relief to a suffering land.

> From out the sunset poured an alien race,
> Who fitted stone to stone again, and Truth,
> Peace, Love, and Justice came and dwelt therein.
>
> TENNYSON.

[1] Certain Muhammadan historical compilations and tolerable paintings in Indo-Persian style were produced.

BOOK V

THE BRITISH OR ANGLO-INDIAN PERIOD; RULE OF THE EAST INDIA COMPANY FROM 1761 TO 1858

SOURCES OF ANGLO-INDIAN HISTORY

Immense mass of authorities. The mass of original authorities for the British period of Indian history is so great as to be practically infinite. No man could explore more than a minute fraction even of the official documents stored in the record-rooms of the Indian Governments in England and India, not to speak of the piles of manuscripts in the British Museum and other collections. In addition to the official documents, many other sources of information exist, including newspapers, memoirs, letters, and the writings of travellers. Some small portion of the official records has been either printed at length or summarily catalogued in print. The Government of India has had prepared many printed hand-lists of manuscripts which are little known and rarely consulted. Considerable blocks of documents have been published more or less fully in *Selections from the Records* issued by various governments. The work of that kind done by Sir George Forrest, C.I.E., is extensive and valuable.

East India Company. Three series of volumes dealing with the early history of the East India Company, eighteen in all, up to date, published at the Clarendon Press, deserve special mention. The titles are: (I) *Letters to the East India Company from its Servants in the East*, 1602–17 (6 volumes); (II) *The English Factories in India*, 1618–50 (8 volumes); and (III) *The Court Minutes of the East India Company*, 1635–54 (4 volumes).

At present, no readable compendious history of the famous Company exists. The volumes mentioned are a quarry of splendid material ready for the hand of a competent historian.

Travellers. The works of travellers during the seventeenth and eighteenth centuries throw much light both on the relations between the European settlers and the native powers, and on the inner life of the settlements. Oaten gives a list to the end of the seventeenth century (*European Travellers in India*, Kegan Paul & Co., 1909).[1] The writings of the eighteenth-century

[1] But Oaten's account of Mandelslo (pp. 177–83) is misleading. Mandelslo wrote little of value. The bulk of the book passing under his name is padding from other authors inserted by Olearius and the French translator, de Wicquefort.

travellers, Ives and the rest, although less important, are of considerable value. 'When the Macaulay of British India history arises, he will enliven the earlier part of his narrative with references to these many travellers' tales.'

No good history of British India. That remark leads me to observe that a well-written, interesting history of British India, on a scale of moderate dimensions, does not exist, and is badly wanted. Mill's great work, even with Wilson's continuation, only comes down to 1835, and has well-known defects, while all the other books—Hunter's, Thornton's, Marshman's, &c.—are either fragmentary or wanting in some important respect. Marshman's work is, perhaps, the most serviceable. Among the small histories I recommend A. D. Innes, *A Short History of the British in India* (Methuen, 1902).

Biographies. Biographies form an important source of Anglo-Indian history, and enshrine or entomb many documents. All the existing Lives of Clive are unsatisfactory, and the same may be said of those of Warren Hastings. Sir George Forrest, who promises a Life of Clive, which should supersede its predecessors, has provided much material for the biography of Hastings in various publications, especially his *Selections from the State Papers of the Governors-General of India : Warren Hastings* (2 vols., 8vo, Oxford, Blackwell, 1910).

Letters. Numerous immense collections of letters and dispatches have been published. The most generally useful books of the kind are Mr. Sidney Owen's volumes entitled *A Selection from Wellesley's Despatches* (Clarendon Press, 1877), and *A Selection from the Wellington Despatches* (1880), which are well edited.

Lord Minto I. The interesting and little-known story of Lord Minto I may be read at first hand in the two volumes of his *Life and Letters* (1874, 1880). Unfortunately, Lord Minto was not given a place in the Rulers of India series, although much more worthy of it than several persons who were included in that most serviceable collection of short biographies.

Marquess of Hastings : Marāthās. Several contemporary books, notably H. T. Prinsep's *History of the Political and Military Transactions in India during the Administration of the Marquess of Hastings*, 1813-23 (published in 1825), tell the events of the government of that eminent Governor-General.

Grant Duff's *History of the Mahrattas* (1826 and reprint) ranks as an original authority, because it is founded on personal knowledge and documents now lost.

Lord William Bentinck, &c. The only biography of Lord William Cavendish-Bentinck is Mr. Demetrius Boulger's excellent little volume (1897) in the Rulers of India series.

The Sikh wars form the subject of a considerable literature. Cunningham's *History of the Sikhs* (1st edition, 1849) may be specified.

For Lord Dalhousie's administration, the *Life* by Sir W. Lee-Warner and other works may be consulted.

The Mutiny. The books about the Mutiny would fill a large library.

The work by Holmes, which has reached several editions, is the best short history. The latest, and presumably the most accurate, of the large histories is that by Sir George Forrest. Good biographies of the Lawrences and other heroes of the period exist.

Afghan wars. Among the numerous books treating of the Afghan wars the work of Lady Betty Balfour, entitled *The Indian Administration of Lord Lytton* (1899), may be named, because it includes many original documents.

The later Viceroys. Sir William Hunter treated Lord Mayo satisfactorily. Mr. Lovat Fraser's work, *India under Curzon and After* (1912), is useful.

Lord Minto II and Lord Hardinge II await their biographers.

The foregoing notes, which might be extended indefinitely, will, it is hoped, be of some use to teachers. A fuller list of books will be found in Appendix II of the *Short History* by Mr. Innes, cited above.

CHAPTER XXII

Transitional period: conflict of French and English in Southern India; Dupleix, &c.: Haidar Alī and Mysore.

The epoch of 1761. The selection by historians of the year 1761 as marking the dividing line between the Mughal and British periods does not rest solely upon the occurrence of the battle of Pānīpat in that year. Four years earlier, in 1757, Clive's victory at Plassey had laid Bengal and its dependencies at the feet of the East India Company, the military position of which was secured in 1764 by the battle of Buxar, and legalized in 1765 by the grant under imperial seal to the Company of the Diwānī, or revenue jurisdiction over the province. In the year of Pānīpat, the fall of Pondicherry, the capital of the French possessions, completed the ruin of the French, who had been routed at Wandiwash in the preceding year In June, 1761, Haidar Alī made himself master of Mysore, and so founded a power which lasted until the close of the eighteenth century, while in 1764 the Sikhs occupied Lahore, and became independent. Thus, from every point of view, we may take 1761, or, more precisely, the years 1760–5, as the end of the old and the beginning of the new era.

Nominal survival of the Mughal empire. The Mughal empire continued to exist as the shadow of a great name until 1858, when the last titular emperor was exiled as the penalty for his share in the Mutiny. But all the princes who bore the imperial titles during the century extending from 1759 to 1858 were equally insignificant, and the course of events was little affected by the succession of one nonentity to another.[1] The real power was in the hands of the Marāthās, the British, the Sikhs, and the Muhammadan states of Oudh, Bengal, and the Deccan. India continued to be a mass of conflicting, unstable states until 1818, when the settlement made by the Marquess of Hastings definitely established the British government of the East India Company as the supreme, controlling power. But it is true to affirm that from 1761 the Company was the most important and influential authority in India.

The transitional period. In the following pages we shall trace in outline the process by which the dominion over India passed from the hands of the Hindu and Muhammadan powers to those of the East India Company, and thence to the Crown. In order to make the subject intelligible we must depart from strict chronological order and go back for some years, dealing first with the south, where the growing strength of the European settlers first made itself distinctly felt. The history of this period of transition cannot be presented in a single continuous narrative, because India in those days was merely a geographical expression and had no unity within herself.

Conflict between French and English. The competition between the French and English settlements on the Madras coasts for the control of the sea-borne trade developed into

[1] Their names are: Shah Ālam II, Dec. 1759–Nov. 1806; Akbar II, Nov. 1806–Oct. 1837; and Bahādur Shah II, Oct. 1837–March 1858. Other pretenders were Shahjahān III, Dec. 1758–Oct. 1760; and Bīdār Bakht, Aug.–Oct. 1788. Shah Ālam at the time of his predecessor's murder was a fugitive, under the protection of the Nawāb-Vazīr of Oudh. He tried, unsuccessfully, to establish himself in Bihār, and from 1765 to 1771 was the dependant of the English at Allahabad. From 1771 to 1803 he was generally under the control of Marāthā chiefs. In 1788 he was cruelly blinded by an Afghan ruffian named Ghulām Kādir. From the time of Lord Lake's entry into Delhi in 1803 he became simply a pensioner of the British Government, and his successors occupied the same position.

a struggle for political mastery, in which the native powers allied with one side or the other played only a secondary part. In that struggle the naval superiority of England was the decisive factor. From Madras, where he had already done much for his country, Robert Clive transferred the conflict to Bengal, and there too was victorious by the aid of sea-power. On the Bombay side the Marāthās were too strong to allow the European settlements much scope for expansion. The British empire in India was founded in Madras and Bengal, the English traders being first forced into political action by French rivalry in the south.

Pondicherry ; Governors Dumas and Dupleix. The French settlement of Pondicherry, about a hundred miles to the south of Madras, founded in 1674, was greatly developed under the government of M. Dumas (1735–41), who won a high reputation by his repulse of a large Marāthā force. His successor, M. Dupleix, who had already distinguished himself as head of the Chandernagore settlement near Calcutta, found in the south a larger field for the exercise of his abilities, and devised an ambitious policy based on interference in the affairs of the native states and aimed at the destruction of the English settlements.

First Anglo-French war. In 1746, war between France and England having been declared, on account of a dispute about the succession to the throne of Austria, a fleet from the island of Mauritius in the Indian Ocean, then a French colony, captured Madras, which was held by France until 1749, when it was restored to England under the treaty of Aix-la-Chapelle. During the interval the English possessions in the south were reduced to the one small fort of St. David, near Cuddalore.

Origin of the second Anglo-French war. The second war between the French and English settlers arose out of disputed successions to the thrones of two Indian princes, the Sūbadār or Nizam of the Deccan at Hyderabad, and his vassal, the Nawāb of the Carnatic, at Arcot.

Disputed succession in the Deccan. As far back as 1724,

Āsaf Jāh, Sūbadār of the Deccan, had ceased to pay allegiance to the emperor at Delhi, and had become practically an independent king. When he died at a great age in 1748 he left six sons. The eldest, who was employed at Delhi as prime minister, did not trouble about his father's dominions. Nāsir Jang, the second son, claimed the throne of the Deccan, and was opposed by his nephew, Muzaffar Jang, son of a daughter of old Āsaf Jāh. War ensued between the rival claimants, with the result that within about three years (1751) both Nāsir Jang and Muzaffar Jang had been killed. Salābat Jang, third son of Āsaf Jāh, then became Nizam and retained his position for eleven years. He was deposed in 1762 by his next brother, Āsaf Jāh's fourth son, Nizām Alī, the ancestor of the present Nizam of Hyderabad.

So much account of the disputes concerning the throne of the Deccan may suffice.

Disputed succession in the Carnatic. The business was complicated by another quarrel concerning the succession to Anwār-ud-dīn Khan, Nawāb of the Carnatic, who had been appointed by Āsaf Jāh in 1744 and had been killed in 1749. The claimants to the succession were Muhammad Alī, son of Anwār-ud-dīn, and Chanda Sahib (Husain Dost Khan), son-in-law of a former Nawāb.

French and English take sides. The French, for reasons of their own, backed Muzaffar Jang in his claim to be Nizam, and Chanda Sāhib in his claim to be Nawāb, while the English supported the respective rival claimants, Nāsir Jang and Muhammad Alī. The quarrels between these two sets of claimants are not of the slightest interest or importance in themselves. Their only right to remembrance is that they served as the occasion for the French and English to fight out their struggle for the empire of India. The French, as we know, were beaten, and the English were victorious. In that way the disputes between the claimants to the two South Indian thrones may be said to have brought about the foundation of the British empire in India.

Ambition of Dupleix. Dupleix, the able head of the French settlement at Pondicherry, aimed definitely at the total expulsion of the English and the establishment of French rule. His intrigues and alliances with native claimants or states were all directed to those ends. The English naturally objected to being driven out, and necessarily sided with the princes opposed to the friends of Dupleix.

Unofficial war. The treaty of Aix-la-Chapelle in 1748 having established formal peace between France and England, and Madras having been restored accordingly to the English in the following year, the officials of the French and English rival Companies had no business to mix themselves up with the quarrels of Indian princes and go to war with each other. But they paid no heed to the treaty made in Europe, and were guided solely by the needs of the local situation in India, which seemed to require fighting.

Trichinopoly. The first conflict in the unofficial war occurred in 1751 at Trichinopoly, where Muhammad Alī and his English allies were besieged by Chanda Sāhib and the French. At the moment it seemed that the French would succeed in driving out the English. Muzaffar Jang had become Nizam and had appointed Dupleix to be governor of the peninsula from the Krishnā (Kistna) river to Cape Comorin. The resources of Madras did not suffice to effect directly the relief of distant Trichinopoly.

Capture and defence of Arcot. Robert Clive, a young 'writer' in the Company's service, who had recently accepted a commission as captain in the army, under his old friend Major Stringer Lawrence, saw that the proper way to relieve Trichinopoly was to attack Arcot, the capital of the Carnatic, and so force Chanda Sāhib to withdraw troops from the siege of the southern town.[1] He persuaded his superiors to allow him to make the attack with an absurdly small force, comprising only 200 British soldiers, 300 sepoys, and three small field-pieces. Clive being, as Pitt called him, 'a heaven-born

[1] Arcot is 65 miles WSW. from Madras.

general', succeeded not only in taking Arcot, but in holding it for fifty-four days against 3,000 of Chanda Sāhib's best troops aided by 150 Frenchmen. Thus Trichinopoly was relieved indirectly, and the fame of the British arms was spread throughout India. The sepoys showed the utmost devotion to Clive as their leader, and generously offered the scanty supply of rice to their British comrades, saying that the water in which it was boiled would suffice for themselves. The French and their allies finally surrendered all claims to Trichinopoly in 1752. Further victories at Kāveripāk, to the east of Arcot, and certain other places resulted in the driving out of Chanda Sāhib. Muhammad Alī became undisputed Nawāb of the Carnatic, and retained the rank to the end of his long and worthless life in 1795. Clive was thus free to return to England for rest in 1753.

Ruin of Dupleix. The career of Dupleix and all his schemes of lofty ambition were ruined by the victories of Clive and Stringer Lawrence in the unofficial war. The Governments of England and France disapproved of their subjects fighting in India while the nations were officially at peace in Europe. An envoy sent from France superseded Dupleix, who was recalled and allowed to die in poverty, the great private fortune which he had amassed having been expended by him in financing the plans he had formed for making France the ruling power in Southern India.

Lally ; battle of Wandiwash ; fall of Pondicherry. In 1756 the outbreak of the Seven Years' War in Europe set the French and English in Southern India fighting again, this time with official authority. The French Government appointed as their governor and commander-in-chief a distinguished officer, Count de Lally. Voyages in those days being slow, he did not arrive in India until May, 1758. At first he gained some small successes, notably the capture of Fort St. David, but the English fleet protected Madras and forced him to retire to Pondicherry in 1760. On land the French forces were routed by Sir Eyre Coote at Wandiwash in that year. In January, 1761,

Pondicherry surrendered after a gallant defence for nine months. Lally was taken prisoner, and later sent to France. His countrymen treated him badly, and after some years' imprisonment, he was executed in 1766 on conviction for having 'betrayed the interest of the [French] King and the India Company, for abuse of authority and exactions against the subjects of the King and the foreign residents of Pondicherry'. Although Lally was a foolish and ill-tempered man he was not a traitor to his King, and ought not to have been executed. After some years the sentence was annulled, and his estates were restored to his son.

Ruin of the French. The Seven Years' War was ended in 1763 by the Treaty of Paris. In India the result of the operations was ruinous to the French, who were left without any regular military force, or any local possessions, except their factories of Calicut and Surat, which were mere trading stations. The fortifications of Pondicherry and the buildings within them were destroyed, so that, as Orme puts it, 'not a roof was left standing in this once fair and flourishing city'. The town was rebuilt subsequently.

De Bussy and the 'Northern Circars'. When Lally arrived in India, a countryman of his, Monsieur de Bussy, controlled the Nizam's court at Hyderabad, and had taken possession of the districts then known as the 'Northern Circars' (Sarkārs).[1] Colonel Forde, marching from Bengal, turned the French out of those districts in 1758 and 1759, while de Lally's ill-judged interference destroyed de Bussy's influence in the Deccan, so that the Nizam was brought over to the English side. Meantime the battle of Plassey had been fought, and the English had become masters of Bengal, as will be narrated in the next chapter.

Summary. The outline of the leading events in the three

[1] The Northern Sarkārs in Mughal times were Guntūr, Kondapalli, Ellore, Rajahmundry, and Chicacole, the chief town being Masulipatam. The corresponding Districts in the Madras Presidency are Guntūr, Godāvarī, Kistna (Krishnā), Ganjām, and Vizagapatam. But Guntūr was not acquired by the East India Company until the time of Lord Cornwallis.

Anglo-French wars waged in the south of India may be conveniently summarized in the following statement, which makes no mention of the contemporary events in Bengal and elsewhere:

The Anglo-French Wars in the South.

I. *War of the Austrian Succession*, declaration of war by France against England 1744
Capture of Madras by the French 1746
Peace of Aix-la-Chapelle 1748
Restoration of Madras to the English 1749

II. *Unofficial War.*
Siege of Trichinopoly by Chanda Sāhib and the French: capture and defence of Arcot by Clive 1751
Surrender of Trichinopoly by the French: other British successes 1752
Return of Clive to England 1753
Recall of Dupleix 1754

III. *The Seven Years' War.*—Began 1756
Occupation of 'Northern Circars' by de Bussy . . . 1757
Arrival of Count de Lally; the French capture Fort St. David and attack Madras; Colonel Forde occupies the 'Northern Circars' 1758–9
Battle of Wandiwash 1760
Fall of Pondicherry . . . . . . January 1761
Treaty of Paris, end of the Seven Years' War . . . 1763

In 1782–3 Admiral de Suffren fought actions with a British fleet off the Madras coast, which may be called a fourth Anglo-French war. Those actions were indecisive, and operations were stopped by the Treaty of Versailles in 1783. The armies in Hindustan, led by French officers, were destroyed by Lord Lake in 1803.

Effect of sea power. The French ill success in these wars was partly due to the incompetence of Count de Lally, the capacity of Major Stringer Lawrence, and the genius of Robert Clive; but those personal accidents are not the whole explanation. The most essential element in the French failure and the British victory was, as already observed, the superior English naval power. The small land forces of the Madras authorities were well supported by the British fleet, which, as a rule, was able to beat the French squadrons. Pondicherry might have held out against the land forces alone, but it could not resist them and the navy together. The ambitious schemes of Dupleix really never had a chance of lasting success, because he lacked the support of a fleet strong enough to bring him a constant supply of men and stores, while preventing the English from receiving, as they did, such supplies in abundance.

The kingdom of Mysore. When the kingdom of Vijayanagar was broken up after the battle of Talikota in 1565 (*ante*, p. 142), its component parts passed under the rule of various chieftains. One of those parts—the province of Mysore, varying in extent from time to time—continued to be governed by a dynasty of Hindu Rājās who had been feudatories of the Vijayanagar kings.

Haidar Ali becomes master of Mysore. In 1749 Haidar Ali, then twenty-seven years of age, joined as a volunteer horseman the corps under the command of his elder brother Shahbāz, an officer in the service of the Mysore Rājā. The young man, having attracted notice during the defence of a fort, was appointed to the command of a small force with the rank of Nāyak; and in due course was promoted to be Faujdar of Dindigal. He used his authority to raise a large body of organized plunderers, and thus became a power in the state. A treacherous palace intrigue drove him from office, but by various stratagems he recovered his position, and in June 1761 had made himself practically master of both the Rājā and Mysore. The weakness of the Marāthās after the battle of Pānīpat in that year gave him his opportunity, and the capture of Bednore with treasure extravagantly valued at twelve millions sterling supplied him with funds.

First Mysore war. The Marāthās could not willingly brook the rise of a new and aggressive power. In 1765 they inflicted a severe defeat on Haidar Ali and compelled him to pay a heavy indemnity. Next year he compensated himself by the conquest of Malabar. The Nizām, who at first had opposed Haidar Ali, now joined him against the English, but the allies

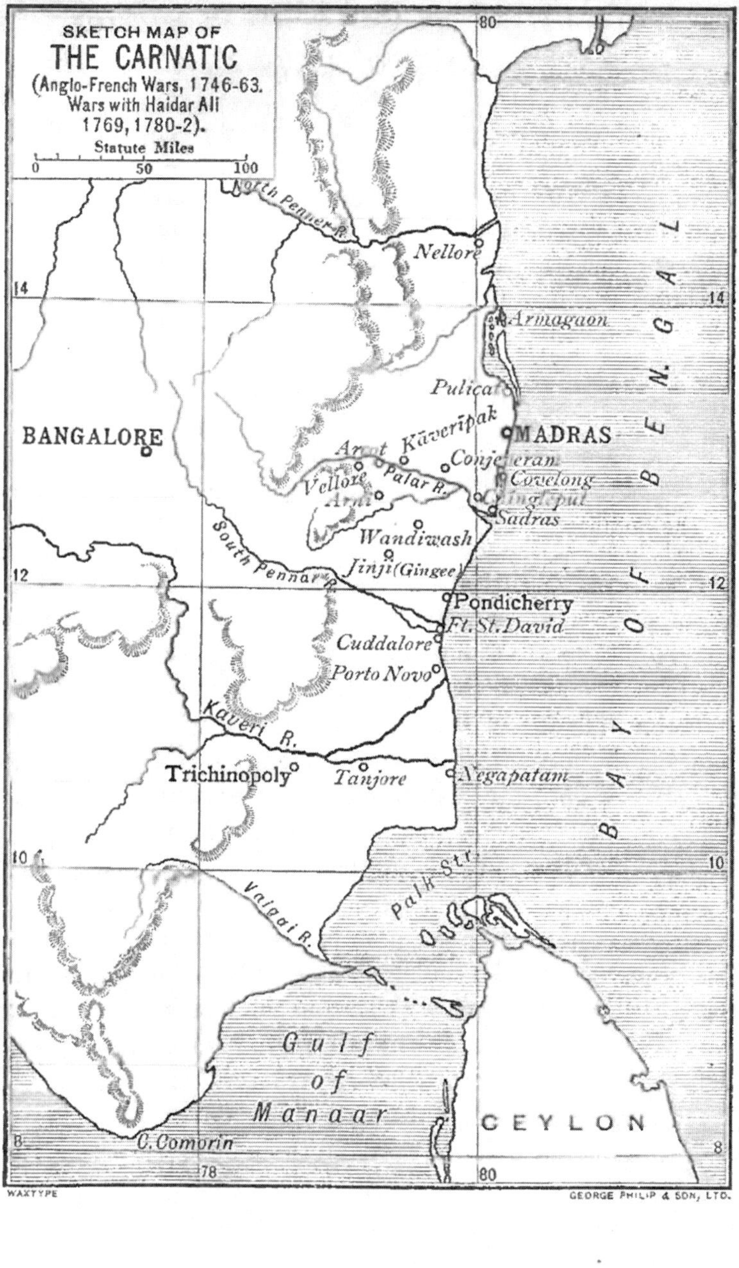

SKETCH MAP OF
THE CARNATIC
(Anglo-French Wars, 1746-63.
Wars with Haidar Ali
1769, 1780-2).
Statute Miles
0
50
100
North Penner R.
Nellore
Armagaon
Pulicat
Kāveripak
MADRAS
BANGALORE
Arcot
Conjeveram
Covelong
Vellore
Palar R.
Arni
Chingleput
Sadras
Wandiwash
South Pennar R.
Jinji (Gingee)
Pondicherry
Ft. St. David
Cuddalore
Porto Novo
Kaveri R.
Trichinopoly
Tanjore
Negapatam
Palk Str.
Vaigai R.
Gulf of Manaar
CEYLON
C. Comorin
BAY OF BENGAL
80
78
14
12
10
8
WAXTYPE
GEORGE PHILIP & SON, LTD.

were defeated by Colonel Smith. In 1769 Haidar Ali appeared before Madras and frightened the incompetent local government into making a treaty with him, on the basis of mutual restitution of conquests, exchange of prisoners, and reciprocal assistance in defensive war. The conflict thus ended is known as the first Mysore war. Three years later the Marāthās again proved themselves too strong for him and forced him to buy them off at a high price.

CHAPTER XXIII

The English in Bengal; Sirāj-ud-daula; battle of Plassey; the Company as sovereign of Bengal.

The Company's war with Aurangzeb, 1685. The beginnings of European settlement on the Indian coasts and the early stages in the history of the East India Company have been recorded in chapter xvii (*ante*, pp. 159–68). The first deliberate bid by the Company for political power in India was made in 1685, when the Directors, in pursuance of a quarrel with the Sūbadār of Bengal, obtained the sanction of King James II to the dispatch of armed squadrons to operate against the ports of both the eastern and western coasts. The expedition to the Hooghly not only failed, but resulted in the temporary expulsion of the English from Bengal (*ante*, p. 166). On the western side the English fleet caused so much annoyance by stopping the pilgrim ships sailing from Surat that in 1690 Aurangzeb, who had no navy and was busy with the Marāthās, came to terms with his assailants on both coasts and permitted Job Charnock to return to the Hooghly and found Calcutta. Soon afterwards, Fort William was built, and the merchants, feeling safe within its walls, devoted themselves to making money and put away all thoughts of empire.

Independence of Bengal; Allahvardi Khan. The government of Bengal, Bihār, and Orissa became practically independent of Delhi in 1740, when the lawful sūbadār or nawāb of those provinces was treacherously slain by a Turkoman officer named Allahvardi (Alivardi) Khan, who usurped the dead man's place. Lavish bribes to the value of about seventeen millions of rupees secured the approval of the imperial court, and the usurper retained office until his death. Once he was established as ruler of the provinces he never sent anything more to Delhi, and was really, although not in name, king of his dominions. The titular emperor at Delhi exercised no control over Bengal after 1741. For several years (1742–51), Allahvardi Khan was much troubled by Marāthā invasions. The atrocious murder by the sūbadār of a Marāthā general and his officers did not stop the plague, and ultimately Allahvardi Khan was obliged to buy off the marauders by ceding the Cuttack province in Orissa and engaging to pay twelve lakhs of rupees yearly as *chauth* for Bengal.

When his power was concerned, Allahvardi Khan was as unscrupulous as the other politicians of his day, but as a ruler of his people he was far above his contemporaries. Stewart, the British historian of Bengal, declares that he was 'affable in manners, wise in state affairs, courageous as a general. He possessed every noble quality'. Orme is equally complimentary, and gives him the quaint praise that he 'remained, perhaps, the only prince in the East whom none of his subjects wished to assassinate'. In his old age, however, he made a bad mistake by naming as his successor his grand-nephew, Mirzā Mahmūd, better known by his title of Sirāj-ud-daula, who was a debauched, cruel, and utterly worthless young man, seventeen years of age when he succeeded his grand-uncle in 1756.[1]

Capture of Calcutta by Sirāj-ud-daula. The officials of the East India Company at Calcutta offended the young Nawāb by sheltering one Kishan Dās, a rich Hindu, whom the Nawāb desired to rob. Moreover, news having been received

[1] Sirāj-ud-daula means 'lamp' or 'sun of the state'. The title is usually written in incorrect forms. It has even appeared as 'Sir Roger Dowler'.

of the approaching outbreak of the Seven Years' War in Europe, the Calcutta people thought it prudent to strengthen their fort, and so gave further offence. Sirāj-ud-daula believed Calcutta to be much richer than it really was, and resolved to loot the place and drive out the English.

The Calcutta merchants, who had been living quietly without thought of anything but business for more than half a century, did not know how to defend themselves properly. When Sirāj-ud-daula came near with a large army, Mr. Drake, the governor had an extremely weak force, including only 174 Europeans, with which to resist. He did something at first, but soon took fright, and slipped away down the river with other cowards.

The deserted garrison elected Mr. Holwell, a brave man, as their leader. He did all that was possible to defend his charge for three days, but on the fourth day was overwhelmed by the greatly superior numbers of the enemy and forced to surrender.

The Black Hole. The prisoners, 146 in number, were carelessly thrust into a tiny lock-up room on a hot night in June, and left there to live or die. Next morning, when the door was opened, only twenty-three were taken out alive, including Mr. Holwell. This tragedy is known to English writers as the affair of the Black Hole of Calcutta. Sirāj-ud-daula, who was in no way concerned about the death of his prisoners, confiscated all the Company's property, and the English for the second time lost their footing in Bengal.

Relief by Admiral Watson and Clive. But, happily for the British reputation, the services of the Company included men who were not cowards. It so happened that an expedition under the command of Admiral Watson and Robert Clive, then on his way out from England, had been operating successfully against the pirates of the Bombay coast, and had just returned to Madras when the news arrived of the capture of Calcutta. Some people in Madras wished to keep what resources they had in order to fight the French. The matter was hotly debated for two months, but ultimately the right decision was taken, and the available force, consisting of Admiral Watson's fleet, with 900 European soldiers, and 1,500 sepoys under Clive's command, was dispatched to Bengal in October, and sailed up the Hooghly in December 1756.

Action at Dum-dum and capture of Chandernagore. In February 1757 the Nawāb was badly defeated in an action at Dum-dum, and obliged to agree to the return of the English, the fortification of Calcutta, and the establishment of a mint there. But, when he heard of the outbreak in Europe of the contest known as the Seven Years' War, his hopes of receiving French aid revived, and he invited the French general, de Bussy, to come up from the south. By way of reply, Clive and Watson took possession of Chandernagore, the French settlement.

Misgovernment of Sirāj-ud-daula; Omichand. The misgovernment of Sirāj-ud-daula, a good-for-nothing youth, provoked discontent, directed by Mīr Jāfar, brother-in-law of Allahvardi Khan, who entered into negotiations with Clive. The English officers agreed to place Mīr Jāfar on the throne of Bengal in return for a payment of 175 lakhs of rupees besides compensation for losses. In order to secure the indispensable support of Amīnchand (Omichand), an influential Sikh banker, Clive descended to the meanness of inserting in a forged copy of the agreement with the Nawāb a promise to pay the banker a large sum, which was omitted from the genuine document. Amīnchand naturally was overwhelmed when Clive coolly confessed to the deception, but the current story that he lost his reason from the shock and died an imbecile is false. The old Calcutta records prove that after an interval he resumed business and engaged in several transactions with the English. As Mr. Marshman observes, 'this is the only act in the bold and arduous career of Clive which does not admit of vindication, though he himself always defended it and declared that he was ready to do it a hundred times over'. Admiral Watson refused to sign the false document, but allowed Mr. Lushington to sign in his name. Negotiations between the

English and the Nawāb followed without satisfactory results. On June 13 Clive advanced, informing the Nawāb that he had 'found it necessary to wait upon him immediately'.

Battle of Plassey, June 23, 1757. On the 23rd of June, 1757, a year after the tragedy of the Black Hole, Clive met the army of the Nawāb at Plassey, in the Nadiyā District, near Kāsimbazar, and not far from Murshīdābād. The English commander's force consisted of a little more than 3,000 men, including about 950 Europeans, and his guns were few and light. His opponent had at his disposal 50,000 infantry, 18,000 cavalry, and fifty-three guns, mostly of heavy calibre, besides some forty or fifty Frenchmen with four light field-pieces. The Nawāb displayed abject personal cowardice, and, after many hours' feeble fighting, his huge host was utterly routed. The handful of 'vagabond Frenchmen', as Orme calls them, under the command of a man named St. Frais, made a brave stand, but were unable to save the cause of the coward whom they served. The loss on the British side was trifling, amounting to only twenty-two killed and forty-nine wounded. The Nawāb's losses were supposed to be about a thousand men killed and wounded. Shortly after the battle, which hardly deserves the name, Sirāj-ud-daula was captured and put to death by a follower of Mīr Jāfar. In accordance with the agreement made, Mīr Jāfar was recognized by the English authorities as Nawāb, the title generally given at that period to the sūbadār, and was compelled to pay heavily for his promotion.

Conquest of the Northern Sarkārs (Circars). In 1758 Clive took a bold step, by dispatching Colonel Forde, with a force which Bengal could ill spare, to wrest the Northern Sarkārs (*ante*, p. 244) from the French, whose hold on the province had been weakened by Count de Lally's orders recalling de Bussy. The expedition, which was well managed and wholly successful, resulted in the acquisition of valuable territory by the Company, and the transference by the Nizam of his alliance from the French to the English side.

Defeat of the Dutch. Mīr Jāfar, the new Nawāb, having soon found that his English patrons were disposed to be masters, resented the position and sought deliverance by negotiations with the Dutch. But Clive put a stop to them by inflicting a severe defeat on the Hollanders at their settlement of Chinsurah, adjoining Hooghly (1759). Next year he returned to England, where he was received with honour by King George, and Mr. Pitt, the Prime Minister, and given an Irish peerage as Baron Clive of Plassey.[1]

Massacre of Patna. During Clive's absence the Company's affairs in Bengal were ill managed by Mr. Vansittart, a weak but tolerably honest man, who had the misfortune to be surrounded by colleagues not at all honest. These men oppressed the people by means of a cruelly worked salt monopoly and other devices for their own enrichment. They replaced Mīr Jāfar as Nawāb by his son-in-law, Mīr Kāsim, making a good profit out of the transaction, and obtaining for the Company the cession of Bardwān, Midnapur, and Chittagong. The misconduct of Mr. Ellis, a civil official at Patna, resulted in the outbreak of war with the Nawāb, who, having been defeated in actions at Katwā (Cutwa) and other places, took refuge in Oudh, and some years later died at Delhi in extreme poverty.

On the other hand, the British lost Mr. Ellis and a number of other officials and soldiers, about 200 in all, who had been taken prisoners, and were barbarously massacred. Most of them (148) were slaughtered at Patna by Walter Reinhardt, nicknamed Sumroo or Sombre, a German soldier of fortune then in the service of Mīr Kāsim (October 1763).

Battle of Buxar, 1764. A year later (October 1764) Major, afterwards Sir Hector, Munro encountered at Buxar, on the Ganges, the combined forces of Mīr Kāsim and the Nawāb-Vazīr of Oudh, who had united in an effort to expel the

[1] An Irish peer does not become, as such, a member of the House of Lords, and may sit in the House of Commons, as Clive actually did. Twelve representative peers, elected by the Irish peerage, have seats in the House of Lords.

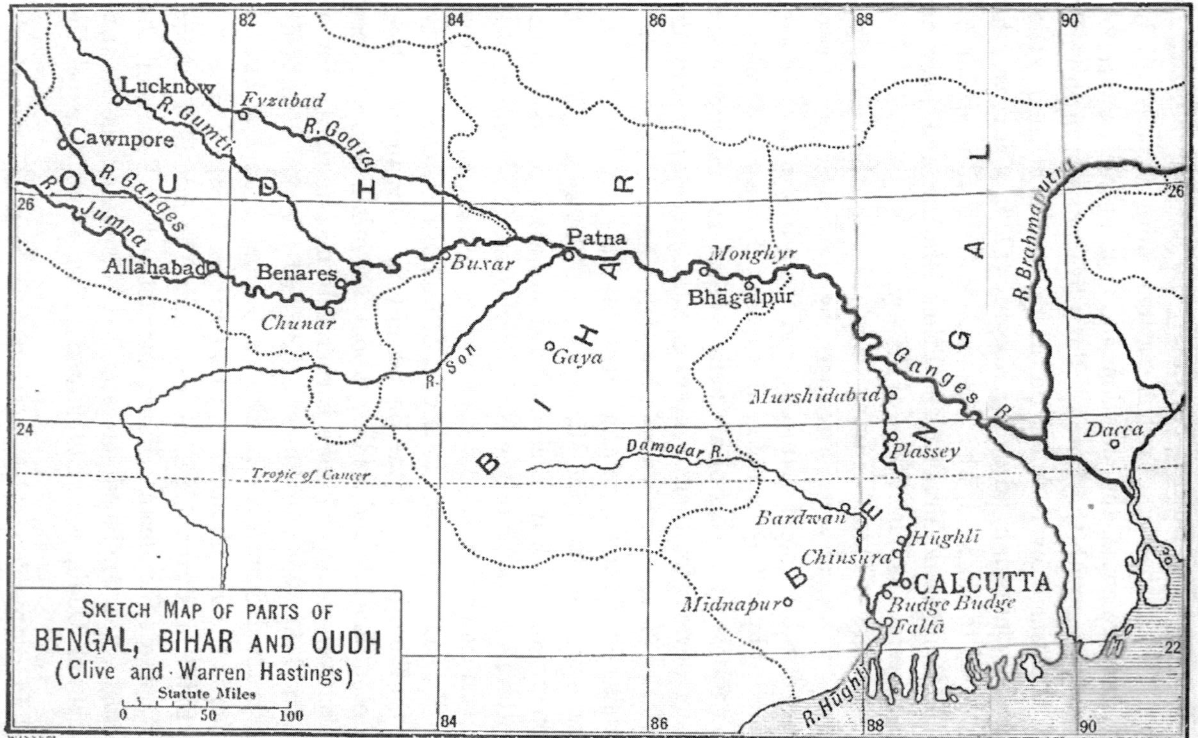

SKETCH MAP OF PARTS OF
BENGAL, BIHAR AND OUDH
(Clive and Warren Hastings)

GEORGE PHILIP & SON, LTD.

foreigners. The allies were decisively defeated, after a real hard-fought battle, in which the Company's force lost 847 killed and wounded, and the country as far west as Allahabad lay at the disposal of the victor. The emperor Shah Ālam took no part in the action, and came into the British camp on the next day. Buxar completed the work of Plassey, and finished once for all the military subjugation of Bengal and Bihār. The Marāthās at that date had not recovered from the effects of the disaster at Pānīpat, and hardly counted among the Indian powers.

Clive's return to India ; his non-aggressive policy. In May 1765 Clive, who had been sent out again from England to settle the disorder in Bengal, returned to Calcutta. He found, to use his own words, 'a presidency divided, headstrong, and licentious, a government without nerves, a treasury without money, and a service without subordination, discipline, or public spirit'. He knew well that the empire of Hindustan was within his grasp, if he chose to take it.

> 'We have at last arrived', he wrote, 'at that critical period which I have long foreseen, that period which renders it necessary to determine whether we can or shall take the whole to ourselves. . . . It is scarcely hyperbole to say that to-morrow the whole Moghul empire is in our power.'

But he disapproved of a policy of adventure, and refused the empire which was to be had for the taking.

Grant of the Dīwānī, Aug. 12, 1765. He was content to legalize the Company's position in Bengal, Bihār, and Orissa (' Orissa ' including only the Midnapur District and part of Hūglī) by accepting from the titular emperor a grant of the Dīwānī, that is to say, power to collect and administer the revenues of those provinces.[1] The Company was thus placed in the legal position of the dīwān or civil colleague of a sūbadār under the Mughal system. It undertook to pay twenty-six lakhs of rupees annually to the imperial treasury. Some

[1] The Cuttack (Katak) province in Orissa was then in the hands of the Marāthās in virtue of the cession made by Allahvardi Khan in 1751.

months earlier the emperor had granted the sarkārs of Benares and Ghazīpur as fiefs to be held direct by the Company.

Double government; Oudh. In his anxiety to disturb traditional arrangements as little as possible, Clive worked the Dīwānī or revenue administration through native agents, and left all police and executive business in the hands of the sūbadār, or Nawāb, as he was then generally called. This system, essentially weak, worked badly in practice, and was defensible only on the ground that nothing better was possible at the time. The Company did not possess the staff necessary for a regular administration. Oudh was left in the possession of the Nawāb-Vazīr, subject to the cession to the emperor of the Allahabad and Karā Sūba (excluding Ghāzīpur and Benares), as the equivalent of tribute due, which had never been paid. This arrangement was agreeable to Shah Ālam, who, on his part, granted to the Company the 'Northern Circars', of which he was not in possession. He took up his residence at Allahabad, and remained there for six years, practically as a pensioner of the English.

Mutiny of British officers (1766); reforms. Certain reductions in the allowances (*batta*) to the British officers having been retrenched under orders from the Directors, great discontent arose among the persons affected, and most of the officers in Bengal so far forgot their duty as to form mutinous combinations. This dangerous movement was met by Clive with inflexible firmness and frustrated within a fortnight. Civil as well as military reforms were pressed with vigour, civil officers being required to sign covenants and abstain from accepting gifts. A scheme was devised for giving the officials adequate legitimate pay, but met with only partial acceptance from the Directors. All these measures of reform aroused much hostility among persons whose pecuniary gains were diminished.

Clive's return to England and death. In 1767 illness compelled Clive to return home, leaving his work unfinished. On arrival in England he was at first received with due honour, but

Lord Clive

after a time his enemies began to pursue him with malignant calumny. Ultimately the House of Commons, while unable to approve of all his acts, resolved that 'Robert, Lord Clive, did, at the same time, render great and meritorious services to his country'. The attacks on him then ceased, but his health had suffered, and he was afflicted by sleeplessness. In November, 1774, weary of an ungrateful world, he cut his throat with a penknife, in his fiftieth year.

Character of Clive. Throughout his brief life of action (1751–67) Clive retained the qualities which he had displayed as a young man in the defence of Arcot. No danger could daunt his calm courage, no difficulties could exceed his resources, no resistance could shake his will. In his youth, although absolutely untaught in the science of war, he had proved himself to be 'a heaven-born general', and in the maturity of his powers he displayed the gifts of a far-seeing statesman. Posterity has endorsed the verdict of the House of Commons that he 'did render great and meritorious services to his country', and the rider may now be added that during his second administration he did his best to serve India as well as England, to protect the weak and restrain the strong.[1]

Misgovernment and famine, 1767–72. The interval of five years between the departure of Clive in 1767 and the appointment of Warren Hastings as Governor of Bengal in 1772 was marked by shocking misgovernment, due to the division of authority, the rapacity of the Company's officials when freed from the strong controlling hand, and general demoralization. In 1769 and 1770 an awful famine, still remembered, desolated the land, and is believed to have destroyed at least one-third of the population. In all ages India has been familiar with the horrors of famine, and several visitations of the kind have been alluded to in previous pages, but, so far as is known, none

[1] The story of Clive is most agreeably read in Macaulay's well-known essay, which is trustworthy on the whole. Certain minor errors are corrected in the notes, by the author of this history, appended to the edition published by the Clarendon Press, Oxford, 1911.

of them surpassed, or perhaps equalled, the famine of 1770, which extended far beyond the limits of Bengal.[1] The ill-compacted system of 'double government' then existing was not competent to deal with a tremendous emergency. Neither the English nor the native authorities held the knowledge requisite for working adequate measures of relief, which were not seriously attempted. The effects of the calamity were still felt forty years later.

The Company sovereign of Bengal. Having thus traced the process by which the East India Company acquired the sovereignty of Bengal, Bihār, Ghāzīpur, Benares, Orissa, and the 'Northern Circars', with a controlling influence over the politics of all Northern India, we proceed to narrate the steps by which Warren Hastings, the first and, perhaps, the greatest of the Governors-General, laid the foundations of a regular system of government.

CHAPTER XXIV

Bengal affairs: the Regulating Act; Warren Hastings, the first Governor-General; the first Marāthā war.

Confusion in Bengal. When Clive quitted India in 1767, only eleven years had elapsed since the English had been expelled from Calcutta with contumely. During that short interval the East India Company was surprised to find that it had become the actual sovereign of Bengal, Bihār, the 'Northern Circars', and Orissa, in the limited sense meaning Midnapur and part of Hūghlī, with a commanding influence over the policy of the ruler of Oudh.[2] The Company was not prepared for this sudden increase of responsibility. Its officials were merchants ill qualified to undertake the duties of

[1] The best printed account is that in Sir William Hunter's *Annals of Rural Bengal*, first published in 1866.

[2] Ghāzīpur and Benares had been restored to Oudh in 1765 by order of the Directors. The rest of Orissa was not annexed until 1803.

government. Clive, as we have seen, tried to administer the country on the old Mughal lines, but the experiment failed, and the consequent disorder made new arrangements absolutely necessary. The Directors sought for a strong man who could be trusted to remedy the miseries of Bengal and to introduce the elements of civilized government. They found him in the person of Warren Hastings, who took over charge of the office of Governor of Bengal in April 1772.

Early life of Warren Hastings. Warren Hastings, the son of an impoverished member of an ancient English family, had joined the Company's service as a lad eighteen years of age in 1750, and afterwards had done good work under Clive, enjoying a high reputation for 'great ability and unblemished character', as certified by the Directors. Early in 1765 he returned to England, where he stayed until the beginning of 1769. The Directors then sent him out to Madras as member of Council at that settlement, where he conducted himself with such discretion in difficult circumstances that he was selected to fill the more arduous position of ruler of Bengal. He enjoyed his employers' 'perfect confidence' and was given secret orders expressing their 'singular trust and dependence upon' his impartiality and prudence.

Hastings as Governor of Bengal; internal reforms, 1772–4. The new Governor lost no time in carrying out his instructions, and in taking measures to introduce effective government under the avowed authority of the Company. The two Indian officials, Muhammad Razā in Bengal and Rājā Shitāb Rāi in Bihār, who had despotically managed the revenue affairs of the two provinces as deputies of the Nawāb, were removed, and a Revenue Board was created at Calcutta, which became the capital. British officers were appointed as Collectors of Districts and Divisional Commissioners, the foundation thus being laid of the administrative system which exists to this day. Hastings found himself obliged to construct a government from top to bottom. He had practically no foundations on which to build. He had to create every department, and do the best possible with the few ill-trained men at his disposal. The collections were farmed for five years, an unsatisfactory settlement of the revenue difficulty, but the best that could be made at the time. Civil and criminal courts were established at Calcutta and in the provinces, and arrangements were made for translating works on Indian law. Large economies were effected by reductions in the allowances paid to the titular Nawāb of Bengal, residing at Murshīdabad, and severe measures were taken to check the ravages of the dacoits or gangs of robbers. During this period Hastings usually enjoyed the support of his colleagues, and was able to carry out his reforms without factious opposition. His zeal, industry, and integrity deserve all the praise that can be given. Throughout his long life he felt a warm interest in literature, art, and science, and was eager to take any possible measures for the moral, intellectual, and material advancement of India. It is impossible to go into details here, but we may note that he was a good Persian scholar, encouraged the study of the Indian languages, patronized artists liberally, promoted Major Rennell's scientific surveys, opened up intercourse with Tibet, and established for a time overland communication with Europe. All such matters engaged his sympathies from the first.

Oudh and the Emperor Shah Ālam. Clive in 1765 had made over to the Emperor Shah Ālam the districts of Allahabad and Karā in the hope that he would be able to hold them and keep out the Marāthās. But the Marāthās, although hit hard by the disaster of Pānīpat, soon began to recover power, and at the close of 1770 Māhādajī Sindia occupied Delhi. He persuaded Shah Ālam to quit Allahabad and return to the capital. The emperor thus became a dependant of the Marāthās, and Hastings was justified in withholding payment of the Bengal tribute, and in treating Allahabad and Karā as abandoned by the emperor. He was not at liberty to take over the government of those provinces, being bound by strict orders to abstain from annexation. He came, therefore, to the conclusion that

Warren Hastings

the best thing he could do was to assign them for payment to the Nawāb-Vazīr of Oudh, who had formerly held them. In 1773, accordingly, Allahabad and Karā were made over to that potentate in exchange for fifty lakhs of rupees, and arrangements were made for supplying a British brigade as an auxiliary force whenever needed by the Oudh Government. When the necessities and difficulties of Hastings's position are realized and the urgency of the Marāthā menace is rightly estimated, these transactions were fully justified, as the Directors held them to be. In 1774, when the Rohilla war was undertaken, the emperor gave formal sanction to the transfer of Allahabad and Karā to Oudh.

The Rohilla war, 1773–4. The provinces of Katehar and Sambhal, north of the Ganges, which were then, and had been for about thirty-five years, ruled by the Rohillas, a clan of Afghan adventurers, consequently had become known as Rohilkhand. The country, being fertile, was an object of desire to both the Marāthās and the ruler of Oudh. The Marāthās already had begun to make raids in it, and the Nawāb-Vazīr was eager to annex it. Hastings, who had long regarded the Rohillas as being dangerous to the Vazīr, the only useful ally of the Company, had reason to fear that they might join the Marāthās, and then destroy the buffer state of Oudh. He therefore held that the threatened danger could be averted only by the conquest of Rohilkhand, and when his ally of Oudh asked for help in that undertaking, Hastings lent him a brigade under the command of Colonel Champion. The enterprise succeeded in its purpose. Rohilkhand was annexed to Oudh, and the Bengal frontier was secured against Marāthā invasion. But the transaction was criticized severely because troops under a British commander were placed in exchange for a money payment at the disposal of an Indian ruler, whose forces were alleged to have permitted themselves a degree of licence forbidden by the customs of civilized warfare. Many of the Rohillas quitted the province, but one chief was permitted to retain his fief, now the small state of Rāmpur, near

Bareilly, and still governed by a Rohilla Nawāb, a prince of approved loyalty. The villagers of the province, Hindus for the most part, once the storm of war had passed, simply had to accept a change of masters, a matter of little concern to them. They went on tilling their lands as usual, and the province suffered little injury, although some villages were burned in the course of the operations. Hastings's conduct in the affair of the Rohilla war, which offers no real occasion for blame, was grossly misrepresented by his enemies in Parliament, and subsequently by Macaulay.

The Regulating Act, 1773. The irregular acquisition of a wide dominion in India by a mercantile company necessarily engaged the attention of Parliament and the King's Government in England, and all parties were agreed that the proceedings of the East India Company must be regulated by law. Discussion resulted in the passing by Lord North's Government of the measure known as the Regulating Act. This statute, the foundation of the existing system of government, limited the powers of the proprietors of the Company, required the submission of dispatches to the King's ministers for information, transformed the Governor of Bengal into a Governor-General in Council with partial controlling powers over all British establishments in India, and constituted a Supreme Court of Judicature consisting of a chief justice and three judges. The council, which under Clive's government had consisted of eleven or twelve members, was reduced to four only, or five including the Governor-General.

Hastings first Governor-General, 1774. Warren Hastings was appointed the first Governor-General of Bengal, with ill-defined powers of control over other settlements, in matters of peace, war, and alliances, retaining his position also as Governor of Bengal. The councillors appointed to assist him were Richard Barwell, a servant of the Company and a member of the old Bengal council, General Clavering, Colonel Monson, and Philip Francis. The Governor-General and his councillors were appointed by name for five years certain. The new

Government took over charge in October, 1774. The chief justice was Sir Elijah Impey, an old schoolfellow and friend of Hastings, and at one time counsel to the East India Company.

Hostile Councillors. When the council met, Hastings found that he could rely on the support of Mr. Barwell alone, the other members being hostile. The Act having given him no power to overrule his colleagues, the Governor-General was always in a minority. This state of affairs resulted in constant friction and some scandalous scenes, which lasted for nearly two years, until Colonel Monson died and Hastings became master in his own house by means of his casting vote as president. A year later General Clavering passed away, and the subsequent official changes did not seriously limit the power of the Governor-General, who was able during the eight subsequent years of his government to give effect to his far-seeing policy without much official opposition.

Rājā Nandkumār. The most famous and disputed incident of the personal struggle between the Governor-General and his councillors is that of the death of Rājā Nandkumār (Nuncomar), a clever and influential Brahman, who had long been an enemy of Hastings, while intimate with his opponents. In 1775 Hastings instituted a charge of conspiracy against the Rājā. While that was pending a private person accused Nandkumār of uttering a forged bond. The forgery case, which was tried with exceptional care by the full Supreme Court and a jury, resulted in the conviction and execution of the Rājā, in accordance with the stern English law of the time, under which forgery was treated as a capital crime. The result of the trial was so advantageous to Hastings that naturally he has been suspected of influencing it. But he denied on oath that he had any concern in the business, and no particle of evidence connecting him with it has been discovered. The Nandkumār affair, which occupies so much space in the biographies of Hastings, was of little importance as an event of Indian history, the course of which was not materially affected by either the life or the death of the Brahman.

Conflict with the Supreme Court. The prolonged struggle between the Governor-General and his council revealed one fault of the Regulating Act, in that it allowed the responsible head of the administration to be overruled by his colleagues. The second defect of the statute was its failure to define either the powers of the Supreme Court or its relations with the Executive. The court asserted extravagant claims to jurisdiction, which if allowed would have made the Government powerless, and the unseemly contest which followed was not stilled until Hastings hit on the device of appointing Sir Elijah Impey to be head of the Company's courts as well as Chief Justice of the Supreme Court. The arrangement, although disallowed by the Home Government, put an end to the scandal of open conflict between the Court and the Executive. An amending Act of Parliament passed in 1781 duly defined the duties of the Supreme Court as limited to Calcutta and the jurisdiction over British subjects elsewhere. The same Act legalized the Company's courts. The modern High Court possesses the powers of both the Supreme Court and the tribunal of the Company.

The first Marāthā war. The war known as the first Marāthā war arose out of a disputed succession to the office of Peshwā. Mādho (Mādhava) Rāo, the fourth Peshwā, died in 1772, the year in which Hastings became Governor of Bengal, and was replaced by his brother Nārāyan Rāo, who, nine months later, was murdered by his uncle Raghoba (Raghunath). The succession was contested between the murderer and the supporters of his victim's posthumous child, who set up a regency. The English authorities at Bombay promised their support to Raghoba at the price of the cession of Salsette and Bassein, and an agreement to that effect, the Treaty of Surat (1775), was concluded without the knowledge of the Governor-General.[1] But he found himself obliged to support the Bombay President in the war which ensued. In 1779 Commissioner

[1] The Treaty of Purandhar, substituted for the Treaty of Surat by Hastings and his colleagues, never took effect, and need not be noticed in detail.

Carnac concluded with the Marāthās, guided by Nānā Farnavīs, an arrangement known as the Convention of Wargāon, the provisions of which were considered so disgraceful that Carnac and other officers concerned were dismissed the service. Hastings saved the Bombay settlement from destruction by the dispatch of an expedition under Colonel Goddard, which marched right across India from Bengal to Surat, a remarkable achievement in those days. The alliance then concluded between the British Government and the Gaikwār of Baroda has never been broken. In the following year (1780) the fortress of Gwalior, supposed to be impregnable, was taken by Major Popham without the loss of a single man. This brilliant feat did much to wipe out the disgrace of the 'infamous' Convention of Wargāon.

Treaty of Sālbāi. Towards the close of 1779 the Nizam had organized a coalition embracing all the Marāthā princes, except the Gaikwār, and including Haidar Ali of Mysore, for the purpose of destroying the growing British power. War followed, in which the principal Marāthā army was defeated. The Rājā of Nāgpur was cleverly bought off without fighting. Haidar Ali, who had attacked the Carnatic fiercely in 1780, was menaced by the dispatch of a Bengal force under Colonel Pearse, which marched by land through seven hundred miles of unknown country to the aid of Sir Eyre Coote. That exploit was second only to Goddard's wonderful march across India to Surat.

Ultimately peace with the Marāthās was arranged through the aid of Māhādajī Sindia, the ablest of the Marāthā chiefs, who treated on their behalf with full powers and guaranteed the execution of the treaty.[1] The document, signed at Sālbāi in Sindia's territory, secured Salsette for the English at Bombay, provided Raghoba with a pension, and in most other respects restored the former state of affairs. The terms thus stated may seem to be of small moment, but the Treaty of

[1] The correct spelling of the name is Māhādajī (माहादजी). The forms Mādho and Mādhava, given in some books, are incorrect.

Sālbāi in 1782 deserves to be remembered as one of the landmarks of Indian history, because it secured peace with the formidable Marāthā power for twenty years, and plainly signified that the East India Company had already become the leading authority in the country.

Māhādajī Sindia. Māhādajī Sindia, who took such a prominent part in bringing about the peace so much needed by Hastings, was the illegitimate son of a village headman named Ranojī, who had begun life as slipper-bearer to the Peshwā, but had risen in the world, as often happened in those stirring times. Māhādajī had taken part in the battle of Pānīpat and was one of the few Marāthā chiefs who escaped with life from that field of death. He succeeded to his father's *jāgīrs*, and quickly became the most prominent of the Marāthā chieftains. In those days the glory of the Peshwā had become obscured, and the real power of the Marāthā confederacy was shared mostly by four territorial princes: Sindia of Gwalior, Holkar of Indore, the Rājā of Nāgpur or Berār, and the Gaikwār of Baroda. In 1771, when Shah Ālam, the titular emperor, had quitted British protection and returned to Delhi, he came under the control of Māhādajī Sindia, whose importance was thus increased. Māhādajī was so much impressed by the military successes gained by the officers under Hastings in 1780 and 1781 that he thought it safer to treat with the British than to fight them. That was the reason which induced him to take so much trouble in carrying through the Treaty of Sālbāi. He died in February, 1794.

Second Mysore war; defeat of Baillie. We must now turn our attention to the south, where the rapid growth of Haidar Ali's power had become a constant menace. The rise of the Mysore adventurer up to 1772 has been narrated in brief (*ante*, p. 246). When the war with France began in 1778, Hastings, acting under orders from home, and against the advice of Sir Thomas Rumbold, the Governor of Madras, seized the French settlements, including the little port of Mahé on the Malabar coast, which Haidar Ali had used for the entry of supplies, and claimed as his. He, being deeply offended at that act and for other reasons, prepared a mighty force of about 90,000 men, with 100 guns, directed by Europeans, to drive out the English. Hastings was then busy with the Marāthās and hoped that the threatened storm in the south might blow over. But it burst with awful suddenness. In July, 1780, Haidar Ali's host swept down on the Carnatic plain, slaying, maiming, burning, and ravaging with fiendish cruelty. He overwhelmed and destroyed a gallant force of 2,500 men under Colonel Baillie near Conjeeveram, and so inflicted on the English the greatest disaster which they had yet suffered in India. Sir Hector Munro, the victor at Buxar in 1764 (*ante*, p. 253), who was no longer as competent as he had been when younger, shut himself up with the few troops remaining in Madras, and did nothing. An urgent appeal for help was sent to Calcutta.

Energy of Hastings. This calamity was a terrible addition to the heavy load of trouble already resting on the shoulders of Hastings. His spirit rose to the occasion. He superseded the acting Governor of Madras, persuaded old Sir Eyre Coote to resume command, sent every available soldier and rupee from Bengal, and abandoned all other plans in order to meet the urgent danger. He succeeded, but not until a year later.

Battle of Porto Novo. The incompetence of the Madras Government put difficulties of all sorts in the way of Sir Eyre Coote, who was in bad health, but at last he was able to venture on a general engagement. On July 1, 1781, at Porto Novo on the coast, he decisively defeated Haidar Ali, who lost about 10,000 men, while the Company's loss did not exceed 300. The brigade under Colonel Pearse which Hastings had sent overland from Bengal joined Coote, who gained some further minor successes.

Effect of command of the sea. Notwithstanding another British disaster, the defeat of Colonel Braithwaite and a force of 2,000 men by Haidar Ali's son Tippoo, Haidar Ali began to feel that the war was too much for him. Shortly before his death he acknowledged in remarkable words the effect of England's command of the sea.

'I have committed', he said 'a great error; I have purchased a draught of spirits at the price of a lakh of pagodas; I shall pay dearly for my arrogance; between the English and me there were perhaps mutual grounds of dissatisfaction, but not sufficient cause for war, and I might have made them my friends in spite of Muhammad Ali [Nawāb of the Carnatic], the most treacherous of men. The defeat of many Braithwaites and Baillies will not destroy them. I can ruin their resources by land, but I cannot dry up the sea; and I must be the first to weary of a war in which I can gain nothing by fighting.'

Death and character of Haidar Ali. In December, 1782, Haidar Ali died, at the age of sixty, and was succeeded by his son Tippoo (Tīpū), a man much inferior in ability.[1] Haidar Ali, by far the most remarkable man evolved from the chaos of the eighteenth century in Southern India, possessed abilities and fertility of resource which enabled him to overcome the caprices of fortune and build up a military state strong enough to threaten the stability of the growing British Empire. Although unable to read or write beyond signing his initial upside down, he spoke five Indian languages fluently, and his conduct of business was a model of regularity and dispatch.

He is described as being never for a moment idle from morning to night. He relied for success on strict personal supervision of every act of government and on a system of ferocious tyranny.

'By his power', writes a contemporary historian, 'mankind were held in fear and trembling; and from his severity God's creatures, day and night, were thrown into apprehension and terror. . . . No person of respectability ever left his house with the expectation of returning safe to it.'

The English officers and soldiers who had the misfortune to

[1] Haidar Ali was born in 1722, not 1702, and when he died, was not 'an old man of eighty', as alleged in several books.

be taken prisoners suffered agonies from his unfeeling cruelty. He had no religion, no morals, no compassion.

The subsequent history of Mysore will be dealt with in connexion with the administrations of Lord Cornwallis and Lord Wellesley.

Failure of promised French help. Haidar Ali had always relied much on hopes of effective French support, and had always been disappointed. The arrival on the coast in 1782 of a French fleet under Admiral de Suffren revived his hopes, but the actions fought by that officer with Admiral Hughes proved indecisive, and the Mysore government did not benefit. Still, the British affairs seemed to be in a very gloomy position in 1782, a year of great events.[1] Good fortune, or an overruling Providence, dispelled the clouds. A victory gained by Rodney in Europe restored the British command of the sea, which had been endangered and for a short time lost. In 1783 the Treaty of Versailles ended the war. France never again attempted to attack the Indian coast.

Treaty of Mangalore. Tippoo, who was not a party to the Treaty of Versailles, continued the war in the south and captured Mangalore, where Colonel Fullarton had made a gallant defence no less notable than the more famous defence of Arcot by Clive. The war with Tippoo was ended in 1784 by the Treaty of Mangalore, arranged by the Government of Madras, whose officers were subjected to the most galling insults. The basis was the mutual restitution of conquests and the exchange of prisoners. The prisoners in Mysore had been treated with the utmost brutality. The contemporary accounts of their sufferings are painful reading. Hastings loathed the treaty and the conduct of the Madras Government, but at the time was restrained from interference by orders from England and a certain amount of opposition in his own

[1] Other events in that year were the resignation of Lord North, who had been Prime Minister of England from 1770; the repulse of the main attack by the French and Spaniards on Gibraltar; and the establishment of 'Grattan's Parliament' in Ireland.

Council. The peace concluded at Mangalore lasted for six years.

Two disputable incidents. From 1778 to 1782 the burden cast upon Hastings was almost more than a man could bear. It is not surprising, therefore, that some of his actions in that critical time, when submitted to close scrutiny, should be open to hostile criticism. The critics forget that his conduct should be judged as that of a sovereign beset by unscrupulous enemies, and not as that of a private person or subordinate official. In those days the Governor-General was obliged to bear his own burdens and to act on his own responsibility. Modern financial facilities were not available, and when war was on, a supply of ready cash was indispensable. That urgent need of cash for public purposes, not for private gain, gave rise to the two incidents—the affair of Rājā Chait Singh and the transactions with the Bēgams of Oudh—which furnished much material to the accusers of Hastings, and cannot be commended without reserve.

The affair of Rājā Chait Singh. In 1775 the fief of Rājā Chait Singh of Benares, illegitimate son of an upstart chief, had been transferred by his suzerain, the Nawāb-Vazīr of Oudh, to the Company and the Rājā thus became bound to render customary service to his new lords When called upon in 1778 to pay a contribution of five lakhs for military purposes he complied grudgingly. The similar demands made in the next two years were partially evaded, and in 1781 Hastings, being pressed for money, determined to make an example of the Rājā, who had given him offence in other ways. A fine of forty or fifty lakhs, about half a million sterling, was decided on, and Hastings went to Benares, intending to impose and levy it. Although escorted by an inadequate force, he rashly and without sufficient reason arrested Chait Singh, whose people rose, slew the Governor-General's sepoys, and forced Hastings to flee for his life to Chunar. The Rājā raised an army of 40,000 men, but Hastings never lost his head, and quickly made arrangements which resulted in the total defeat of the enemy. The main purpose of the dangerous adventure, however, failed, because the victorious army appropriated as prize-money the forty lakhs of rupees taken in the Rājā's stronghold. The Company gained no direct advantage except a nearly doubled assessment on the estates of Chait Singh, which were made over to his nephew and are still held by a descendant, H.H. the Mahārāja of Benares, a much respected and loyal prince. It is impossible either to deny a certain amount of harshness in the proceedings of Hastings against Chait Singh, or to acquit him of rashness in the execution of his plans.

The affair of the Bēgams of Oudh, 1782. The second incident arose out of the failure to secure Chait Singh's cash. At that time the Nawāb-Vazīr of Oudh, Āsaf-ud-daula, was deeply in debt to the British Government for the pay of the auxiliary troops supplied to him, and was unable to raise the money required, unless he could lay hands on the treasures held adversely to him by his mother and grandmother, known as the Bēgams of Oudh. Those treasures undoubtedly should have been treated as State property, but Hastings's hostile Councillors had guaranteed them to the Bēgams as personal belongings, and had rejected the just claims of the Nawāb-Vazīr. The Bēgams having actively supported the cause of Chait Singh, Hastings felt justified in revoking the guarantee given by the Council improperly and against his opinion. Troops were sent to Fyzabad, where the ladies resided, the palace eunuchs were thrown into chains and half-starved, and seventy-five lakhs of rupees were extracted. At the trial of Hastings in England these censurable facts were enormously exaggerated by the rhetoric of his accusers, made familiar to all readers in Macaulay's brilliant but untrustworthy essay. The seventy-five lakhs did not nearly exhaust the accumulations of the Bēgams, the younger of whom was 'alive and hearty and very rich' twenty-one years later, when one of the roughly treated eunuchs also was still living, 'well, fat, and enormously rich.' Sir Alfred Lyall's judgement may be accepted, that 'the employment of personal severities, under the superintendence of British officers, in order to extract money from women and eunuchs, is an ignoble kind of undertaking'; but his award of 'serious blame' to Hastings is partly met by the answer that Hastings did not actually order the severities.

Close of the career of Hastings. The conclusion of the treaties of Versailles and Mangalore left Hastings free to return to England, after thirteen years of rule, as Governor of Bengal for two years and a half, and as Governor-General for the rest of the time. His activity was so incessant and his services to the country so many that it is impossible to present a really fair picture of his work in small compass. But what has been said may suffice to satisfy the junior student that Warren Hastings was one of the greatest of men and a true friend of India, notwithstanding his rare errors.

Impeachment and death of Hastings. His proceedings, some of which undoubtedly were open to adverse criticism, had raised up many enemies. The opposition to his policy, stimulated by motives of English party politics, resulted in the impeachment of the ex-Governor-General by the House of Commons at the bar of the House of Lords.[1] The court sitting only for a few days in each year, the trial dragged on for seven years. At last, in April 1795, Hastings was acquitted on all the charges which had been pressed. The Directors having made the necessary provision for his expenses and support, he lived at Daylesford as a benevolent country gentleman until 1818, when he died in his eighty-sixth year.

Character of Warren Hastings. The character of Warren Hastings has given rise to so much bitter controversy that even now it is difficult to pass a judgement likely to command universal assent. Perhaps a general agreement may be assumed that his acquittal was right, and that his errors were not of the kind deserving of judicial penalties. Undoubtedly he was

[1] In an impeachment the House of Commons orders and directs the prosecution, while the House of Lords sits as a court and judges the case. The process is now obsolete. The last case was that of Lord Melville in 1805.

a great Englishman, devoted to the service of his country, and not unmindful of his duty to the land in which he did so much to make his nation supreme. In labour he was unwearied, in resolve inflexible, in adversity patient, in danger imperturbable, and in policy far-seeing. If he displayed at times somewhat of arrogance, or intolerance of opposition, his consciousness of superior knowledge and capacity must be his excuse. In a greedy age and surrounded by men whose god was money, he was distinguished by clean hands which scorned to grasp polluted riches. In private life he was a well-bred gentleman, of amiable manners, refined taste, and generous beyond the bounds of prudence.

British India in 1785. Annexation was not in favour with Hastings, whose acquisitions were limited to the Ghāzīpur and Benares districts on the Ganges, and the small islands of Salsette and Elephanta, close to Bombay. When he went home, British India comprised Bengal, Bihār, a small area of Orissa, Ghāzīpur, Benares, the 'Northern Circars' (except Guntūr),[1] Madras, and a limited area adjoining, with Fort St. David and some other little settlements on the east, besides Bombay, Surat, and a few other places on the west coast. Orissa (excluding Midnapur and part of Hūglī) although included in the imperial grant of the Dīwānī, was held by the Marāthās of Nāgpur, and did not come into the Company's effective possession until 1803.

CHAPTER XXV

Mr. Macpherson; Lord Cornwallis; Pitt's India Act; Permanent Settlement and reforms; the third Mysore war; Sir John Shore.

Mr. Macpherson; Lord Cornwallis. Pending the arrival of a permanent successor, Warren Hastings made over charge to Mr. Macpherson (afterwards Sir John), the senior member of Council, as acting Governor General. The Home Government deeming it necessary to appoint a statesman of reputation, unconnected with the East India Company, to take charge of

[1] Ceded by the Nizām to Lord Cornwallis.

the now extensive British dominions in India, selected Earl Cornwallis. A special Act was passed in 1786 conferring upon the Governor-General that power of overruling his Council which Hastings had so much missed.

Pitt's India Act, 1784. The system of the Home Government was changed by Mr. Pitt's India Act of 1784, which placed Indian affairs in the hands of a secret committee consisting of the chairman, vice-chairman, and senior member of the Court of Directors, acting under the supervision of a board of six commissioners, commonly called the Board of Control, appointed by the Crown. The Directors were allowed to retain the patronage, but the real power now passed to the King's ministers, of whom the President of the Board was one. Mr. Dundas was appointed first President, and practically became the Minister for Indian Affairs. After a short time the Board never met, the President taking action in its name. That system lasted without substantial change until 1858, when the Crown assumed the direct administration, and a Secretary of State for India was substituted for the President of the Board of Control.

Administrative reforms of Lord Cornwallis. Lord Cornwallis, when he assumed charge at Calcutta in September, 1786, was vested with full authority as both Governor-General and Commander-in-Chief to control all civil and military affairs of the British settlements in India, and, if necessary, to overrule opposition by his colleagues. He also enjoyed the confidence of the Ministry at home, and thus started his work with advantages never possessed by Hastings. The first three years of his administration were devoted to internal reforms, and especially to the organization of a regular Civil Service properly paid by fixed salaries, and not by fluctuating commissions or irregular trading profits. The beginnings of this necessary reform were the work of Clive and Hastings, but neither was able to complete the change, which was effected by Lord Cornwallis with comparative ease, owing to his more favourable position.

The Permanent Settlement. The most famous measure of

Lord Cornwallis

Lord Cornwallis is the Permanent Settlement of Bengal, Bihār, and Orissa, concluded in 1793, when the then existing assessment of land revenue, which had been made for ten years, was declared to be perpetual. Two years later the same supposed boon was conferred upon the province of Benares.[1] The policy of the Permanent Settlement, carried out by Lord Cornwallis against the advice, but with the help, of his most esteemed councillor, Sir John Shore (Lord Teignmouth), and with the full approval of Mr. Pitt and the Board of Control, is undoubtedly open to the criticism that it was adopted with undue haste, and that it has imposed an unequal burden on the less favoured parts of the empire. No attempt was made to follow the example of Todar Mall by surveying the lands or calculating their value. The assessment was made roughly on the basis of accounts of previous collections, and was necessarily done in a haphazard fashion. Probably most competent judges, not being personally interested, are of opinion both that the measure was a mistake and that now it is too late to rectify the error. The author of the Permanent Settlement fancied that he would create a race of ideal landlords, eager to improve their estates, and was not sufficiently acquainted with the facts of Indian life to know the baselessness of such a fancy. He also designed to protect the subordinate tenure-holders and cultivating tenants against the oppression of their lords, and, so far as words went, the regulations gave such protection. But, in practice, tenants with grievances had little chance of redress until long afterwards, when Act x of 1859 was passed, and provided more or less effective remedies. The difficulty of reconciling the conflicting interests of landlords and tenants in Bengal and elsewhere still continues acute in spite of much modern legislation. Of course, the provinces permanently settled have received many obvious advantages from the hasty benevolence of Lord Cornwallis, but those benefits have been gained at the expense of other provinces not less meritorious.

[1] Now included in the United Provinces of Agra and Oudh. 'Orissa' meant Midnapur and part of Hūglī.

The Cornwallis Code. Lord Cornwallis also carried out judicial reforms, supplementing the work begun by Hastings. The new courts were provided with a bulky code, prepared by Mr. George Barlow, which is a monument of good intentions. But it was far too elaborate, being loaded with formalities and technical rules ill suited to a people only just delivered from the rude simplicity of Mughal jurisprudence and procedure. The courts of appeal established by Lord Cornwallis were abolished long ago, and all his detailed judicial arrangements have been modified by later legislation, but the existing system is built on his foundations. The criminal courts under his regulations were governed by the Muhammadan law, shorn of some of its more barbarous peculiarities; mutilation, for instance, being forbidden. The English civil courts were assisted by a Hindu pundit as adviser on Hindu, and a Musalman Kāzī or Maulavī as adviser on Muhammadan law. The administrative arrangements of Lord Cornwallis were marred by his excessive distrust of Indian agency. The natives of the country were excluded from office except of the most petty kind, and a burden greater than it could bear was thrown on the covenanted Civil Service, which at that time comprised only about three hundred members and had to supply all the executive and judicial appointments of any importance.

The third Mysore war. At the time of passing the India Act Parliament had declared that 'to pursue schemes of conquest and acquisition of territory was contrary to the wish, the honour, and the policy of the British nation'. The Governor-General was also forbidden, in the absence of express sanction from home, to enter upon or make any treaty with any of the Indian princes, except in defence of the British dominions or the territory of an ally. Such a strict rule, considering the length of the voyage between England and India in those days, was absurd and could not possibly be obeyed. Absolute necessity compelled every Governor-General to either evade or violate it. Instructions given by the Directors in accordance with the Act of Parliament were honestly accepted at first by Lord Cornwallis, but long before his rule ended he had to bow to necessity and lead in person a victorious army to extensive conquests. In 1790, only thirty-three years after the battle of Plassey, an attack by Tippoo, the ruler of Mysore, on distant Travancore, an ally of the British Government, compelled the Governor-General to declare war. An alliance with the Nizām and the Peshwā was arranged on the condition that all conquests should be divided equally among the three allied powers. The earlier operations of the war were unsatisfactory owing to the failure of the Madras authorities to provide supplies, and Lord Cornwallis found himself constrained to use his special powers and take command himself. In the third season's operations the British force, assisted by a contingent from Bombay, captured the outworks of Seringapatam, Tippoo's capital (1792). The sultan was forced to accept the hard terms dictated by the victor, which exacted the cession of half his dominions, the payment of three hundred lakhs (thirty millions) of rupees, and the delivery of two of his sons as hostages. The districts thus acquired by the Company, namely, Malabar, Coorg, and part of Salem, forming the nucleus of the existing Presidency of Madras, yielded a revenue of forty lakhs of rupees, about four millions sterling. The Home Government confirmed the proceedings of the Governor-General, and the King raised Lord Cornwallis to the rank of marquess.

Various events; death of Māhādajī Sindia. In 1793 the long war between France and England, caused by the French Revolution, began. In India the immediate result was the capture without difficulty of Pondicherry and the other French settlements. In the same year the charter of the East India Company was renewed for a period of twenty years, the Company's monopoly of trade being confirmed, with a small exception. While Lord Cornwallis, with the nominal help of the Peshwā, was crushing Tippoo, the Marāthā chiefs in Northern India were fighting among themselves. Māhādajī Sindia in those days was the most powerful prince in the country (*ante*, p. 268), having made himself irresistible by means of an army organized by the Savoyard de Boigne, and other foreign officers. He inflicted a signal defeat on his rival Holkar, who also had utilized the services of European adventurers. In February, 1794, Māhādajī Sindia died suddenly, bequeathing to his grand-nephew Daulat Rāo, the dominant position in a large part of Malwā and the Deccan, as well as in Hindustan, from the Sutlaj to Allahabad. In October, 1793, Lord Cornwallis quitted India, making over charge to his trusted colleague Sir John Shore, and leaving behind him a high reputation for industry, dignity, honour, and integrity.

Administration of Sir John Shore; Sikhs and Afghans. Sir John Shore, a man of peace, failed to support the Nizām, and allowed that prince to be defeated decisively by the Marāthās under the direction of Nānā Farnavīs, an able minister, at the battle known by the name of Kardlā in 1795.[1] This weak policy of non-intervention dangerously enhanced the Marāthā power, and, of course, ensured the hostility of the Nizām. It also stimulated the ambition of Tippoo, who sent embassies to the French, Afghans, and other powers, in the hope of forming a combination strong enough to expel the English from India. Shah Zamān, the ruler of Afghanistan, actually entered the Panjāb in 1797 and occupied Lahore, but luckily was compelled to retire quickly on account of a Persian attack on his western provinces. Ordinarily during this period the hostility between the Sikhs and the Afghans protected India from invasion through the north-western passes. Sir Alfred Lyall has pointed out that 'the effect was to maintain among the fighting powers in Northern India an equilibrium that was of signal advantage to the English by preserving their north-west frontier unmolested during the last quarter of the eighteenth century, a critical period when they were fully occupied by Mysore and the western Marāthās'.

[1] Farnavīs is a corruption of the Persian *fard-navīs*, and meant 'finance minister' in the Marāthā system of government. All the histories give the name of the battle-field as Kardlā, but it is Khardā, now in the Ahmadnagar District, Bombay.

CHAPTER XXVI

Lord Wellesley; fourth Mysore war; second Marāthā war; subsidiary alliances.

Lord Wellesley assumes charge, 1798. In May, 1798, Sir John Shore, who had been created an Irish peer as Lord Teignmouth, made way for a man of a different type, Richard, Earl of Mornington in the peerage of Ireland, and Baron Wellesley in that of Great Britain, who had been for four years a member of the Board of Control. Lord Wellesley, when he assumed charge, was thirty-seven years of age, in the full vigour of his powers, and thoroughly well informed on Indian affairs as seen by the Home Government. His younger brother, Arthur, afterwards the famous Duke of Wellington, already was serving at Madras in the army. The rule of Lord Wellesley, which lasted for a little more than seven years, until July, 1805, has been pronounced to have been 'the most memorable in the annals of the Company', and good reasons may be alleged in support of that opinion.

Preparations for war with Mysore. Immediately after his arrival the news of Tippoo's intrigues with the revolutionary government of France determined him to crush the power of Mysore and to finish the work of Lord Cornwallis. The Governor-General's plans from the first were definite, comprising a march on the capital of Mysore, the seizure of the sultan's conquests in Malabar, the appointment of a British Resident at his court, the expulsion of all Frenchmen from his service, and the compulsion on him to defray the whole expense of the war. As a preliminary the Nizām, then much weakened by the Marāthā victory at Kardlā (properly Khardā), was induced to accept a treaty which imposed on him the support of a British sepoy force of six thousand men, and required the dismissal of all the French officers in his employ. The Nizām took some part in the campaign, and was handsomely rewarded.

THE MARQUESS WELLESLEY

Fourth and last Mysore war, 1799; restoration of Hindu dynasty. The war when it came was short and sharp. General Harris took command on February 3, 1799, and on the 5th of the following month his troops entered Mysore. On the 4th of April Tippoo lay dead inside the breach in the walls of Seringapatam, which had been stormed by General Baird and his men in seven minutes. Thus was fulfilled the saying that Haidar Ali was born to win, and Tippoo to lose, a kingdom. This one exploit practically ended the war, which had carried the Governor-General farther than he had anticipated. He had planned to bridle the power of Mysore, and found that he had utterly destroyed it. The sultan's territory was divided. The Company took Kanara, the entire sea-coast, and other districts which gave them an uninterrupted dominion from sea to sea. The Nizām received a considerable amount of lands to the north, while the Marāthās were offered, on conditions which they declined, certain smaller areas adjoining their territories. On their refusal, those lands were divided between the Nizām and the British.[1] The rest of the kingdom was assigned to a youthful representative of the old dynasty of Hindu Rājās, dispossessed by Haidar Ali. The new State thus constituted was placed under the control of a Resident. The young chief, Krishna Rājā Wodeyar, did well at first, but lapsed into evil ways, and in 1831 the Government of India was obliged to deprive him of all authority, and to confide the administration directly to British officers.

Rendition of Mysore, 1881. That arrangement, with various changes of form, lasted until 1881, when Lord Ripon felt justified in again making over the State to a native government. This event, known as the Rendition of Mysore, took place on the 25th of March, 1881, when Mahārāja Chāma Rajendra Wodeyar, adopted son of Krishna Rājā, was installed with befitting ceremony, and the disinterested good faith of the British Government was triumphantly vindicated. The

[1] The territories acquired by the Nizām in 1792 and 1799 were given up to the Company in 1800 to pay for the support of a subsidiary force.

WAXTYPE

GEORGE PHILIP & SON, LTD.

subsequent excellent administration of the state has justified the confidence and generosity exhibited by Lord Ripon and the Home Government.

Significance of the destruction of Tippoo's power. The splendid success of the Mysore war roused enthusiasm in all parts of British India, and the news was received in England with universal applause. The Governor-General was promoted to the rank of marquess in the peerage of Ireland, and endowed by the Directors of the Company with an annuity of £5,000 for twenty years. The destruction of Tippoo's power was rightly recognized as being a serious blow to the schemes of Napoleon Bonaparte, whose dream of an Eastern empire was finally dissipated in August of the same year (1799) by Nelson's naval victory at the battle of the Nile.

Wellesley's policy ; subsidiary alliances. The Mysore war finally pacified the south. The north and west continued to be unquiet in consequence of the domination of the restless Marāthā chiefs. Lord Wellesley aimed avowedly at the establishment of British supremacy in the whole of India, and so necessarily came into conflict with the Marāthā power. He sought to gain his end by a system of subsidiary alliances, involving the subordination of the Indian princes to the British Government in all matters of external policy, the dismissal of officers belonging to other European nations, and the acceptance of the services of a contingent of troops under the orders of the Government of India, and usually paid by an assignment of territory.

Annexation of the Carnatic. Muhammad Alī, the old Nawāb of the Carnatic, died in 1795. Six years later the Governor-General very properly annexed his territory and so got rid of the 'double government' which had lasted so long in Southern India and had caused untold misery to the people, as well as grave corruption in high places. Muhammad Alī was a thoroughly worthless person throughout his long life.

Treaty of Bassein, 1802. The wars between the rival Marāthā chiefs gave the opportunity and created the necessity for British intervention. In 1795 Ahalyā Bāī, the saintly Marāthā lady who had guided the affairs of Holkar's dominions with wisdom and justice for nearly thirty years, died, and in the scramble for the succession which followed, Jaswant Rāo Holkar, a wild and unscrupulous leader of banditti, made himself master of the state. His defeat of the Peshwā, Bājī Rāo, at Poona in 1802 constrained that prince to seek British protection, and to accept from Lord Wellesley a treaty of subsidiary alliance in the usual form. The document recording the agreement is known as the Treaty of Bassein, and marks the extinction of the independent power of the Peshwās. Daulat Rāo Sindia, who had succeeded the great Māhādajī in 1794, and the Bhonslā of Nāgpur, also known as the Rājā of Berār, at once prepared for war with the Company.

Second Marāthā war; Assaye, Laswāri, &c. General Arthur Wellesley defeated the army of Sindia, at least seven times more numerous than his own, at Assaye near Aurangabad, on September 23, 1803. A little later the Bhonslā was defeated even more decisively at Argāon in Berār. The capture of the ancient Bahmanī fortress of Gāwilgarh, also in Berār, followed, and the Bhonslā was brought to his knees. By the Treaty of Deogāon he accepted a subsidiary alliance, and gave up the province of Cuttack (Katak) in Orissa. The war in Hindustan was in the competent hands of General Lake, who captured Aligarh, defeated the army under the command of Monsieur Perron, the successor of de Boigne (*ante*, p. 281), and entered Delhi in September, 1803. In the following month the remaining troops of Sindia were defeated at Laswāri in the Alwar state with great slaughter. By the Treaty of Surji Arjangāon, concluded at the end of the year, that prince surrendered all the territory in the Doāb between the Ganges and Jumna, recognized the rights of several Rājpūt chiefs, and submitted to a subsidiary alliance. Holkar remained to be subdued, and an expedition was sent against him, but he gained an unexpected advantage by the folly of Colonel Monson, a relative of his namesake, Hastings's opponent, who 'advanced without

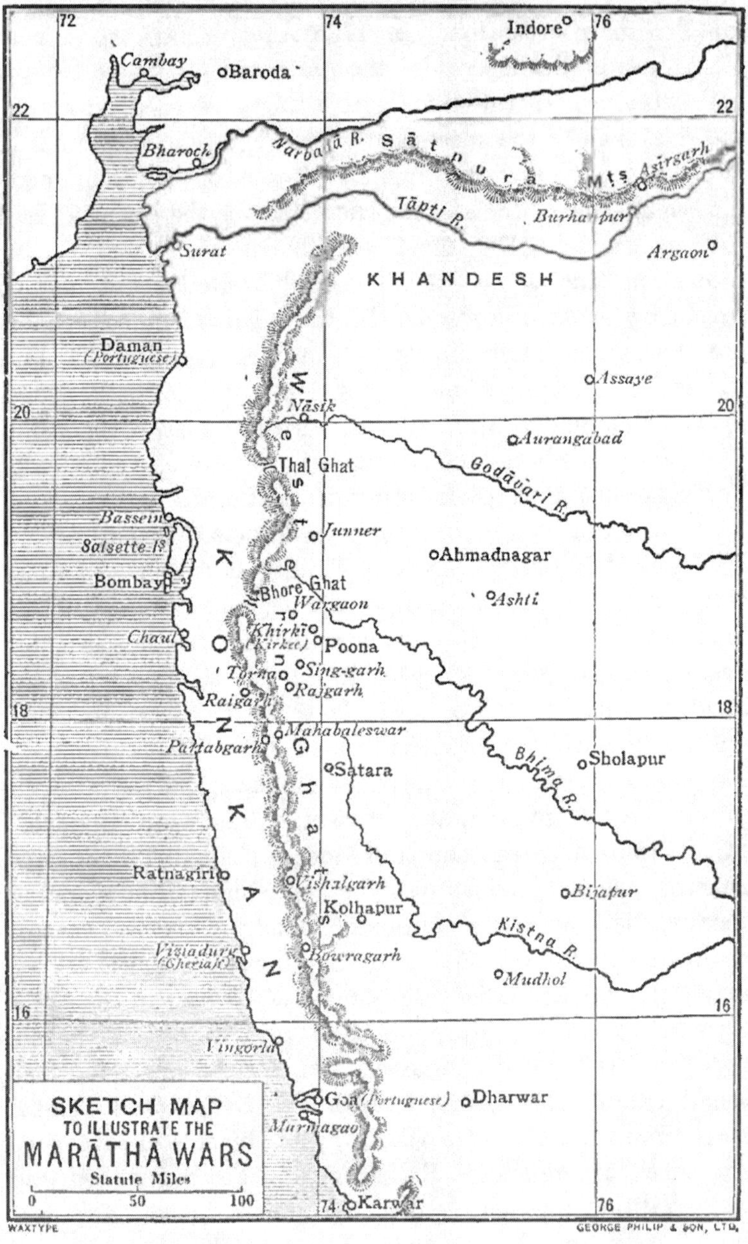
Indore
Cambay
Baroda
Bharoch
Narbada R.
Sātpura Mts
Asirgarh
Tāpti R.
Burhanpur
Surat
Argaon
KHANDESH
Daman (Portuguese)
Assaye
Western Ghats
Nāsik
Aurangabad
Thal Ghat
Godāvari R.
Bassein
Junner
Salsette Is.
Ahmadnagar
Bombay
Bhore Ghat
Wargaon
Ashti
Chaul
Khirki (Kirkee)
Poona
Torna
Sing-garh
Rajgarh
Raigarh
KONKAN
Mahabaleswar
Partabgarh
Satara
Sholapur
Bhima R.
Ratnagiri
Vishalgarh
Bijapur
Kolhapur
Kistna R.
Vigiadurg (Gheriah)
Bowragarh
Mudhol
Vingorla
Goa (Portuguese)
Dharwar
Murmagao
Karwar
SKETCH MAP TO ILLUSTRATE THE MARĀTHĀ WARS
Statute Miles
0 50 100
WAXTYPE
GEORGE PHILIP & SON, LTD.

reason, and retreated in the same manner ', in south-eastern Rājputāna (1804), losing thereby nearly the whole of his force. Holkar next suffered a severe defeat at Dīg (Deeg), but was not yet wholly subjugated. General Lake, who did not well understand siege operations, was repulsed in repeated attempts to storm the Jāt fort of Bhurtpore (Bharathpur) in 1805. The Rājā, although he succeeded in holding the fort, submitted to a treaty. The titular emperor, poor old blind Shah Ālam, was handsomely pensioned, and all pretence of regarding him as a power in the land was avowedly dropped.

Recall of Lord Wellesley. The authorities at home had long been restive at Lord Wellesley's bold policy, which seemed to them needlessly expensive, while the tone of his dispatches was not calculated to soothe their feelings. The disaster suffered by Colonel Monson's force filled the cup. On receipt of the news, the Directors and the Board of Control resolved to recall the Governor-General, and reverse his policy through the agency of Lord Cornwallis, who was persuaded to accept office at Calcutta for the second time. As has happened so often to timid Governments, the event proved that the home authorities in seeking peace had been preparing war. Their shortsighted, although natural, caution plunged a large area of India into acute misery for many years, and resulted in a formidable war in the time of the Marquess of Hastings. Great Britain, having become the paramount power, could not enjoy the gains without assuming the duties of the position. The recall of Wellesley left the Marāthā power still face to face with the English. The struggle for mastery was bound to come.

Lord Wellesley's internal reforms and character. The primary importance of Lord Wellesley's wars in settling to a large extent the fate of India must not make us forget that the Governor-General was a scholarly man of many interests, as keen to devise internal reforms as he was determined to assert the inevitable British supremacy. The college founded by him at Fort William for the training of young civil servants was reduced by the Directors to the rank of a school of Oriental languages, but even as such it was a valuable institution. Calcutta is indebted to him for Government House, modelled on the lines of Lord Scarsdale's mansion at Kedleston, and for sundry civic improvements. In spite of his costly wars, he improved the public credit, and brought the finances into order with the aid of Mr. Tucker. Lord Wellesley's solid merits were to some extent obscured by his imperious temper, a tendency to inflated language in speech and writing, and an excessive fondness for ceremonial display. He lived until 1842, when he died at the age of eighty-two, having filled many important positions after his retirement from India.

Wars with Mysore.

First, 1767–9, ended by treaty dictated by Haidar Ali under the walls of Madras.

Second, 1780–4, ended by Treaty of Mangalore, based on mutual cession of conquests.

Third, 1790–2, ended by peace dictated by Lord Cornwallis under the walls of Seringapatam, which deprived Tippoo of half his kingdom.

Fourth, March to May, 1799, ending in the death of Tippoo, the capture of Seringapatam, and the partition of his kingdom, part of which was formed into a protected Hindu state.

CHAPTER XXVII

Lord Cornwallis again; Sir George Barlow; Lord Minto; abolition of trade monopoly.

Lord Cornwallis; Sir George Barlow; and Lord Minto. Lord Cornwallis, when summoned to resume charge of the Indian Government in order to carry out the policy of non-intervention, was in the sixty-seventh year of his age and feeble health, and consequently unfitted for the task imposed upon him. He reached Calcutta on July 30, 1805, and having proceeded up country, died at Ghāzīpur on October 5. In the short interval he found time to address letters to the Directors and Lord Lake expressing in distinct terms his resolve to reverse the policy of Lord Wellesley. He found a willing disciple in Sir George Barlow, the senior member of Council, who succeeded him as Governor-General, pending an appointment from home. Ultimately Lord Minto, President of the Board of Control, and great-grandfather of the Viceroy who succeeded Lord Curzon in 1905, was appointed Governor-General.

Mutiny of Vellore, 1806. Even Sir George Barlow could not bring himself to carry out the desire of the Directors to withdraw from the Treaty of Bassein (*ante*, p. 287), and to permit the resumption by the Peshwā of his old position as head of the Marāthā states. He also insisted on maintaining the control of the Resident over the policy of the Nizām. His period of rule was marked by the mutiny of the sepoys at Vellore, where the sons of Tippoo had been assigned a residence. Those princes had been rashly allowed to assemble a following of eighteen hundred men, besides some three thousand other immigrants from Mysore. Such a gathering of refugees from a recently conquered kingdom, and close to its frontier, necessarily became a centre of disaffection, and encouraged the mutiny of the troops, which was provoked directly by injudicious orders prescribing a new form of turban and other matters of the kind. During the disturbances 113 Europeans, including fourteen officers, were massacred. The Directors blamed Lord William Bentinck, the Governor of Madras, for his policy, and recalled him, a decision which he always resented as unjust.

Travancore rebellion; mutiny of officers. The new Governor-General soon discovered that, whatever his prejudices and instructions might be, he could not avoid interference with the native states. In 1808 the minister of the Rājā of Travancore in the extreme south engaged in a mad rebellion, attacking the British Resident and murdering a surgeon and thirty-three privates of the 12th Regiment. The rising was put down early in the following year. During the same year (1809) much anxiety was caused by the mutinous conduct of the officers of the army of Madras, where Sir George Barlow had been appointed Governor. Lord Minto went down to the south, but the trouble had passed before his arrival.

Bundelkhand. In Bundelkhand, as in Travancore, the Governor-General found the policy of non-intervention to be impracticable. The anarchy in that province, which had been ceded by the Marāthās, forced him to declare that 'it was essential, not only to the preservation of political influence over the chiefs of Bundelkhand, but to the dignity and reputation of the British Government, to interfere for the suppression of intestine disorder'. The ensuing military operations resulted in the surrender of the fort of Ajaygarh and the capture of the famous fortress of Kālanjar after a difficult siege. The suppression of the growing Pindāri outrages in Central India, and the checking of Gūrkha and Burmese encroachments on the northern and north-eastern frontiers, were recognized by Lord Minto as necessary measures, but he was obliged to leave their execution to his successor, his own action in these matters being hindered by the disposition of the Home Government.

Lord Minto and the Sikhs. On the north-western frontier he acted with uncompromising firmness, and did not allow himself to be deterred by the non-intervention bogy from defining the line of the Sutlaj as the frontier separating the British dominions from those of Ranjit Singh, the lord of the Panjāb. We have already noticed the early history of the Sikh sect (*ante*, p. 226), which was gradually hammered into the shape of an organized military power by its conflicts with the Afghans during the eighteenth century. After the last invasion and withdrawal of Ahmad Shah Durrānī in 1767 the Sikhs occupied the country between the Jumna and Rāwalpindi. Their progress was then checked by the Marāthās, but when the Marāthā power in Hindustan was broken by Lord Lake in 1803 (*ante*, p. 287), some of the Sikh chiefs between the Sutlaj and the Jumna tendered their allegiance to the victor, and all looked to the British Government as their protector.

Rise of Ranjit Singh. At that time the Sikh community was organized into twelve sections or fraternities called *misls*. One of these came under the rule of Ranjit Singh, who, in 1799, when nineteen years of age, had helped Zamān Shah of Kābul in his invasion of the Panjāb. The Afghan ruler, who claimed the sovereignty of the country, appointed Ranjit Singh governor of Lahore. From that vantage ground the young chief gradually made himself master of the Panjāb and Kashmīr, retaining his power until his death in 1839. He followed the example of the more southern princes by engaging European adventurers to train his troops, and thus organized the fine army which fought the British so stoutly in 1846 and 1849.

Treaty of Amritsar, 1809. In 1809, encouraged by Sir George Barlow's non-intervention policy, Ranjit Singh claimed control of all the Sikh principalities between the Sutlaj and Jumna. Lord Minto, without waiting to refer home for orders, made up his mind that Ranjit Singh's pretensions could not be admitted without breach of faith to allies and imminent danger to the British possessions. The Sikh ruler naturally was unwilling to submit to dictation, but the arrival of a British army on the Sutlaj put an end to his hesitation, and on April 25, 1809, at Amritsar, he signed a brief treaty of fifteen lines establishing 'perpetual amity between the British Government and the state of Lahore'. During the remaining thirty years of his life Ranjit Singh observed this engagement with honourable fidelity. A British garrison was posted at Lūdiāna, which now became the frontier station, and so it happened that a Governor-General, appointed to carry out the non-intervention policy, practically advanced the British boundary from the Jumna to the Sutlaj.

Foreign embassies outside India. During the whole of Lord Minto's term of office Great Britain was engaged in the deadly, world-wide struggle with Napoleon, in which the ruler of India had to take his share. His predecessors had extinguished the French power in India; Lord Minto made it his business to curb it in the adjoining countries and surrounding seas. His Panjāb policy was partly based on the fear of French interference, and the embassies sent by him under Malcolm to Persia and Mountstuart Elphinstone to Kābul were decided on solely with the object of checkmating Napoleon's plans. A treaty with Persia was arranged, but the results hardly justified the heavy cost of the mission. The embassy intended for Kābul never arrived there in consequence of the deposition of Shah Shujā (Soojah), the Afghan ruler to whom it had been dispatched. We shall meet Shah Shujā again.

Expeditions by sea. Lord Minto's expeditions by sea were more fruitful, and testify to his broad grasp of political problems. In those days Mauritius and the neighbouring islands in the Indian Ocean to the east of Madagascar formed a French colony, which was used as the base of a privateer fleet to prey on Indian commerce. In the course of fifteen years the Mauritius privateers had plundered property of Calcutta merchants worth three millions sterling. The Governor-General determined to stop this, and in 1810 a fleet acting under his orders captured Mauritius and its dependencies. Mauritius still is a British Crown Colony, but the neighbouring island of Bourbon or Réunion was restored to France at the peace of 1815. Lord Minto's expedition to Java and the Spice Islands, Dutch colonies then under French control, was even more daring and brilliantly successful. The Governor-General, who accompanied the force intended for the reduction of Java, which was under the command of Sir Samuel Auchmuty, made suitable arrangements for the civil government of the island. Batavia, the capital of Java, was taken after a hard fight at the end of August 1811, and the operations, naval and military, being admirably arranged, were successful at all points. The valuable conquests so gallantly won were unfortunately surrendered at the general peace.

Abolition of the Company's monopoly of the Indian trade. The renewal of the East India Company's charter, granted in 1793 (*ante*, p. 280), was to hold good for only twenty years. As the end of the term fixed drew near, a lively discussion took place, the Directors fighting to keep their monopoly, while the general public in Great Britain demanded liberty for all to take part in Eastern commerce. In the end Parliament decided to throw open the Indian trade to all comers, while maintaining the Company's exclusive rights in the China seas. On these terms the charter was renewed in 1813 for twenty years longer. At the same time permission was given for missionaries to enter India as freely as merchants, a reform also resisted strenuously by the Directors.

CHAPTER XXVIII

Lord Hastings: Nepalese, Pindāri, and Marāthā wars; Lord Amherst; first Burmese war.

The Earl of Moira, Marquess of Hastings. Lord Minto was succeeded by the Earl of Moira, better known by his later title as the Marquess of Hastings, who was fifty-nine years of age and had seen much service in high military and political employ. He came out full of the doctrines of the non-intervention school then in fashion, but soon found himself constrained to act as a disciple of Lord Wellesley. He assumed charge on October 4, 1813, and ruled India until January, 1823, for nine years and a quarter, without rest or holiday. After his retirement he became Governor of Malta, where he died in November, 1826.

Result of non-intervention. Lord Minto, as we have seen, had done brilliant service for his country by defeating French hostility in foreign lands and beyond the seas, where he was able to act with a free hand. But within the limits of India his action had been hampered by instructions which he could not venture to disregard altogether. The result was the accumulation of internal difficulties and the tying of knots which must be cut by the sword. Lord Hastings, consequently, when he took over the reins of government, found 'seven different quarrels likely to demand the decision of arms' thrust upon him, and six years of his term of office were spent in constant and unavoidable war.

Nepalese encroachments. The most pressing of the pending quarrels was that with the Gūrkhas of Nepāl, whose encroachments on British territory could not be longer endured. A Gūrkha chief having overcome the ancient principalities of the valley of Nepāl in 1768, he and his successors subsequently extended their power over the whole hill region from the frontier of Bhutan on the east to the Sutlaj on the west, and constantly sought expansion of their dominion in the richer regions of the plains. The cession of the Gorakhpur territory by the Nawāb-Vazīr of Oudh in Lord Wellesley's time had brought the British boundary to the frontier of Nepāl, and unceasing difficulties arose on the border. Before 1813 the Nepalese had seized more than two hundred villages on the British side of the ill-defined frontier. Their annexation of the districts of Būtwal and Sheorāj brought the quarrel to a head, and their refusal of restitution made war inevitable. Hostilities began in October 1814.

War with Nepāl, 1814–16. Lord Hastings, who was his own commander-in-chief, worked out an excellent plan of operations, providing for the attack on the Gūrkha positions at four widely separated points. The British force was superior to the enemy in numbers, and, in spite of the difficult nature of the country, speedy success should have been secured but for the incapacity of most of the generals employed. One of them, General Gillespie, a brilliant officer, who had distinguished himself in Java, lost his life in making a rash frontal attack on a stockade contrary to orders, and three others muddled away their opportunities through sheer imbecility. Many lives were needlessly thrown away and little progress was made, except in Kumaon, where Colonels Nicholls and Gardner occupied Almora by a force of irregulars, and in the territories along the Upper Sutlaj, which had been invaded by a force from Lūdīana, under the command of General (afterwards Sir David) Ochterlony, a highly capable leader. In

May, 1815, Ochterlony compelled the brave Gūrkha commander, Amar Singh, to surrender the fort of Malaon. The success of these operations inclined the Nepalese Government to peace, and a treaty was signed. But on second thoughts the Darbār refused to ratify it and the war began again.

Treaty of Sagauli, 1816. In February, 1816, Ochterlony penetrated the hills by a daring night march and attained a position threatening Kathmāndu, the capital. The Gūrkhas then gave in and the Treaty of Sagauli was signed in March. It provided for the cession by the Nepalese of Kumaon to the west of the Kālī river, their withdrawal from Sikkim, the surrender of most of the Tarāi, or lowlands below the hills, and the acceptance of a British Resident at the court of Kathmāndu. The treaty has been observed faithfully ever since, and friendship, although with considerable reserve, has been maintained unbroken between the contracting Governments. The Gūrkha regiments recruited in Nepāl are a most valuable element in the Indian Army, and during the troubled times of the Mutiny a Nepalese force gave welcome aid to the British authorities. In the great war of 1914 they have again freely shed their blood in the cause of the British Rāj. The sites of the hill stations of Almora, Naini Tal, Mussoorie, Simla, &c., were acquired by the cession of Kumaon.

General unrest. The news of the British failures during the earlier stages of the Nepalese war excited every court in India and raised hopes of the expulsion of the foreigner. Ranjit Singh moved troops towards the Sutlaj; Amīr Khan, the leader of the roving Pathān bands in Rājputāna, watched events with a force of 30,000 men and 125 guns, while the Marāthā chiefs, the Peshwā, the Bhonslā of Nāgpur, Sindia, and Holkar, all began to arm. If the jealousies of these powers had permitted their effective combination at the right moment, the Governor-General had not the force to withstand them. But the 'Company's *ikbāl*', or good luck, prevailed; the effective combination did not take place, and each of the hostile powers was overcome in due course.

The Pindāris. Still more urgent than the danger from all those territorial powers was the peril caused by the Pindāri hordes of marauders, who, starting from a central position in Mālwā and the Narbadā valley, where they were loosely attached to the armies of Sindia and Holkar, ravaged India with fiendish cruelty from Gujarāt to Ganjām. The Pindāris, first heard of during the struggles between Sivājī and Aurangzeb, had grown enormously in numbers and strength during the century of anarchy which followed the death of the Great Mogul.[1] They were bands of lawless men, drawn from all castes and classes, who took advantage of the absence of a strong government to make their living by organized plunder. Mounted on hardy ponies, a body of two or three thousand men could cover fifty miles in a day, harry a district, and be far away with their booty long before any regular troops could appear. They worked in conjunction with the Marāthās, one division being specially connected with Holkar and another with Sindia. Towards the end of 1815 the Pindāris laid waste the Nizām's dominions as far south as the Kistna (Krishnā) river, and early in the next year ravaged the Northern Circars, which had enjoyed security for half a century. The Governor-General reported the case of a village in which the inhabitants had been driven to the

> 'desperate resolution of burning themselves with their wives and children. . . . Hundreds of women belonging to other villages have drowned themselves in the wells, not being able to survive the pollution they had suffered. All the young girls are carried off by the Pindāris, tied three or four, like calves, on a horse, to be sold. . . . They carried off booty to the value of more than a million sterling'.

Nevertheless, the authorities in England, fearing a war with Sindia, hesitated to permit the punishment of the villains, and their timidity was shared by Lord Hastings's Councillors at Calcutta. But at last, early in 1817, the Council could no longer shirk the decision that 'vigorous measures for the

[1] The origin of the word Pindāri is uncertain.

suppression of the Pindāris had become an indispensable object of public duty'. Lord Hastings then took the necessary measures to organize his forces and to smooth their path by diplomacy.

Plan of campaign. The plan devised provided for the surrounding of the Pindāri lair in Mālwā, by a converging force of about 120,000 men, divided into eight sections or divisions, comprised in two armies, the southern under the command of Sir Thomas Hislop, and the northern led by the Governor-General in person. The force, the largest ever collected up to that time under the British flag in India, was provided with 300 guns, and comprised about 13,000 Europeans. A skilful movement subjected Sindia to such pressure that he reluctantly signed a treaty binding him to assist the English, and the circle was closed round the Pindāris. But the operations of the Governor-General were much hindered by the sudden outbreak of an epidemic of cholera, and some of the ruffians broke through the line.[1]

Third Marāthā war. Operations were prolonged by a general rising of the Marāthā powers, excepting Sindia and the Gaikwār, and the hunt of the Pindāris became merged in the third Marāthā war. During November and December, 1817, the Peshwā, the Bhonslā, and Holkar successively took up arms. Bājī Rāo, the Peshwā, having been decisively beaten by a small British force at Kirkī near Poona (November 13, 1817), was driven as a fugitive from his capital. The Bhonslā was defeated on the 26th of the same month at Sītābaldī, near Nāgpur, in one of the most brilliant actions ever fought; and Holkar was routed at Mahīdpur on the Sipra river, to the north of Ujjain (December 21, 1817). Amīr Khan, the leader of the Pathan host of rovers, was induced to settle down as Nawāb of Tonk in Rājputāna, where his successors still flourish. Karīm Khan, one of the Pindāri leaders, was given an estate in Gorakhpur, still enjoyed by his descendants;[2] another

[1] The common belief that cholera first appeared in India in 1817 is mistaken.

[2] Now in the Bastī District, separated from Gorakhpur in 1865.

leader, weary of being hunted, ended his life by poison, and Chītū, the most famous of all the bandit captains, was driven into a jungle, where he was killed by a tiger. On January 1, 1818, the Peshwā suffered another defeat at Koregāon near Poona, and, a few days later, yet another at Ashti, where his gallant general, Gokula, met a soldier's death. The Peshwā, who was no hero, surrendered to Sir John Malcolm, whom he persuaded into promising him the extravagant pension of eight lakhs a year. With this allowance he was sent into retirement at Bithūr, near Cawnpore. Nānā Sahib, notorious for his cruelty in the Mutiny, was the adopted son of Bājī Rāo, the last Peshwā. Lord Hastings, following the Mysore precedent, sought out a descendant of Sivājī, and presented him with a portion of the Marāthā dominion under the title of Rājā of Sātārā. The rest of the country was annexed to the British dominions, and the Presidency of Bombay thus was extended to nearly its present dimensions in India Proper. The Bhonslā's territory also was annexed in part, and in part made a protected state. It now forms the Central Provinces. Holkar, treated with less severity, was allowed to retain the districts which constitute the state of Indore. The final operation in the war was the capture in 1819 of Asīrgarh, the famous stronghold in Khāndēsh, but the contest had been decided early in 1818.

Achievement of Lord Hastings. In the long roll of brilliant Governors-General the name of the Marquess of Hastings deserves a place of the highest honour in virtue of personal achievement. In October 1817 he was confronted by forces of more than 150,000 men—Pindāris, Marāthās, and Pathans—with 500 guns. Four months later the power of Sindia was paralysed; that of Holkar broken; the Pathan armies of Amīr Khan and Ghafūr Khan had ceased to exist; the Rājā of Nāgpur was a captive; the Peshwā was a fugitive, and the Pindāris had disappeared. The campaign finally extinguished the Marāthā empire, at which Lord Wellesley had struck the first blow. This great and necessary work, by which countless millions were delivered from cruel tyranny, was done by Lord Hastings alone, in the teeth of opposition from colleagues and superiors.

Fall of the Marāthā empire. The Marāthā empire thus ended in 1818 its brief career, perishing deservedly, because it had never deserved to exist. The government of the Marāthā confederacy, whether before or after the Treaty of Bassein, was organized solely for the purposes of plunder and blackmail. It fulfilled none of the proper functions of a government, and in its latter days had not even the merit of being national. The armies defeated by Lord Lake, Sir Arthur Wellesley, and the Marquess of Hastings had little distinct Marāthā character, being filled up with Musalmans, vagabond Europeans, and rascals of all sorts. Those armies were closely associated with the purely criminal gangs of Pindārī marauders, 'the refuse of the Mahratta armies', as Grant Duff calls them. The connexion was so close that the operations of the Marquess of Hastings, directed primarily against the Pindārī hordes, passed almost insensibly into war with the Marāthā governments, which willingly shared in all the Pindārī atrocities. The Marāthā chiefs never did any good for India, and left behind them nothing but ruin and devastation.

The student should realize that the year 1818 marks an epoch in the history of India.

Internal administration. The internal administration of the marquess achieved notable progress. Laying down the maxim that 'it would be treason against British sentiment to imagine that it ever could be the principle of this Government to perpetuate ignorance in order to secure paltry and dishonest advantages over the blindness of the multitude', he established and encouraged schools and colleges, and permitted the issue of the first vernacular newspaper. The 'ryotwari' settlement of the Madras territories was carried out by Sir Thomas Munro, and the imperial finances were administered with success and enhanced credit. Much was done to improve Calcutta; the ancient Jumna canal near Delhi (*ante*, p. 125) was reopened, and many other works of public utility were executed.

Lord Amherst; Barrackpore mutiny; Bhurtpore. The government was carried on for seven months after Lord Hastings's departure (January 1 to August 1, 1823) by Mr. Adam, the senior member of Council. He was relieved by Lord Amherst, who, like most of the Governors-General, sought peace and found war. Before narrating the story of the Burmese war, the principal event of his term of office, we must notice the two other most memorable incidents—the mutiny at Barrackpore and the capture of Bhurtpore (Bharathpur). The mutiny of the 47th Native Infantry at Barrackpore, under the windows of the Governor-General's country house, caused by the unwillingness of the sepoys to proceed to Burma, was promptly suppressed (October, 1824). The operations against Bhurtpore arose out of a disputed succession to the principality, which rendered necessary the intervention of the Government of India. It is to be noted that on this occasion the Governor-General in Council stood forth avowedly as 'the paramount power and conservators of the general peace'. After a short siege the fortress, before which Lord Lake had failed in 1805 (*ante*, p. 289), was stormed by Lord Combermere, and the general belief that it could never be taken was destroyed (January, 1826).

First Burmese war. At about the same time as the English conquered Bengal, an adventurer named Alaungprā (Alompra) founded an aggressive dynasty in Burma (1752–60). He and his successors extended their conquests into Assam, Cāchār, and Manipur, and threatened the British frontier Districts of Sylhet and Chittagong. The Burmese had an unbounded conceit of themselves, and went so far as to require the Marquess of Hastings to surrender Eastern Bengal, including Dacca and Murshīdābād. In 1824 their defiant seizure of a British outpost compelled Lord Amherst to declare war, which the Burmese awaited with eager confidence. The Governor-General, who did not possess his predecessor's military genius, was advised that the occupation of the port of Rangoon by a naval expedition would quickly prove decisive. The occupation was easily effected by a force sent from Madras, but sickness and the want of supplies crippled the troops. Assam was occupied early in 1825 by General Richards, but attempts to enter Burma overland failed, and a detachment was cut up at Rāmū on the Chittagong frontier. The campaign, as a whole, was badly planned, and much preventible loss was incurred; ultimately, however, when Prome was occupied, and the Burmese capital threatened, the king was forced to sue for peace. In February 1826 the Treaty of Yandabo was signed, which ceded to Great Britain the provinces of Assam, Arakan, and Tenasserim. The king further agreed to abstain from all interference in Cāchār, Jaintia, and Manipur, and to pay an indemnity.[1] Thus, in spite of many errors in planning and execution, the war ended in a triumphant success for British arms, and the acquisition of extensive provinces then little esteemed, but now recognized as possessing high value. The annexation closed up the north-eastern frontier of the empire and protected it against foreign aggression.

The Marāthā Wars

First, 1775–82: Warren Hastings Governor-General; Convention of Wargāon, 1778; capture of Gwalior, 1780; ended by Treaty of Sālbāi, 1782. (Some writers treat this war as two wars, namely, the first, up to the Treaty of Surat, and the second, from 1778 to 1782.)

Second, 1803: Lord Wellesley Governor-General; battles of Assaye, Argāon, and Laswāri; occupation of Delhi; ended by Treaties of Surji Arjangāon and Dēogāon.

Third, 1817–19: Lord Hastings Governor-General; battles of Kirkī, Sītabaldī, Mahīdpur, Ashti, and Koregaon; ended by capture of Asīrgarh, and general pacification by nineteen treaties.

Sindia was subsequently defeated in 1843. His descendant is now a loyal supporter of the King-Emperor.

---

[1] Assam and Arakan were attached to Bengal. Tenasserim was placed under a Commissioner responsible directly to the Government of India

THE FAMILY OF THE SEVEN PESHWĀS

- (1) Bālājī Visvanāth (1707–20)
  - (2) Bājī Rāo I (1720–40)
    - (3) Bālājī Bājī Rāo (1740–61)
      - Visvās Rāo (killed at Pānīpat)
      - (4) Mādho Rāo (1761–72) (civil war followed his death)
      - (5) Narāyan Rāo (1772–3; murdered by Raghoba)
        - (6) Mādho Rāo Narāyan (1774–95, committed suicide; never exercised power)
    - Raghunāth Rāo (Raghoba; claimant, 1773–4)
      - Amritā Rāo
      - (7) Bājī Rāo II (Dec., 1796–1818)
        - Nānā Sahib (adopted son, disappeared in 1858)
      - Chimnājī Appa
  - Chimnājī Appa (took Bassein)
    - Sadāsheo Rāo, 'the Bhāo' (killed at Pānīpat, 1761)

CHAPTER XXIX

Lord William Cavendish-Bentinck, commonly called Lord William Bentinck: reforms; charter of 1833; Sir Charles Metcalfe and the press.

Lord William Bentinck. After the departure of Lord Amherst, Mr. Butterworth Bayley acted as Governor-General until the arrival, in July, 1828, of Lord William Bentinck, who had been recalled from Madras twenty-one years earlier, and had since held various appointments. The India of 1828 was very different from the India of 1807, and Lord William, during his long term of office, nearly seven years, was able to devote himself almost exclusively to the business of internal administration and reform. When he became Governor-General the only independent powers left in India were the Sikhs of the Panjāb and the Amīrs of Sind, whose subjugation was reserved for his successors. The friendship between the Government of India and Ranjit Singh was solemnly affirmed in 1831, when Lord William Bentinck met the Sikh potentate at Rūpar on the Sutlaj with splendid ceremony.

Annexation of Cāchār and Coorg; Mysore. But even the most peaceful of the rulers of India was unable to escape the necessity for small annexations. The Rājā of the principality of Cāchār, to the east of Sylhet, given up by the Burmese under the provisions of the Treaty of Yandabo, having been murdered, leaving no heirs, the Governor-General acceded to the prayers of the inhabitants and annexed the country. It now forms a valuable District in the prosperous province of Assam, and is largely occupied by European tea-planters. The little province of Coorg, lying between Mysore and the Malabar coast, had the misfortune to come under the rule of a mad Rājā, who treated his people with ferocious cruelty and exterminated all his male relatives. Lord William Bentinck was obliged to occupy the province, and, with the full consent of the people, to depose the Rājā, in May, 1834. Coorg is now governed by a Commissioner, subordinate to the

Resident of Mysore as Chief Commissioner under the Government of India.

The action of Lord William's Government in Mysore has been noticed above (*ante*, p. 284).

Opinions on Lord William's policy. In dealing with the protected states Lord William Bentinck showed hesitation and was not always successful, but the significance of his term of office lies in his internal administration, of which we must now give a brief account. Like all reformers he excited bitter hostility, which has found expression in Thornton's *History*, but general opinion has settled down to a favourable verdict on his policy, and on the whole endorses the eulogium recorded in the inscription on his statue at Calcutta, composed by Lord Macaulay, his friend and colleague, which extols him as the man who 'ruled India with eminent prudence, integrity, and benevolence', and 'whose constant study it was to elevate the intellectual and moral character of the nation committed to his charge'.

Finance. The Burmese war having caused a deficit of a million sterling, the Governor-General was constrained to pay close attention to finance. Additions to revenue were obtained by improved organization of the opium monopoly and by the revision of land settlements in the Agra provinces and in Madras. The precedent of the Permanent Settlement of Bengal was not followed in either the north or the south. The Madras assessments had been made under the able supervision of Sir Thomas Munro on the 'ryotwari' system of direct contracts between the Government and the cultivators for a term of years. The assessments of the Agra or North-Western Provinces were generally confirmed for thirty years, and the contracts were made, not with large proprietors as in Bengal, but with the village zemindars, or their representatives.

Army, &c. Extensive economies were effected in both the civil and military services. The cessation of war gave opportunities for profitable retrenchments, and in 1831 Lord William Bentinck took a free hand by assuming the office of

Lord William Cavendish-Bentinck

Commander-in-Chief in addition to that of Governor-General. His studies of military organization led him to form a poor opinion of the Indian army, which he stigmatized in a confidential minute as 'the least efficient and most expensive in the world'. After the general settlement effected by the Marquess of Hastings in 1818 the spirit of the sepoys had rapidly declined, and the army was not nearly as good as it had been in Lord Lake's time. The events of the Mutiny in 1857 proved that Lord William understood the defects of the Indian system much better than most people. He appreciated the strategical advantages given by steam power in navigation, at that time a novelty, and did much to develop communication with Europe by the Rea Sea and Suez route. He also formed a just estimate of the importance of Singapore in Malacca, acquired finally by treaty with the Dutch in 1824, and made it the capital of the Straits Settlements. Constant tours enabled Lord William to exercise supervision over all branches of the administration and to acquire personal knowledge of local needs.

Prohibition of suttee. The most famous reform associated with his name is the prohibition of suttee (*satī*), enacted in 1829. The Regulation declared 'the practice of suttee, or burning or burying alive the widows of Hindus, illegal and punishable by the Criminal Courts', and rightly pronounced it to be 'revolting to the feelings of human nature, and nowhere enjoined by the religion of the people as an imperative duty'. The practice had attained terrible prevalence in Bengal, where in some years eight hundred or more women had been sacrificed, and the only strenuous opposition to Lord William's measure came from Bengal. A better feeling on the subject exists now, and it is to be hoped that it is no longer necessary to defend the prohibition, which was enacted owing to the zeal and courage of the Governor-General.

Thuggee. Another social reform was effected by the suppression of thuggee (*ṭhagī*), the practice of wholesale strangling for the sake of plunder by strong armed gangs who infested the highways of every province in India except the Konkan, and inveigled unwary travellers to their death. More than three thousand of the Thugs were arrested, and an elaborate system of detection and punishment was organized, under the control of Major (Sir William) Sleeman, which extirpated the system almost completely.

Employment of Indians and judicial reforms. Lord William Bentinck's judicial reforms and arrangements for the employment of natives of the country in appointments hitherto reserved for Europeans were intimately associated with his financial economies. The practical exclusion of the native races from all official employment except of the most humble kind, which was the blot on the arrangements of Lord Cornwallis, had, in addition to its other demerits the objection of expense. Lord William's measures threw open to Indian candidates responsible employment in the judicial and executive service, with the ultimate result that now Indian judges have seats in all the High Courts as well as the Judicial Committee of the Privy Council, and the bulk of the judicial business of the country is done by the natives of it. In 1910 Indians were appointed to the Executive Councils of the Supreme and Provincial Governments. The dilatory Provincial Courts of Appeal and Circuit established by Lord Cornwallis were abolished and replaced by a more workable system, which need not be described in detail.

English education. Important as were the reforms indicated in the preceding pages, some observers give an even higher place to 'the momentous decision to make the English language the official and literary language' of the country, and regard that decision as the event which makes the administration of Lord William Bentinck a landmark in Indian history. Previous Governors, Warren Hastings and the Marquess of Hastings especially, had not been unmindful of the claims of Oriental literature on the attention of the rulers of India, but the idea of a general system of education was first brought forward during the discussions concerning the renewal of the Company's charter in 1833. Among other things, the new charter provided for the appointment of a Law Member to the Governor-General's Council. The first holder of the office was Mr. Thomas (Lord) Macaulay, afterwards famous as the historian of England. His influence decided the Government, as against the advocates of purely Oriental learning, to accept his view that 'it is possible to make natives of this country thoroughly good English scholars, and that to this end our efforts ought to be directed'. The possibility has been abundantly demonstrated, and the existing system of education in India is based on the lines laid down by Macaulay. That system is open to much criticism, but few of its critics will dispute the propriety of the decision to make the English language the vehicle for higher instruction.

The charter of 1833. In 1813 the Indian trade had been thrown open to all comers (*ante*, p. 295), and the Company had been allowed to retain its monopoly only in the commerce with China. As the time approached for another renewal of the charter, reform of all kinds was in the air, the English Reform Act having been passed in 1832, and it was clear that the last vestige of monopoly must go. The main question at issue was whether the Crown should take over the direct administration of the Indian Empire, now an established fact, or continue to exercise its powers through the medium of the Company. The Ministry of the day not feeling ready to undertake the direct government, Parliament preferred to continue the use of the Company's machinery. But the Company ceased to exist as a commercial body; its assets were bought at a valuation, and its organization became merely an extra wheel in the mechanism of the Imperial Government. That was the main effect of the legislation of 1833, although other important changes were effected. The Government of India was now formally empowered to pass laws, and its statutes were given the title of Acts instead of Regulations. At the same time Madras and Bombay were deprived of the legislative power,[1] and, as already mentioned, a Law Member was added to the Governor-General's Council. A Commission was appointed to devise a system of Anglo-Indian law, and after many years its labours resulted in the existing Codes. The North-Western Provinces (now the Agra Province) were formed into a fourth Presidency, but soon afterwards they were reduced to the standing of a lieutenant-governorship. Europeans were permitted to hold lands, and a declaration was recorded that 'no native of India, nor any natural-born subject of His Majesty, should be disabled from holding any place, office, or employment by reason of his religion, place of birth, descent, or colour'. As everybody knows, the liberty so granted was confirmed by Queen Victoria's Proclamation in 1858 and has been freely used. Two Indians now sit on the Secretary of State's Council, which takes the place of the Secret Committee of the Court of Directors under Pitt's India Act and subsequent charters.

Eminent men of the period. The review of Lord William Bentinck's memorable administration may be closed by mentioning the names of some of the illustrious men, British and Indian, who adorned the period. The Indian career of Mountstuart Elphinstone ended in the year of Lord William's arrival, when he was succeeded as Governor of Bombay by Sir John Malcolm. Elphinstone's history of India during the Muhammadan period, although no longer adequate, has not yet been superseded, and Malcolm's account of Central India and other works are still standard authorities. James Prinsep laid the foundation for the scientific study of Indian antiquities and early history; Horace Hayman Wilson and other scholars handed on the torch of Sanskrit learning received from the hands of Sir William Jones and Colebrooke. Colonel James Tod, author of the inimitable *Annals of Rajasthan*, retired in 1823 and died twelve years later. Another famous historian of the period is Grant Duff, who told the story of the Marāthās in a work which ranks as an original authority.

[1] Afterwards restored.

His namesake, the Rev. Alexander Duff, was one of many eminent missionaries who were the pioneers of education in India. Rājā Rāmmohan Rāi, the founder of the Brahmo Samāj, died in England in 1833; and Isvar Chandra Gupta, editor of a Bengali newspaper in 1830, is famous as a poet in his mother tongue.

Sir Charles Metcalfe and the press. The short term of office of Sir Charles Metcalfe, one of the ablest of the Company's servants, who held charge pending the arrival of Lord William Bentinck's successor, is memorable for the Act repealing all restrictions on the press, which at that time was almost wholly confined to Calcutta and in European hands. The censorship, introduced during the French wars in order to prevent communication of intelligence to the enemy, was withdrawn in 1818 by Lord Hastings, and replaced by the issue of rules, which editors were required to obey. Mr. Adam, who deported the editor of the *Calcutta Journal*, made the rules more stringent. Lord William Bentinck, while making no change of system and maintaining that the press should be subject to 'rigid control', ordinarily allowed the journalists a free hand. Sir Charles Metcalfe, believing in absolute freedom, passed an Act applicable to the whole of India, removing all checks on the press. Recent experience having shown the dangers of 'the liberty of unlicensed printing', both the Government of India and the protected States have been obliged to reimpose certain restrictions.

CHAPTER XXX

Lords Auckland, Ellenborough, and Hardinge: first Afghan war; conquest of Sind; war with Sindia; first Sikh war.

Lord Auckland; first Afghan war. Changes in the English Ministry caused some delay in choosing a successor to Lord William Bentinck. Ultimately the choice fell on Lord Auckland, a respectable Whig politician, who arrived in Calcutta on March 5, 1837. He proved himself, in my judgement, the weakest and most mischievous of the Governors-General. On more than one occasion he showed a disregard for honest, truthful dealing. In Lord Minto's time, when Napoleon was at the height of his power and the Tsar of Russia was his humble servant, embassies had been sent from Calcutta to Kābul, Sind, and Persia with the object of securing the North-western frontier against French ambition working through Russian agency. When Lord Auckland came out, Napoleon was dead, French dreams of interference in the affairs of Asia had vanished, and Russia had recovered freedom of action.[1] She had used that freedom on her own behalf to extend her dominion in Central Asia to the east of the Caspian Sea and to acquire a commanding influence at the court of Persia. The Russian advance was regarded by some politicians in both England and India as a menace to India, and when the Persians besieged Herat, Lord Auckland was much alarmed. He came to the conclusion, in agreement with Lord Palmerston and other Ministers in England, that the best way to check Russia was to support Shah Shujā, then living as an exile in the Panjāb (*ante*, p. 294), in his claim to the Afghan throne, at that time occupied by Dost Muhammad Barakzai, who was believed to be under Russian influence. In 1838 a 'tripartite treaty' was drawn up between the Government of India, Shah Shujā, and Ranjit Singh, and an army was sent into Afghanistan. The troops advanced through both the Bolān and Khyber Passes with great difficulty, and occupied Kandahar, Ghaznī, and Kābul. Dost Muhammad surrendered, and Shah Shujā was enthroned. But the Afghans did not want him, and in 1841 they rose, murdered Sir William Macnaghten, the Political Agent, and forced the British out of Kābul. The English commanders and political officers were incompetent, the troops lost heart, and in January, 1842, the entire Kābul force of about 15,000 souls, including followers, when trying to retire through the Khyber Pass, was utterly destroyed, excepting about 120 prisoners and one officer, Dr. Brydon, who made his

[1] Napoleon died at St. Helena in 1821, having been confined in the island since 1815.

way, wounded and exhausted, to Jalālabad, where General Sale held out.

Lord Ellenborough; the avenging army. After this disaster, the worst which has ever befallen the British in India, Lord Auckland was relieved in the ordinary course by Lord Ellenborough. With some hesitation he sanctioned the advance of General Nott from Kandahar and General Pollock through the Khyber to Kābul. The great bazaar there was blown up, the prisoners were recovered, and the avenging army returned to India. Meantime Shah Shujā had been killed, and the Government of India wisely resolved not to meddle any more in Afghanistan. Dost Muhammad was allowed to return to the vacant throne without conditions, and retained it until his death at a great age in 1863. Everybody is now agreed that the policy of Lord Auckland and Lord Palmerston was mistaken. Lord Ellenborough welcomed the returning army with unbecoming festivities and boastful proclamations, which produced an unfavourable impression in India and Europe.

Conquest of Sind. The Governor-General, who was dissatisfied with the Amīrs of Sind for their conduct during the Afghan war, was anxious to annex that province, and his sentiments were shared by his agent, Sir Charles Napier, who conducted the negotiations with the chiefs in a provocative spirit, which goaded the people into open hostility. In February, 1843, the Residency was attacked by a mob of Balochis, and war began. The Amīrs having been defeated in a fiercely contested battle at Miānī, near Hyderabad, and in other fights, the country was annexed and subsequently attached to the Presidency of Bombay. The military operations were well managed, but the crooked policy which led to the war cannot be justified. The annexation was followed by mutinies of the sepoy regiments stationed in the province, which were dealt with in a feeble fashion.

Gwalior affairs. About the same time trouble arose in Gwalior, owing to the death of Jankajī Sindia without issue. A son having been adopted by the widow, Tārā Bāi, a regent was appointed with the sanction of the Government of India. Palace intrigues expelled the regent, and the Resident was obliged to withdraw. The peace of the country being threatened by the arrogance of the Gwalior army, which was too strong for the state, Lord Ellenborough and the Commander-in-Chief, Sir Hugh Gough, brought up troops as a precaution, and demanded the reduction of the local force. Negotiations failed, and the inevitable conflict took place at Mahārājpur, near Gwalior (December 29, 1843). The army of Sindia was defeated after a hard fight, and on the same day another battle took place at Paniār. The requisite steps were then taken to ensure the subordination of the Gwalior state to the paramount power, but no territory was annexed.

Sir Henry Hardinge (Lord Hardinge). The Directors, with good reason, being dissatisfied with Lord Ellenborough's conduct of affairs, recalled him, and appointed in his place Sir Henry Hardinge, a distinguished military officer, who was fifty-nine years of age, and, like all his predecessors, came out as the friend of peace. But, like most of them, he found his business to be not peace but war. From the moment of his arrival he was compelled to take precautions against the threatening attitude of the Sikh army in the Panjāb, and to strengthen the garrisons on the frontier.

The Sikhs after Ranjit Singh's death. When Ranjit Singh died in 1839, during the Afghan war, he was nominally succeeded by his imbecile son, Kharak Singh. A series of intrigues and murders ensued, resulting in the proclamation as Mahārāja of Dilīp (Dhuleep) Singh, a child five years of age, falsely reputed to be a son of Ranjit Singh. But all real authority was in the hands of the *panchāyats*, or committees, commanding the powerful army of the Khālsā, as the Sikh community was called. At last the Rānī, the mother of Dilīp Singh, and two of her friends, Lāl Singh and Tej Singh, were constrained to tempt the army which was beyond their control by holding out the promise of the plunder of Delhi, and to give the order to cross the Sutlaj. Early in December, 1845, a force of 60,000 Sikhs, with numerous camp-followers and guns, crossed the river, the boundary fixed by Lord Minto in 1809, and so declared war.

The Sutlaj campaign: four battles, 1845–6. On December 18, 1845, the British army, taken by surprise and attacked at Mudkī (Moodkee), was victorious, but at a heavy cost. Three days later, the same force, strengthened by fresh troops, attacked the Sikh entrenchments at Ferozeshah (properly Pharūshahr), in the Fīrōzpur district about twelve miles from the Sutlaj. The battle lasted for two days, and after a desperate struggle, in which the British army lost 2,415 in killed and wounded, the entrenchments were carried and the Sikhs compelled to retreat. In this battle the Governor-General, in order to encourage the men, chivalrously served as second in command to Sir Hugh Gough, the Commander-in-Chief. Five of his aides-de-camp were killed and four wounded. A few days later a third battle was fought at Aliwāl in the Lūdiāna district, and again the Sikhs were worsted. The fourth and final struggle took place at Sobrāon on the bank of the Sutlaj, where the Sikhs were strongly entrenched and defended by powerful artillery. They were driven into and across the river with a loss of about 10,000 men. The casualties on the British side also were heavy, nearly 2,400. Thus, in less than two months four great battles had been fought and won, and the Panjāb lay at the disposal of the victors. The Governor-General and Commander-in-Chief received peerages, and honours never were more hardly earned or better deserved.

Treaties of Lahore. Lord Hardinge did not wish to annex the whole province, nor at the time had he the means to do so. A treaty concluded at Lahore stipulated for the reduction of the Sikh army and the surrender of the guns used in the war. Major Henry Lawrence was left at the capital with a British force, and after a short time a fresh treaty was drawn up providing for a regency under British control during the Mahārāja's minority. Gulāb Singh, an upstart chief who was already in possession of Jamū, was guaranteed in his position

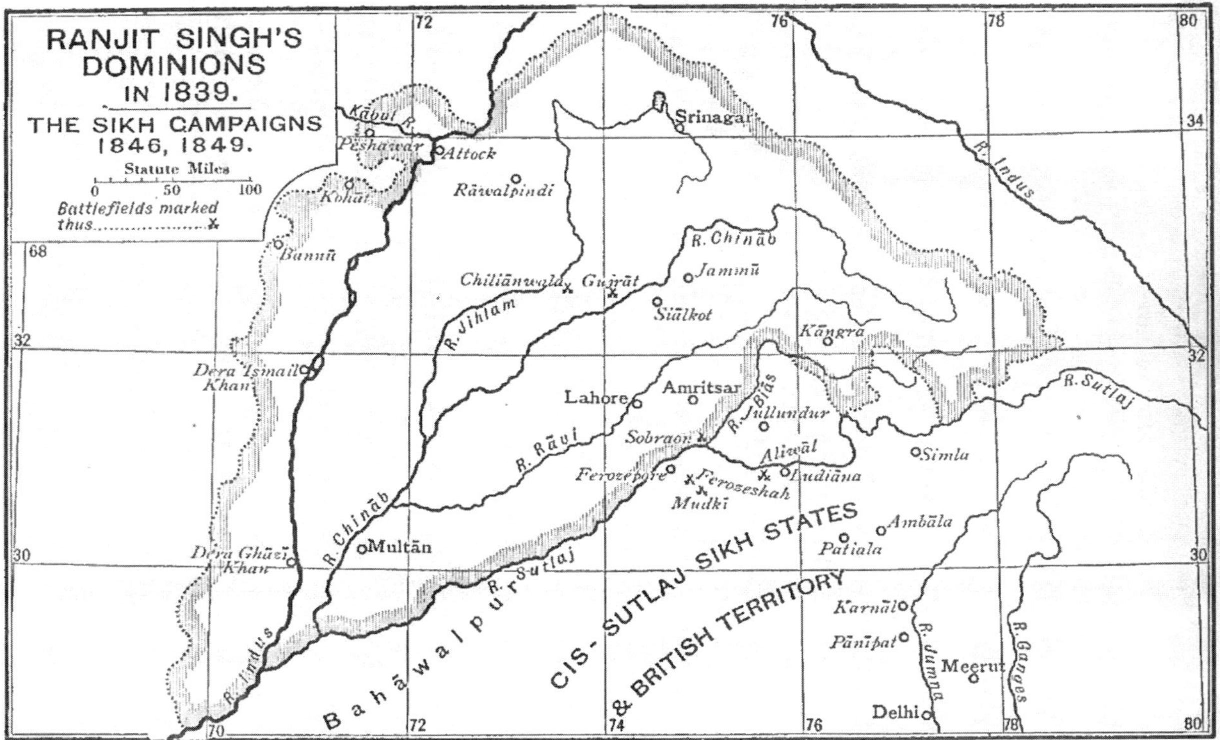

WAXTYPE

GEORGE PHILIP & SON, LTD.

as ruler of that country and allowed to occupy Kashmīr on payment of seventy-five lakhs of rupees. The Sikhs thus lost the control of the hill regions, and were further weakened by the cession to the Company of the tract between the Sutlaj and Biās. At the beginning of 1848 Lord Hardinge returned to England, and was succeeded by Lord Dalhousie.

Civil reforms. Amid the clash of arms the voice of the reformer is little heard. The whole history of Lord Auckland's administration is contained in that of the Afghan disaster, but some civil progress was effected in the time of his successors. Lord Ellenborough's Government carried out two notable reforms, the abolition of slavery and the prohibition of state lotteries. Lord Hardinge is entitled to the credit of having pushed on the construction of the Ganges Canal, and taken effective steps to check the practice of suttee in the protected states.

CHAPTER XXXI

Lord Dalhousie: second Sikh war; second Burmese war; doctrine of lapse; annexations; material progress.

Lord Dalhousie. Lord Dalhousie, a brilliant young Scotch nobleman with some official experience, and only thirty-five years of age, took over charge at Calcutta in January, 1848, receiving from his predecessor an assurance that so far as human foresight could predict, 'it would not be necessary to fire a gun in India for seven years to come'. A year later the Governor-General's army fought the Sikhs in two deadly battles, and the Panjāb became British territory. Then for three years there was peace, followed by the second Burmese war and the annexation of Pegu. Such is human foresight.

Second Sikh war; battles of Chilianwāla and Gujrāt. The arrangements for the government of the Punjāb made by Lord Hardinge on the lines of the Wellesley policy, and obviously unstable, temporary makeshifts, did not last long. The trouble began at Multān, held by a governor named Mūlrāj in practical

MARQUESS OF DALHOUSIE

independence. He resigned his office when the new administration came into power, and two young British officers were sent to take over charge. Disputes having arisen, the officers were attacked and murdered, and Mūlrāj went into open rebellion. The revolt quickly spread over the whole province and war became inevitable. 'Unwarned by precedent, uninfluenced by example', said the Governor-General in October, 'the Sikh nation has called for war, and on my word, sirs, they shall have it with a vengeance.' They got it. Multān, after a gallant defence, was taken on January 28, 1849, Lord Gough, the Commander-in-Chief, having fought a bloody battle at Chilianwāla, on the Jihlam, on the 13th. The conflict has been unjustly described as 'an evening battle fought by a brave old man in a passion'. In reality, Lord Gough, who had intended to encamp, was forced to fight by the Sikhs moving from their entrenchments. Darkness coming on, the Sikh army retired a short distance, but the British lost four guns and the colours of three regiments. Both sides claimed the victory, and the contest may be called a drawn battle. The authorities in England blamed Lord Gough, and ordered his supersession by Sir Charles Napier. But before the new Commander-in-Chief could arrive, Lord Gough, on February 21, 1849, retrieved his reputation by winning at Gujrāt, in the district of that name, near the Chināb river, a victory so complete that the Sikhs had no option but unconditional submission.

Annexation of the Panjāb. Lord Dalhousie rightly decided on annexation, suitable provision being made for the young Mahārāja and other people with claims. The annexation of the Panjāb completed the extension of British dominion over the whole of India Proper. The Governor-General practically took over the government himself, working through a board of three commissioners, replaced after a time by a Chief Commissioner, who has since developed into a Lieutenant-Governor. In Lord Dalhousie's time the real authority, even when Sir John Lawrence was Chief Commissioner, vested in the Governor-

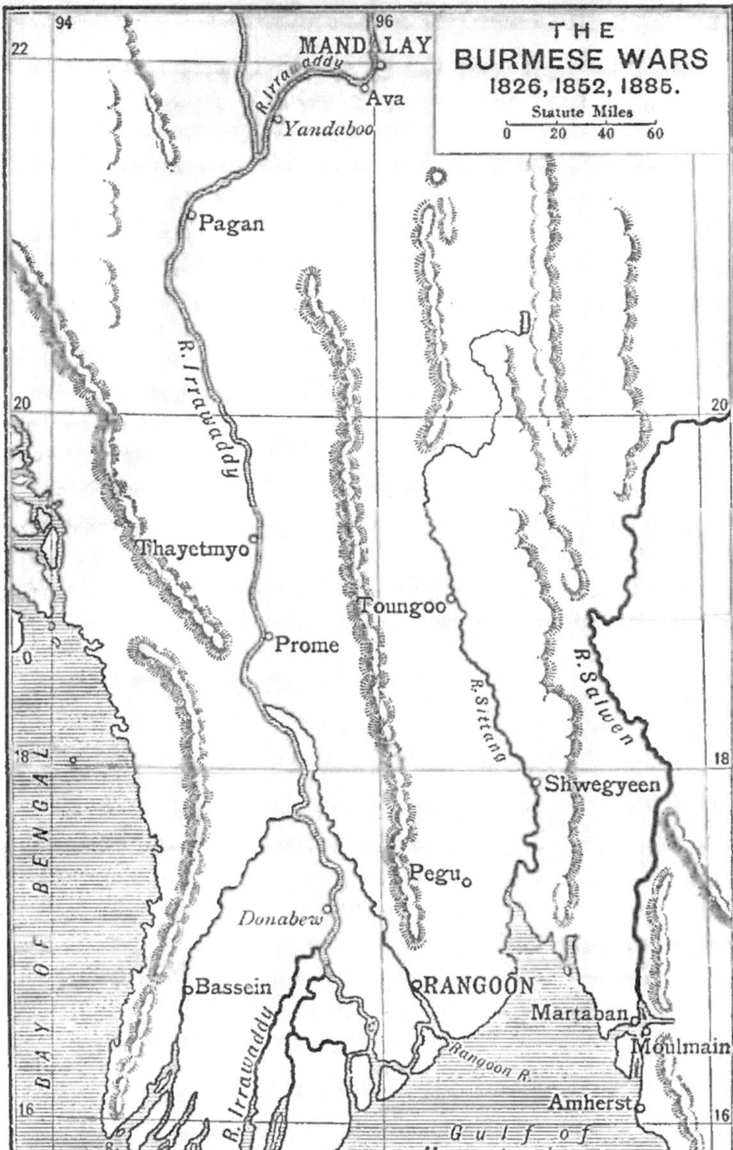

WAXTYPE GEORGE PHILIP & SON, LTD.

General, the local ruler being his agent. Under the fostering care of Lord Dalhousie and the able officers chosen by him, the province rapidly advanced in prosperity, and the Sikh soldiers, who had fought so bravely against the British power, became its loyal supporters. In the Mutiny the Panjāb was a tower of strength to the Government, and since then many of its gallant sons have given their lives on many fields in the cause of their sovereign. A Sikh battalion took part in the Burmese war only three years after the annexation of the Panjāb.

Second Burmese war, 1852. After an interval of three years' peace another war was forced upon Lord Dalhousie by the arrogance of the King of Burmah, who committed various outrages on British subjects, refused redress, and deliberately insulted the officers deputed to demand it. War was declared, and in April, 1852, the pagoda at Rangoon was captured and the town occupied. The taking of Prome followed in October, and in December the war was ended by a proclamation annexing the province of Pegu, the inhabitants of which eagerly accepted deliverance from Burmese cruelties.[1] No treaty was made because the court of Ava declined to negotiate. The conduct of the operations presented a strong contrast to the proceedings of 1826 under the feeble guidance of Lord Amherst. Lord Dalhousie saw to everything himself, and took care that everything should be well done. The annexation of Pegu completely shut off Upper or independent Burma from the sea.

The doctrine of lapse. No ruler of India surpassed, or perhaps equalled, Lord Dalhousie in strength of will, love of justice, and devotion to duty. He gave his life to India and his country. He came out a young man in his prime; after eight years of office he returned a cripple on crutches, fit only for death, which was not long delayed. Those eight years were crowded with unceasing labours, dedicated in large part

[1] Pegu was placed in charge of a Commissioner. The province of Lower Burma, including Arakan, Pegu, and Tenasserim, was not formed until 1862.

to the affairs of the native states. The system of subsidiary alliances, started by Lord Wellesley and continued by his successors, was a necessary stage in the relations between the protected states and the paramount power, but by the middle of the nineteenth century it had served its purpose. Nearly all the princes who occupied their thrones under British protection abused their powers, lived lives of selfish indulgence, and misgoverned their subjects. Lord Dalhousie, therefore, was convinced that the subjects of any native state would benefit immensely by the substitution of direct British government for the rule of a licentious prince, freed by the protection of superior authority from the restraints imposed by the fear of revolt. Wherever he turned—to Oudh, the Panjāb, or elsewhere—he found the same abuses. He was thus led, in the interests of the people, to act systematically on the doctrine of lapse—that is to say, he refused to acknowledge the right of a childless Rājā or Nawāb to pass on the sovereignty of his state to an adopted son, and held that in such a case the sovereignty lapsed to the supreme government. The doctrine was already well established in principle, but Lord Dalhousie applied it with greater strictness than his predecessors. The question first arose with reference to Sātārā (*ante*, p. 300), the Marāthā principality created by Lord Hastings, which was annexed by Lord Dalhousie in the first year of his rule, on the principle above stated. That principle subsequently was applied in the cases of Jhānsī, Nāgpur, the relic of the Bhonslā dominions, and in several others of minor importance. It was also invoked to stop the large pension paid to the ex-Nawāb of the Carnatic. The refusal to continue to the Nānā Sahib of Bithūr, adopted son of Bājī Rāo, the ex-Peshwā, who died in 1851, the pension of eight lakhs granted by Lord Hastings (*ante*, p. 300) was not a case of the application of the doctrine of lapse, for Sir John Malcolm had expressly declared the allowance to Bājī Rāo to be a 'life pension'; and as such it died with him. The Nānā Sahib, as adopted son, admittedly inherited twenty-eight lakhs of rupees, and, as an act of favour, was given a *jāgīr* besides. He had not any just grievance. In all cases where the doctrine of lapse of sovereignty was enforced, the adopted son inherited under Hindu law the private property of the deceased, and the Nānā Sahib received in full everything to which he was entitled. On November 4, 1859, at Cawnpore, Lord Canning announced the withdrawal of the doctrine of lapse, and assured the assembled princes that in future adopted sons would be recognized as heirs to the states.

Annexations otherwise than by lapse or conquest. A portion of Sikkim on the north-eastern frontier was annexed as punishment for the Rājā's ill-treatment of Dr. (Sir John) Hooker and another officer. Sambhalpur, on the south-west of Bengal, was taken over in accordance with the wish of the deceased Rājā, who deliberately abstained from adopting an heir. Oudh was annexed during the closing days of Lord Dalhousie's rule, in consequence of the persistent misgovernment of the country. This drastic measure was taken by express order of the home authorities, and in opposition to the Governor-General's recommendation that the king, in special consideration of the faithfulness of his dynasty to the English alliance, might be maintained in his royal state and dignity, the administration being taken over by the Government of India. The rulers of Oudh, who were allowed to assume the title of king in 1819, had misgoverned the country for a century, and had uniformly refused to listen to the remonstrances pressed by Lord William Bentinck, Lord Hastings, and a long succession of Residents. Sir William Sleeman's *Journey through the Kingdom of Oudh, 1819–50*, gives an appalling picture of the state of the country, which formed an ample moral basis for the decision to annex.

Modern system of government founded. Lord Dalhousie made a beginning in framing a system of government on modern lines, and got rid of absurd traditions which had come down from the old mercantile days of the Company. The first sensible distribution of the work of administration among distinct departments dates from his time, and each department created received his special and ever-watchful attention. Nothing escaped him, and every official felt him to be master.

Railways. The Governor-General, when officially employed in England, had been in touch with the growth of the railway system, then a novelty; and when he came to India, was resolved that India should have railways of her own. The prophets declared that they would not be used, would not pay, and so forth, but Dalhousie persevered and was able to open a short line in 1854.

Postal and telegraph departments. When he assumed charge, India had no postal organization worthy of the name, the mails being conveyed by prehistoric methods under the control of local officers. Dalhousie founded the Postal Department now so efficient, and also introduced the electric telegraph.

Public works. Roads, irrigation works, navigable canals, and, in short, material improvements of every kind, were designed and executed under his personal guidance and supervision. The Grand Trunk Road from Calcutta to the Panjāb was constructed in his time. All this labour was performed in spite of painful bodily suffering and crushing domestic sorrow.

Education. The Governor-General was busy considering the subject of education when he received a dispatch from the Secretary of State, Sir Charles Wood (Lord Halifax), 'containing a scheme of education for all India, far wider and more comprehensive than the local or the Supreme Government could have ventured to suggest'. That celebrated document provided for the establishment of vernacular schools in all Districts, colleges, aided schools, and universities. Lord Dalhousie took action under it without delay, and organized the Department of Public Instruction.

Charter of 1853. The charter of the East India Company was renewed for the last time in 1853, not for any specific period, but during the pleasure of Parliament. The system of government established in 1833 was continued, with the exceptions that certain changes were made in the constitution of the Court of Directors, the Governor-General was relieved of the charge of Bengal and Bihār, a Lieutenant-Governor being provided, and the patronage of the Civil Service was withdrawn from the Directors, the appointments being thrown open to public competition.

CHAPTER XXXII

Lord Canning: the Mutiny; the Queen's Proclamation.

Lord Canning. Lord Canning, son of Mr. George Canning, who was Prime Minister in 1827, relieved Lord Dalhousie on the last day of February, 1856, and remained in office for a little more than six years, until March, 1862. Like Lord Dalhousie, he wore himself out in the service of his country, and returned home only to die. When he assumed charge of the government, England was involved in wars with Persia and China, and the Home Government required India to contribute contingents of European troops, which the country could not spare. The troubles which ensued were largely the result of the reduction of the European garrison of India below the safety point.

Unrest. The history of Lord Canning's administration is the story of the Mutiny, its suppression, and the consequent reorganization. Unrest was in the air when he arrived. The annexation of Oudh, however justifiable on moral grounds, undoubtedly had unsettled men's minds and displeased the Bengal army, which was largely recruited from the ex-king's dominions. England, only just emerging from the long Crimean war with Russia, found herself engaged in lesser conflicts with Persia and China, and it seemed to the numerous classes in India who were dissatisfied for one reason or another with the British rule, that the power of the Government was shaken and might be defied. They could not realize the existence of hidden reserves of strength.

The Mutiny. A panic in the sepoy army was caused in January, 1857, by the discovery that the cartridges for the new Enfield rifle had been greased with animal fat, and that the purity of the sepoy's caste was consequently endangered. The authorities did their best to remedy the blunder ignorantly committed, but the alarm extended throughout the army, and was not to be allayed, the men believing that the Government intended to force them to become Christians. Trouble began with incendiary fires at Barrackpore, followed in February and March by mutinies there and at Berhampore, the cantonment of Murshīdabad. In distant Umballa, too, fires in the lines during March and April indicated the rebellious spirit of the troops. The decisive outbreak occurred at Meerut on May 10, when the native regiments broke out, burnt the station, murdered Christians, and set off for Delhi. The commanding officer at Meerut, an imbecile old man, did nothing with the 2,200 European troops at his disposal, but allowed the revolted regiments to escape and occupy the ancient capital, where the Christian population was slaughtered, and the sepoys tendered their allegiance to the titular emperor, Bahādur Shah, then more than eighty years of age. Within a month nearly every regiment between Allahabad and the Sutlaj had mutinied, and in most districts of the United Provinces of Agra and Oudh civil government was at an end. Those days are still remembered as 'the time of disorder' (*ghadr* or *balwā kā wakt*).

Cawnpore. At Cawnpore, on June 27, General Wheeler, after a gallant defence of an untenable entrenchment for three weeks, was compelled to surrender on terms, which were immediately violated. All the prisoners, men, women, and children, were barbarously massacred under the orders of the Nanā Sahib of Bithūr, adopted son of the late Peshwā (*ante*, p. 300), who caused himself to be proclaimed Peshwā on July 1. 'The great company of Christian people, chiefly women and children', who were slaughtered at the Bībīghar, and cast into a well, are believed to have numbered about 200. The avenging troops, led by Havelock and Neill, who arrived on

July 17, were just too late to prevent this crime, which was perpetrated on the 15th.

Lucknow. The small European garrison and population of Lucknow, including many women and children, held out in the Residency, at first under the command of Sir Henry Lawrence, until he was killed on July 4, and afterwards of his successor, Brigadier-General Inglis. On September 25, when the siege had lasted for eighty-seven days, Generals Outram and Havelock with a relieving force fought their way into the Residency through the streets of the city, and brought a welcome reinforcement to the hard-pressed defenders, who were finally delivered and withdrawn safely by Sir Colin Campbell in November, after standing a siege for five months with unsurpassed heroism. The defence had been materially aided by a small number of gallant, loyal sepoys, including Sikhs, who remained 'true to their salt'.

Battle of Cawnpore; Rānī of Jhānsī and Tantia Topi. The troops which relieved the Residency at Lucknow were obliged to withdraw from the city in order to rescue Cawnpore from the hands of the Gwalior contingent, 25,000 strong, which had occupied that place. Sir Colin gained a complete victory on December 6 over the Marāthā rebel leader, Tantia Topi, who then united the remnant of his forces with those of the Rānī of Jhānsī, the ablest of the rebel leaders. The campaign in Central India against the Rānī and Tantia Topi was conducted by Sir Hugh Rose (Lord Strathnairn) in command of an army brought up from Bombay. The princess was killed in June, 1858, fighting bravely at the head of her troops, like another Chānd Bībī, and in the following year Tantia, who was deeply implicated in the Cawnpore atrocities, was captured and deservedly executed. Lucknow, being held in force by the rebels, was not retaken until March, 1858.

No unity of purpose among the rebels. The rebels did not agree in aiming at any one political object. The mutinous sepoys of the Bengal army tendered their allegiance to Bahādur Shah, and attempted the restoration of the Mughal monarchy,

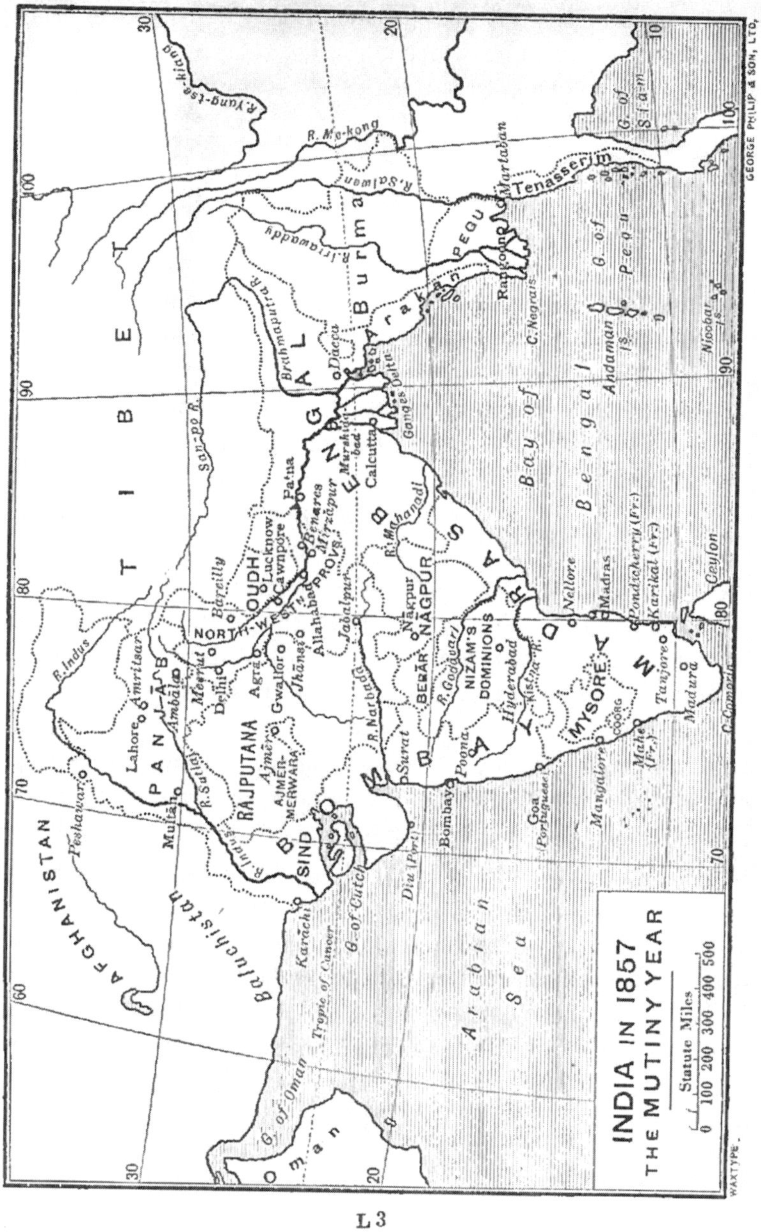
INDIA IN 1857
THE MUTINY YEAR
Statute Miles
0 100 200 300 400 500
GEORGE PHILIP & SON, LTD.
WAXTYPE.
TIBET
AFGHANISTAN
Baluchistan
Oman
G. of Oman
Arabian Sea
Bay of Bengal
G. of Pegu
G. of Siam
BOMBAY
BENGAL
MADRAS
PANJAB
SIND
RAJPUTANA
AJMER-MERWARA
OUDH
NORTH-WEST PROVS.
NAGPUR
BERAR
NIZAM'S DOMINIONS
MYSORE
COORG
Burma
Arakan
PEGU
Tenasserim
Peshawar
Multan
Lahore
Amritsar
Ambala
Meerut
Delhi
Agra
Gwalior
Jhansi
Bareilly
Lucknow
Cawnpore
Allahabad
Benares
Mirzapur
Patna
Murshidabad
Calcutta
Dacca
Jabalpur
Nagpur
Surat
Bombay
Poona
Hyderabad
Goa (Portuguese)
Mangalore
Mahe (Fr.)
Madras
Nellore
Pondicherry (Fr.)
Karikal (Fr.)
Tanjore
Madura
C. Comorin
Ceylon
Karachi
Diu (Port.)
G. of Cutch
Tropic of Cancer
Rangoon
Martaban
C. Negrais
Andaman Is.
Nicobar Is.
Ganges Delta
R. Indus
R. Satlaj
R. Narbada
R. Godavari
Kistna R.
R. Mahanadi
Brahmaputra R.
San-po R.
R. Irrawaddy
R. Salwen
R. Me-kong
R. Yang-tse-kiang
60
70
80
90
100
10
20
30

chiefly because the outbreak of the mutiny happened to occur at Meerut close to Delhi, which offered to them the only possible rallying point. Most of the mutineers were Hindus, who had little cause to love Mughal rule for its own sake. Nānā Sahib, far from supporting the cause of the titular emperor, proclaimed himself as Peshwā, and sought to revive the Marāthā supremacy, destroyed in 1818. The Gwalior contingent and Central Indian rebels generally had more sympathy with the Marāthā than with the Mughal. The Rānī of Jhānsi fought for her own hand, and in other places sundry local interests influenced the rebels. This lack of unity greatly weakened the power of the rebellion, which was never controlled by any one mind, whereas the British operations were guided by the firm hand of the Commander-in-Chief, acting in concert with and under the general supervision of the Governor-General. Each section of the rebels was separately crushed. When all was over, the old Bengal army had ceased to exist.

Delhi. Important as were the operations at Cawnpore, Lucknow, and other places, the critical point was Delhi. A tiny British force had established itself in June on the famous Ridge to the north of the city, but was barely able to hold its ground against the insurgent hosts until reinforcements and a siege train from the Panjāb, collected by Sir John Lawrence at the risk of losing hold on his own province, arrived during August and September. At last, on September 14, 1857, the assault was delivered, the rebels were swept out, and Bahādur Shah was a prisoner. The joy of victory was dimmed by the fall of heroic John Nicholson. The recapture of Delhi was the turning-point of the war, and broke the rebel organization, such as it was. The subsequent operations, some of which have been related, were conducted against detached forces unconnected by any bond of union. By the end of 1858 the authority of the Government had been generally restored, although in some localities the troubles continued into the following year.

The Queen's Proclamation, November 1, 1858. The news

of the rebellion determined Parliament to abolish the powers of the Company and transfer the government of India directly to the Crown,[1] substituting a Secretary of State for India and a Council of fifteen members for the President of the Board of Control and the Secret Committee.[2] At Allahabad, on November 1, 1858, Lord Canning published the Queen's Proclamation, which appointed him to be the 'first Viceroy and Governor-General', and announced the principles on which Her Majesty proposed to govern the Indian empire. The text of this weighty message from the 'mother of her people' to her children in the East is reprinted in Appendix A.[3] A few days after the solemnity at Allahabad, the last of the Mughal emperors passed through on his way to Burma, where he spent the rest of his days in confinement as the penalty for his passive share in the doings of the rebels at Delhi.

Causes of the Mutiny. In the beginning the rebellion was simply the result of the panic caused in the Bengal army by the greased cartridges incident; the Bombay and Madras armies being but slightly affected. The fighting took place almost wholly to the north of the Narbadā, and for the most part was confined to the plains of Hindustan. Oudh was the only province in which the insurrection became general, and nearly every great landholder rebelled. The displeasure at the recent annexation had something to do with this fact, but much of the trouble in Oudh must be attributed to the lawless condition of the kingdom after a century of gross misgovernment. The cause of the Mutiny, expressed in the most general terms and without regard to specific grievances, was the revolt of the old against the new, of Indian conservatism against European innovation. The spirit of revolt undoubtedly had been stimulated by the annexation of Oudh and the trend of

[1] The East India Company was formally dissolved as from January 1, 1874, by an Act of Parliament passed in 1873 (36 Vict. c. 17).

[2] An Act of 1889 authorized the reduction of the Council to ten members.

[3] It has been confirmed and extended by the gracious Message of H.M. the King-Emperor, Edward VII, dated November 2, 1908 (App. B).

Lord Dalhousie's policy, which alarmed men's minds. Every one of his actions was prompted by the highest motives, and each can be justified in detail, but the cumulative effect of them all was profound unrest. Railways, telegraphs, and other material and educational improvements, now matters of course, were in those days unorthodox, disturbing novelties, which contributed largely to unsettle the minds of the people and support the delusion that their religions were in danger. Mutiny in the army was nothing new ; several instances have been mentioned in the preceding pages, and there were others besides. The military organization had become rusty and antiquated, and discipline was lax. The Bengal army, thus ill organized and mutinous, seeing England engaged in distant wars, and the European garrison diminished, believed itself to be master, and in its ignorance rushed blindly to destruction.

Leading Events and Dates of the Mutiny.

I. Delhi area.	1857,	May 10 : Mutiny at Meerut ; rebel occupation of Delhi.
		June 8 : occupation of the Ridge by a small British force.
		Sept. 14 : British recovery of Delhi.
II. Lucknow.		July 1 : defence of Residency began.
		Sept. 25. reinforcement of garrison by Havelock and Outram.
		Nov. 22 : final relief by Sir Colin Campbell and Outram ; withdrawal of the garrison.
	1858,	March 21 : British recovery of city of Lucknow.
III. Cawnpore.	1857,	June 6 : defence of entrenchment began.
		June 27 : defence of entrenchment ended.
		June 27–July 16 : surrender and massacres.
		July 17 : entry of avenging force.
		Nov. 27 : defeat of Windham by Gwalior contingent.
		Dec. 6 : victory of Sir Colin Campbell (battle of Cawnpore).
IV. Central India	1858,	June : death of Rānī of Jhānsi.
and Bundelkhand.	1859,	April : execution of Tantia Topi.
V. Rohilkhand.	1858,	June : recovery of Bareilly by the British.

1858, Nov. 1 : Queen's Proclamation announced.

BOOK VI

THE BRITISH OR ANGLO-INDIAN PERIOD: INDIA UNDER THE CROWN

CHAPTER XXXIII

1858–69: Reconstruction; Lord Canning; Lord Elgin I; Lord Lawrence.

The Mutiny 'a fortunate occurrence'. Sir Lepel Griffin ventured to write, in 1898, that 'perhaps a more fortunate occurrence than the Mutiny of 1857 never occurred in India'. The saying, though a hard one, is, I think, true. If we can place ourselves at the point of view of a general who sends thousands of men to certain death for the sake of their country's cause, and close our eyes to the horrors of Cawnpore and a hundred other places, we can now see that the bloodshed of 1857–9 brought more good than evil. The conflict between the old ideas and the new had to be fought out, and if the struggle had not been begun in 1857 on the question of the greased cartridges, it must have come a little later over some other issue. The proposition that 'without shedding of blood is no remission' has a meaning beyond the theological sense.

'The Mutiny', to continue the quotation from Sir Lepel Griffin, 'swept the Indian sky clear of many clouds. It disbanded a lazy, pampered army, which, though in its hundred years of life it had done splendid service, had become impossible; it replaced an unprogressive, selfish, and commercial system of administration by one liberal and enlightened, and it attached the Sikh people closely to their rulers, and made them what they are to-day, the surest support of the Government. Lastly, it taught India and the world that the English possessed a courage and national spirit which made light of disaster, which never counted whether the odds against them were two or ten to one; and which marched confident to victory, although the conditions of success appeared all but hopeless.'

The tragic events of 1914 give fresh force to those words, and have shown that not only the Sikhs, but all the Indian races, are now to be reckoned among the sure supports of a Government which honestly tries to do its duty to all.

Lord Canning's attitude. Lord Canning, although he could not possibly see the far-reaching effects of the Mutiny as clearly as we see them now, set himself bravely to the work of reconstruction. The dignified calmness of his attitude, undisturbed by much scurrilous abuse, was a wholesome restraint on panic fear and furious passion, which, if left free from control, would have prompted many evil deeds. The Governor-General, like other people, made some mistakes, but, on the whole, he deserves the highest credit for the manner in which he fulfilled the duties of his office, and sought to heal rather than to inflame the wounds inflicted by civil war.

Reform of the army. The reorganization of the army obviously was one of the most pressing duties of the Government. The European force had until then been divided into two bodies, the Queen's and the Company's, an arrangement which often caused much friction. The amalgamation or union of the two was rightly decided on and carried out, in the face of great difficulties. So many changes have occurred since, that it is needless to dwell on details. The Native or Indian Army was reformed at the same time. It, too, has been vastly changed since the days of Lord Canning, and has now proved itself worthy to fight side by side with its British comrades on the huge battlefields of Europe.

Finance. Finance, which lies at the root of all government, claimed equal attention. The immense cost of the military operations had necessarily resulted in a large deficit, the expense much exceeding the income. The old, crude methods of the Company no longer sufficed. Skilled financial experts, at first Mr. James Wilson and then Mr. Samuel Laing, were brought out from England to set things straight. They introduced the income tax and other new imposts, enforced strict economy, and soon converted the deficit into a surplus. The methods of doing financial business were much improved.

Education; Universities. The Education Dispatch sent out by Sir Charles Wood in 1854 (*ante*, p. 325) had borne immediate fruit under Lord Dalhousie's care, in a large extension of village schools. The three universities of Calcutta, Madras, and Bombay were founded by Lord Canning in 1857, the very year of the Mutiny. In those days people thought too much of examinations. The first Indian universities, accordingly, were purely examining bodies, on the model of the University of London as it then existed. Since that time a change of opinion has taken place, and it is recognized that universities should teach as well as examine. New universities have come into being at Allahabad and Lahore, while others are promised or in course of erection at Dacca, Patna, and Rangoon. The proper mode of constituting and managing such institutions is constantly under discussion, and there is reason to hope that, even if perfection be not attained, much improvement will result.

The impulse given by the universities to the study of English and all the subjects taught through the medium of that language has produced an effect on India too profound to be measured.

Codes of law. The useful work of codification began after the Mutiny, during Lord Canning's term of office. The Penal Code, on which Macaulay and other experts had been long at work, saw the light in 1860, and was followed in the next year by the Code of Criminal Procedure. The Penal Code has stood the test of experience wonderfully well, and has needed but slight amendment. The procedure codes naturally require to be re-edited from time to time. In the course of years most branches of Anglo-Indian law have been reduced to the form of codes. The only considerable branch remaining uncodified is that of torts, or civil wrongs.

Other reforms in 1861. The year 1861 was marked by

other important reforms. Chartered High Courts—that is to say, courts constituted under the authority of royal charters—replaced both the old Supreme Court and the Company's courts, known by the Persian names of Sudder Dewanee or Civil, and Nizamat or Criminal, Adawluts. The change got rid of many abuses and legal obscurities.

The Indian Civil Service Act listed the appointments reserved for the Civil Service of India, while throwing open all others, with certain reservations.

Changes were also made in the constitution of the Executive and Legislative Councils of the Governor-General, which have been carried much further in recent years.

The Rent Act. The Rent Act, x of 1859, which applied to Bengal, Bihār, the North-Western Provinces (now the Agra Province), and the Central Provinces, did much to secure the rights of cultivating tenants, which the Regulations of the Permanent Settlement (*ante*, p. 276) had failed to protect. The arbitrary rule that continuous cultivating possession of a field for twelve years should confer tenant-right, or, as the Act called it, 'a right of occupancy', was now laid down for the first time. Experience has revealed many defects in Act x of 1859, which has been superseded by later legislation in the several provinces. The problem involved in trying to give definite legal force to the old vague tenant-right usages is immensely difficult, and the success attained is imperfect.

Death of Lord Canning and Lord Elgin I. The work mentioned, and much besides, wore out and killed Lord Canning, who retired in March, 1862. He survived his retirement for only three months. He was succeeded by the Earl of Elgin, who died at Dharmsala in November, 1863. During the interval pending the arrival of a permanent Viceroy two acting officers carried on the government.

Lord Lawrence appointed Viceroy. At the beginning of 1864, Sir John Lawrence, who, as Chief Commissioner of the Panjāb, had done so much to suppress the Mutiny and recover Delhi, was appointed Viceroy and Governor-General with general approval. The rule that a member of the Civil Service of India should not be promoted to the highest office under the Crown, although recognized to be valid in all ordinary cases, was held not to apply to his special claims. He was subsequently raised to the peerage, and so may be called Lord Lawrence. His term of office may be considered to close the period of reconstruction after the Mutiny. He laid himself out to carry on a purely peaceful, administrative programme, and to keep out of all political and warlike troubles, so far as possible.

'Masterly inactivity.' This disposition led Lord Lawrence to preserve an absolute neutrality in Afghan affairs. When the old Amīr, Dost Muhammad, died, in 1863, various candidates fought for the throne. Lord Lawrence intimated that he would recognize the prince who came out top, whoever he might be. Accordingly, when Sher Ali won the vacant throne, he was duly recognized. This policy, called 'masterly inactivity' by the admirers of the Lawrence system, did not always approve itself as masterly. It was reversed by Lord Lytton, and there is much to be said for his view. At any rate, the inactive policy had the merit of being cheap.

Internal affairs. In internal affairs we may mention the terrible Orissa famine of 1866, which was not well managed, and caused vast loss of life. The want of roads and railways made relief very difficult. Many people were ruined about the same time by the failure of wild speculations in Bombay, where the American Civil War had given occasion for rash dealings in cotton. Lord Lawrence throughout his life took a warm interest in the welfare of the cultivating peasantry, as distinguished from the landlords. He passed a valuable measure for protecting the tenantry in Oudh, and drafted a similar measure for the Panjāb, which was passed after he had left India.

The rule of Lord Lawrence. Lord Lawrence was not quite as successful a Governor-General as he had been a Chief Commissioner of the Panjāb. He carried too far his dislike of pomp and ceremony, and never fully attained the position of mastery over his colleagues which the head of the Government should possess. It is unlikely that a member of the Civil Service of India will ever again be appointed Viceroy. The ministry at home should not have waited to give Sir John Lawrence his peerage until after his retirement, as they did.

CHAPTER XXXIV

1869-84: Lord Mayo; Lord Northbrook; Lord Lytton and the second Afghan war; Lord Ripon and non-intervention; local self-government.

Lord Mayo. The Earl of Mayo, chosen by the Conservative Government as the successor of Lord Lawrence, was a man of a totally different type, gifted with singular charm of manner and lively sympathies—qualities which endeared him to the chiefs of the protected states in a degree never attained by any other Governor-General.

Relations with the Native or Protected States. The taking over of the direct government of India by the Queen had completely changed the position of the Native or Protected States, which now had become parts of the British Empire, although not included in British India. All the chiefs, small and great, from 1858 owed personal allegiance to the Queen of England as their sovereign. No question of annexations, such as had occurred in Lord Dalhousie's time, could possibly again arise. The sovereign could not annex territory forming part of her dominions. But the paramount power necessarily retained the right to change the ruler of a state, in case of grave misgovernment. Lord Mayo fully understood the new conditions and acted on them in the cases of Alwar in Rājputāna and certain small states in Kāthiāwār. His personal qualities assured his success in all such measures. He arranged for the foundation at Ajmēr of a Chiefs' College, which was actually established after his death. Similar institutions now exist at Lahore and at Rājkot in Kāthiāwār.

Friendship with the Amīr of Afghanistan. The Viceroy was successful in establishing friendly relations with Sher Ali, the Amīr of Afghanistan, who had been disgusted by the cold and avowedly selfish policy of Lord Lawrence. In those days the rapid progress of Russian arms in Central Asia made it necessary to watch that Afghanistan should not become a dependency of Russia. Lord Mayo was permitted to promise the Amīr a general support as against Russia, on condition that the Government of India should decide the manner of help to be given.

Visit of H.R.H. the Duke of Edinburgh. The visit to India in 1869 of H.R.H. the late Duke of Edinburgh, second son of Queen Victoria, was an event of high political importance, as marking the beginning of those close relations between the sovereign and her Indian Empire which have been made so much more intimate in later years.

Internal affairs. Lord Mayo was as active and energetic in dealing with internal affairs as he was in other fields. Before his time the Supreme Government used to keep all money matters in its own hands, and every item of expenditure, however trifling, had to be sanctioned by it. The result was that the time of the highest authorities was wasted, and that the provincial Government which gave the most worry got most money. Lord Mayo abolished that absurd system, and made the Government of each province responsible for its own finance within certain limits. His measure is known by the name of decentralization, meaning that much business was transferred from the centre of the government to the branches. The reform has been carried further since Lord Mayo's time. Much attention was given to public works, especially railways and canals. A regular census of Bengal, taken for the first time, revealed the astounding fact that the population of the province as then constituted exceeded the official estimate by twenty-six millions.

Murder of Lord Mayo. Lord Mayo's warm interest in prison administration brought about the sudden end of his useful life. He had gone to the Andaman Islands to visit the penal settlement there, and on January 24, 1872, was getting into his boat after making an inspection tour, when a convict, a desperate frontier Pathan, sprang on his back and stabbed him to death. All India loathed the crime and mourned the victim.

Lord Northbrook. After a short interval, Lord Northbrook, a member of the wealthy banking house of Baring, was appointed as Lord Mayo's successor. The new Viceroy proved himself to be, as might be expected, a good man of business. He was destitute of the personal charm which won affection as well as respect for his predecessor, and he lost the friendship of Sher Ali, Amīr of Afghanistan, who turned away from the British, and showed an inclination to join Russia.

Visit of H.R.H. the Prince of Wales. The visit, in 1875–6, of H.R.H. the Prince of Wales, afterwards King Edward VII, deepened the impression made some years earlier by his brother's visit, and evoked ardent expressions of loyalty to the throne from princes and people.

Deposition of the Gaikwār of Baroda. A disagreeable incident was the trial of H.H. the Gaikwār of Baroda by a special Commission on the charge of having attempted to poison the Resident, Colonel Phayre, by administering diamond dust. The Commissioners differed in opinion, and the Government of India, while refraining from pronouncing a verdict of guilty, held the Gaikwār to be unfit for his position and removed him. A young man, a distant relative, was appointed in his place.

Famine in Bihār. In 1873–4 a serious, although not very severe, famine was experienced in Bihār. The Government was so afraid of repeating the mistake made in Orissa in 1866, when too little was done, that it threw away money with both hands. Seven millions sterling or more were spent, with much waste, but the mortality from starvation was prevented, and there were practically no deaths.

Lord Lytton. Lord Northbrook retired before his term of office was ended. The appointment of Lord Lytton as his successor was a surprise. He was a professional diplomatist, being at the time British Minister in Portugal. Lord Beaconsfield, then Prime Minister, selected him because he believed that India at the moment needed 'a statesman', capable of dealing properly with the dangers threatening from the side of Russia and Afghanistan.

Things have changed so much that it is difficult for the younger generation now living to realize the anxiety concerning the advance of Russia, and her designs for the conquest of India, which prevailed forty years ago. Nobody then could have imagined that in 1914 Russia and England would be the best of friends, closely allied, and fighting together against the hosts of Germany. Nobody now supposes that the Tsar wishes to conquer India. But forty years ago there were very influential people in Russia who did wish to effect the conquest of India, and thought they could do it. All English and Anglo-Indian parties were then agreed that Russia must be prevented from gaining control over Afghanistan, although opinions differed widely concerning the proper means to attain that desired end.

Lord Lytton's policy. Lord Lytton, instructed by Lords Salisbury and Beaconsfield, came to India with perfectly distinct and logical views on the subject. He held that Amīr Sher Ali, if he would not be a friend of the British, should be treated as an enemy, and that the danger threatening from Kābul should be averted by separating Herat and Kandahar so as to form a distinct state. The Viceroy also was convinced that Balochistān must be occupied, and the Bolān and Khojak Passes secured by establishing a garrison at Quetta.

Second Afghan war; Treaty of Gundamuk. Action was taken accordingly. When Sher Ali received Russian envoys while refusing to receive an English mission, war ensued. Sher Ali was driven from his throne. Yākūb Khan, one of his sons, was recognized by the Treaty of Gundamuk (Gandamak, 1879) as Amīr, and was compelled to accept the English mission.

Murder of envoy; renewal of war; resignation of Lord Lytton. Sir Louis Cavagnari, who was sent to Kābul as envoy, was murdered with his escort after a few weeks. That crime, of course, brought on a renewal of the war. General (Lord) Roberts distinguished himself greatly in a series of brilliant military operations, deposed Yākūb Khan, and inflicted severe punishment on Kābul. Lord Lytton, feeling that the frontier had been secured by the occupation of Balochistan and Quetta, did not care what happened at Kābul, and was content to let the Afghans choose an Amīr at their leisure. He arranged for the government of the Kandahar province, and was working out detailed plans, when, in April, 1880, news arrived that Mr. Gladstone had come into power as Prime Minister, and that the Afghan policy of the Conservative Government was disapproved. Lord Lytton, consequently, was obliged to resign. He was relieved by Lord Ripon on June 8, 1880.

Title of Empress of India. Before finishing the story of the Afghan business, we must note certain other events of Lord Lytton's term of office.

In 1876, Lord Beaconsfield had induced Parliament, rather unwillingly, to pass the Imperial Titles Act authorizing Queen Victoria to assume the title of Empress of India (*Kaisar-i-Hind*). The new style of Her Majesty was proclaimed with great pomp at an Imperial Assembly held at Delhi on January 1, 1877, the first of a series of similar displays. The assumption of the title carried further the policy announced in 1858, all the princes being required to do homage to Her Majesty's representative, acting on her behalf.

Famine of 1877 and 1878. A terrible famine ravaged the Deccan and the greater part of the Madras and Bombay Presidencies during 1877 and 1878. In spite of the most zealous exertion and immense expenditure, some five millions of people perished. Lord Lytton showed that he understood the true principles of famine relief, namely (1) perfect freedom of inland trade in grain; (2) the systematic planning and execution of large relief works of lasting usefulness; (3) the preparation of well-considered measures, especially railways and canals, for the prevention of famine.

Abolition of Customs hedge. The abolition of the barbarous customs line or hedge, which ran across India for 1,500 miles, from near Attock to Berār, was a great boon. That hedge, supplemented by others like it in the Bombay Presidency, had been constructed to make easier the collection of the duty on salt. It is surprising that such a monstrous thing should have lasted so long.

Repeal of Vernacular Press Act. Lord Ripon repealed, in 1882, a measure passed by Lord Lytton for the control of the vernacular press. The sedition which followed Lord Curzon's term of office has rendered necessary fresh legislation on the subject, which is too closely connected with the politics of the day to be discussed in this place.

Rendition of Mysore. The restoration of Mysore to the Hindu dynasty in 1881 has been mentioned already (*ante*, p. 284). The present Mahārāja, who attained his majority in 1902, governs his country well, and is an eminently loyal supporter of His Majesty the King-Emperor.

The Ilbert Bill. A great turmoil was raised by a measure known as the Ilbert Bill, from the name of the official who introduced it. The purpose was to make European British subjects triable like natives of India by magistrates of Indian nationality. After much angry controversy the Bill was dropped and the right to claim trial by jury was reserved to European offenders.

Local self-government. Lord Ripon, who was extremely anxious to associate non-official Indians more closely with the administration, passed measures for local self-government, colloquially known in Northern India as 'local sluff', which provided for the establishment of district boards, more or less modelled on English county councils. For many reasons, the success of such measures could only be partial. The Viceroy regarded them as instruments for political and popular education rather than as the means for increased efficiency. How far they have succeeded in their purpose is a matter on which opinions may differ.

Final stages of the Afghan war. When Lord Ripon took over charge, on June 8, he hastened to recognize Sher Ali's nephew, Abdurrahmān, as Amīr, and to make arrangements for restoring Kandahar to him and getting clear of Afghan affairs. But in July 1880 Ayūb Khan, a rival of Abdurrahmān, inflicted a serious defeat at Maiwand, near Kandahar, on a British force, commanded by General Burrows, to whose ill management the reverse was due. The defeated army took refuge in Kandahar, which was relieved by General (Lord) Roberts, who made his celebrated forced march from Kābul with 2,800 European and 7,000 Indian soldiers, besides about 8,000 camp-followers, covering the distance, 318 miles, in twenty-three days. Ayūb Khan was then defeated and Kandahar was made over to the Amīr, Abdurrahmān.

Results of Lord Lytton's policy. It must not be supposed that Lord Lytton's policy, although so far reversed, was barren of results. Balochistan had been brought under British control, and the strong strategical position of Quetta had been permanently garrisoned. Those measures threw open the Bolān and Khojak Passes and exposed the flank of Afghanistan, so that the country could be entered at any moment without troubling about the dangerous Khyber Pass. A few years later the Kurram Pass was occupied, and in due course a railway through the Bolān was made and extended to Chaman beyond Quetta. Thus the Government of India has a hold on Afghanistan such as it never possessed before Lord Lytton's time. The proper way to deal with Afghanistan is still the subject of much difference of opinion. One thing is certain, even at this day, that, as Lady Betty Balfour, Lord Lytton's daughter, wrote in 1899, 'the problem of our permanent relations with Afghanistan is still awaiting a durable and satisfactory solution.' Since 1905, the present ruler, Habībullah, has been recognized as king, and addressed as His Majesty.

Popularity of Lord Ripon. The sympathetic spirit of Lord Ripon's government approved itself to educated Indians, with whom he was popular to a degree never attained by any of his numerous more brilliant predecessors. In England he was never regarded as more than a painstaking, well-trained official of moderate abilities. But in India he aroused burning enthusiasm. When he retired, in December, 1884, 'his journey from Simla to Bombay was a triumphal march such as India has never witnessed—a long procession in which seventy millions of people sang hosannas to their friend'. The time for fixing his final place in history has not yet come.

The Afghan Wars

First.

1838. Tripartite Treaty between the Government of India, Shah Shujā and Ranjit Singh.
Lord Auckland declares war with Dost Muhammad.
1839. Advance of British armies; death of Ranjit Singh.
1840. Surrender of Dost Muhammad.
1841. Rising at Kābul (November).
1842. General Elphinstone capitulates (Jan. 1); British army destroyed (Jan. 6–13).
Defeats of Afghans (March–October); bazaar at Kābul blown up; British withdrawn from Afghanistan.

Second.

1878. Beginning of war (Nov. 21).
Flight of Amīr Sher Ali (Dec. 13).
1879. Treaty of Gundamuk (May 26).
Murder of Sir L. Cavagnari and his escort (Sept. 3).
Retribution; abdication of Amīr Yākūb Khan (October).
1880. British defeat at Maiwand (July 27).
Ayūb Khan defeated by Roberts at Kandahar (Sept. 1).
1881. Kandahar taken over by Amīr Abdurrahmān.

(The operations after the murder of Sir Louis Cavagnari are sometimes called the third Afghan war.)

CHAPTER XXXV

1884-98: Lord Dufferin and the third Burmese war; Lord Lansdowne; Lord Elgin II.

Lord Dufferin. Lord Dufferin, who became Governor-General and Viceroy in 1884, brought to India ripe experience gathered by him in diplomacy during a long career in Russia, Turkey, Egypt, and Syria, and in government as Governor-General of the Dominion of Canada. He was gifted with singular tact, and knew how to get his own way without offending anybody.

The Panjdeh affair. He made friends with Abdurrahmān, Amīr of Afghanistan, whose chief anxiety was to keep British officers and troops out of his country. In 1885 an affray between Russian and Afghan outposts concerning a boundary dispute at a place called Panjdeh, situated between Herat and Merv, nearly brought on war with Russia. But the Amīr remained calm, and the business was amicably settled.

Third Burmese war; annexation of Upper Burma. The most notable event of Lord Dufferin's term of office was the annexation of Upper Burma, following on the third Burmese war. The main cause of the war was the attempt of King Theebaw to put himself under French protection by means of a treaty giving France special consular and commercial privileges. The Viceroy was determined to keep France out of Burma, and was quite prepared to annex the country in order to effect that purpose The king gave further provocation by imposing an enormous fine on a trading company and imprisoning its officials. The resulting war involved no serious fighting and was over in a fortnight, November 14–27, 1885. King Theebaw surrendered and was deported to Ratnagiri on the Bombay coast, where he still lives (1914).

Subsequent disturbances. The real war began after the official war was ended, and lasted for five years. Sundry pretenders to the throne appeared, while the disbanded soldiers and every disorderly person in the country formed themselves into robber gangs, which kept the land in turmoil and committed shocking atrocities. At one time 30,000 regular troops had to be employed. Gradually roads were made, the gangs were hunted down, and peaceful administration was introduced bit by bit. Upper Burma is now quiet and prosperous.

Close of era of conquests. The annexation of Upper Burma completed the list of conquests on a large scale open to the ambition of a Governor-General of India. The settlement made by Lord Hastings in 1818 had brought the whole of India Proper within the control of the British Government, with the exception of the two outlying provinces, Sind and the Panjāb, which were annexed respectively in 1843 and 1849. The Burmese empire, which had no close geographical or historical connexion with India, was taken over in three instalments, in 1826, 1852, and 1885. The final operation completely closed in the Indian frontier in the narrower sense, and at the same time brought the enlarged Indian empire into touch with China, Siam, and the French dominions in the Far East. The Government of India nowadays, whether it likes it or not, must be prepared to deal with external foreign politics.

Internal affairs. Gwalior, the famous fortress in Central India, which had served as the state prison in Mughal times, and had been taken so cleverly by Popham in 1780, had lost all strategical value owing to the changes in the art of war. In 1886 Lord Dufferin did a graceful act by restoring the fortress to Sindia, receiving suitable compensation.

In 1887 Queen Victoria's Jubilee, marking the completion of fifty years of her reign, was celebrated all over India with appropriate festivities and genuine enthusiasm.

Important Rent Acts concerning Bengal, Oudh, and the Panjāb were passed.

Lord Lansdowne. Lord Dufferin retired for personal reasons before the full customary five years of office had elapsed, and was succeeded in 1888 by another distinguished Irish nobleman, Lord Lansdowne, who devoted special attention to questions concerning frontier defence and the reorganization of the army. The Imperial Service troops, which have done splendid service in the Great War, date from his time.

Rising in Manipur. In 1890, during the course of a rising in Manipur, a small hill state on the north-eastern frontier, Mr. Quinton, the Chief Commissioner of Assam, and several other officers were treacherously murdered. The guilty parties were suitably punished and the state was placed under British management for some years.

Currency. In India, for several centuries, the standard of value had been silver—that is to say, the debts, whether of the State or private persons, were payable in silver rupees, not in gold or anything else. From 1874, owing to various causes, the value of silver fell rapidly, and the rupee, which once had been worth the eighth part (2*s.* 6*d.*) of an English gold sovereign, and for many years had been worth the tenth part (2*s.*), decreased until it was worth only about the nineteenth part (1*s.* 0½*d.*) of a sovereign. This fall made it very difficult for India to pay her debts to England and other countries with gold currencies. Arrangements begun by Lord Lansdowne in 1893, and completed in Lord Curzon's time (1899), have made gold a legal tender in India—that is to say, any Indian or the Indian Government may pay a debt in either gold or silver. The rate of exchange was fixed as fifteen silver rupees to the gold sovereign, or, in other words, 1*s.* 4*d.* to the rupee. Little fluctuation in the rate thus fixed has occurred, and the difficulty has been surmounted for the present at all events.

Lord Elgin II; frontiers settled. In 1894, Lord Lansdowne made over charge to Lord Elgin, son of the nobleman who had been Governor-General for a short time in 1862 and 1863. Lord Elgin's Government continued the work of settling disputed frontiers which had been begun by his predecessor. The lines separating the Indian empire from Burma, Siam, and China were marked out, and a Commission defined the Afghan frontier. Disputes with Russia were prevented by a treaty which settled the limits of Russian and British influence in the remote region of the Pāmīrs beyond Kashmīr. Two frontier campaigns were fought during Lord Elgin's term of office, namely, a small though difficult one in Chitrāl, and a series of more extensive operations in the Tirāh country to the south of the Khyber Pass. The valleys of Tirāh were then explored for the first time, but the tribesmen are still far from being subdued.

Plague—the Oriental or bubonic plague—which devastated London in 1665, is no stranger to India, epidemics of the disease being recorded at intervals since the fifteenth century. It seems to exist more or less at most times in Garhwāl. The present epidemic, which began at Bombay in 1896, in the time of Lord Elgin II, is generally believed to have been introduced from China. The most strenuous efforts to stamp out the disease have met with poor success, and we must be content to hope that it may, in the course of time, disappear from India, as it has disappeared from England.

The Burmese Wars

FIRST. 1824-6; Lord Amherst Governor-General; Treaty of Yandabo; annexation of Arakan and Tenasserim, 1826.

SECOND. 1852; Lord Dalhousie Governor-General; annexation of Pegu; no treaty.

THIRD. 1885; Lord Dufferin Governor-General; annexation of Upper Burma (Jan. 1, 1886).

Fighting with gangs lasted for five years longer.

CHAPTER XXXVI

1899-1914: Lord Curzon and his successors.

Lord Curzon. At the beginning of 1899 Lord Elgin was succeeded by Lord Curzon of Kedleston, who was then in his fortieth year, and had achieved high distinction in Parliament and as a traveller in Asia. The whole period since the Mutiny is too recent for historical treatment like that which is applicable to earlier times. When we come to events so near us as those of Lord Curzon's memorable administration it is impossible to approach them in the detached spirit of the impartial historian. His Lordship and many other actors in the scene are still living, the passions and feelings aroused by the acts of the Viceroy are still burning, and the record is necessarily imperfect. Although many years must elapse before documents now confidential can become public property, so that it will be possible to appraise correctly the place of Lord Curzon in Indian history, it is safe to affirm that he proved himself to be one of the ablest in the long series of Governors-General. Consciously or unconsciously, he seems to have taken as his model Lord Dalhousie. Lord Curzon, like his prototype, was masterful, full of consuming energy, and devoted to the attainment of efficiency in all departments. I venture to think that, like Lord Dalhousie, he did too much, and forced the pace of reform too fast. Whatever differences of opinion may exist concerning the merits of Lord Curzon's policy in several matters of high importance, everybody must acknowledge that he approached each problem with an acute intellect, instructed understanding, unwearied industry, and lofty motives. He effected many improvements in administration to which no objection can be taken.

Afghan frontier policy. Lord Curzon's Afghan policy was directed to the object of putting a stop to the costly and unfruitful punitive expeditions which had been going on for so many years. One method adopted to attain that purpose was the withdrawal of British garrisons from the frontier, combined with arrangements for guarding the passes by levies of local tribesmen. He managed to avoid expeditions during his term of office, with one partial exception, the chastisement of the Wazīris. The operations against that tribe were called a 'blockade'. Another measure directed to the same end was the formation of the North-Western Frontier Province, an irregular straggling strip of territory chiefly to the west of the Indus, made up by combining certain districts taken from the Panjāb with sundry tribal territories. The new province was placed directly under the Government of India, which now holds all the threads of frontier policy in its own hand. Lord Curzon's management of the frontier has saved much money and may be fairly described as successful.

Tibet and Persia. The invasion of Tibet in 1904 was brought about by Tibetan intrigues with Russia, obstruction to trade with India, and neglect to answer letters from the Indian Government. The expedition penetrated to Lhasa, the capital of Tibet, which had long been closed to European visitors, and much interesting information was collected. The value of the political results attained seems to be rather doubtful, and everybody is not agreed concerning the supposed necessity for military operations.

Lord Curzon took effective steps to preserve British influence in Persia and the Persian Gulf.

Death of Queen Victoria. On January 22, 1901, Queen Victoria, Empress of India, passed away, and was mourned by the whole world. She had lived for nearly eighty-two and reigned for nearly sixty-four years. During that long time she had enjoyed the love as well as the respect of her subjects, being justly regarded as the 'mother of her people'. She always cherished a special affection for her Indian empire, and liked to have representatives of various Indian races in attendance on her person. Her eldest son, who had visited India as Prince of Wales in 1875 (*ante*, p. 340), succeeded to the throne as King-Emperor Edward VII.

A magnificent Coronation Darbār was held at Delhi in 1903.

The famine of 1900. A grievous and wide-spread famine in 1900 gave ample scope for the exercise of Lord Curzon's remarkable skill in organization and his patient attention to minute details. The calamity was met by efforts on the part of all concerned which could not be surpassed, and led to the preparation of elaborate revised rules regulating measures for the relief of famine or scarcity.

Earlier famines. Foolish people, ignorant of history, are found from time to time who assert that famines are mainly

FROM AN ENGRAVING BY WYON

the result of British misgovernment, and that they were hardly known in the days of independence. Such assertions are ludicrously false. The history of India is full of famines. Several of terrible severity have been mentioned in the pages even of this little book, from which many others have been omitted.[1]

The difference between the old times and the present is that the ancient rulers, so far as appears, never in any instance took really effective steps to relieve famine on a large scale, and very often did nothing at all; whereas the authorities of British India, since 1873 at any rate, fully recognize the duty of preserving life so far as possible and of giving substantial relief, even at the cost of crores of rupees. The Government of India was somewhat slow in recognizing its duty in the matter; but since the comparatively slight local Bihār famine of 1873–4, no person possessing the least knowledge of the facts can honestly accuse the Indian authorities of indifference to the miseries caused by failure of the rains and consequent famine. What is possible is done.. No human agency or lavish expenditure can prevent enormous suffering and numerous deaths when the failure of rain is widespread and famine severe. The opening up of means of communication by roads, railways, and other modern inventions has done much to prevent local famines, and to make relief easier in all cases. The provision in immense areas of facilities for irrigation has protected a large percentage of the best land in the country from all danger of acute famine. We must not, however, expect that the occurrence of famine in India will be or can be prevented altogether.

Finance. No ruler who understands his business can be indifferent to finance. Money, denounced by the moralist as the root of all evil, is certainly the root of all government. Long ago, Kautilya laid down the sound doctrine that 'all undertakings depend upon finance. Hence foremost attention

[1] Balfour's *Cyclopaedia* gives a list of about twenty notable Indian famines prior to 1750. A famine of early date is mentioned in *Jātaka*, No. 199.

shall be paid to the Treasury.' Lord Curzon fully understood that principle. Among other reforms, his Government completed the legislation making gold a legal tender for the payment of debts (*ante*, p. 348), raised the limit of exemption from income tax, and nearly halved the salt tax. From the earliest times Indian Governments have relied for part of their revenue upon a tax on salt, and have retained a right to regulate the production of that necessary article. The tax, when low in rate, cannot be felt severely even by the extremely poor, who form the large majority of the population of India; and it has the merit of taking some contribution for public purposes from everybody. The rate used to be too high.

Since 1894, India has levied a customs duty, usually 5 per cent., on most articles arriving at the ports by sea. The propriety of the way in which duty is levied on cotton goods has been the subject of much controversy, which continued in Lord Curzon's time, and has not yet been settled.

Education. Warren Hastings, a man of large ideas, who saw far into the future, was keenly alive to the necessity for education, and did what he could to promote it. The Marquess of Hastings was able to do something more. His remark that it would be treason to perpetuate ignorance has been quoted (*ante*, p. 301). But no general well-conceived plan for a system of education in all grades throughout the empire existed until the time of Lord Dalhousie. The dispatch sent by the Secretary of State in 1854 laid down the principles to be followed and is the foundation of the Education Department (*ante*, p. 325). Lord Dalhousie gladly gave the fullest possible effect to the instructions then sent out from England.

We have seen how the earliest Indian universities were established in the year of the Mutiny, and that other institutions of the kind have been created, while still more are to come. Lord Curzon devoted the most laborious study, even to the extent of injuring his health, to all aspects of the education problem, and rightly came to the conclusion that in the constitution and management of the universities grave abuses existed. He attempted to correct those abuses and start a better system by means of the Universities Act, 1904. The representatives of the educated classes took up the erroneous notion that the Viceroy was opposed to higher education, whereas his real objects were to convert such education 'into a reality instead of a sham', and to give it 'new life'. A great clamour arose and pursued Lord Curzon for the rest of his stay in India. The turmoil was due largely to the fears of vested interests, and in a measure to mistakes made by the Viceroy. But the opposition also rested on certain grounds of principle. The subsequent appointment of a Minister of Education has raised hopes that the exceedingly difficult question of university education in India may be solved in a manner at least tolerably satisfactory.

The Partition of Bengal. Another act of Lord Curzon's which aroused intense bitterness of feeling, especially in the province immediately concerned, was the so-called Partition of Bengal. There can be no question that the huge area under the jurisdiction of the Lieutenant-Governor of Bengal in 1904 could not be administered properly and that it was absolutely necessary to break up the unwieldy province. Lord Curzon hit on a scheme which unluckily gave deep offence, and awakened in Bengal a violent expression of nationalist feeling which had not been expected by the Government of India. The action of the authorities with regard to the universities and the rearrangement of the Bengal province was made the pretext for a furious seditious agitation resulting in a series of murders and other grave crimes.

At the Imperial Darbar held at the close of 1911, H.M. the King-Emperor announced a different arrangement, which seems to be considered satisfactory. The old Bengal province is now divided into three jurisdictions, namely, Bengal, under a Governor-in-Council, Bihār and Orissa under a Lieutenant-Governor-in-Council, and Assam under a Chief Commissioner. Unfortunately the crimes committed by dangerous secret societies of anarchists have not yet wholly ceased (1914).

The antiquities of India. It is pleasant to turn from these highly contentious subjects to measures of Lord Curzon's which have won, and deservedly won, universal approval. India is full of memorials of olden times. Lord Curzon not only passed an Act for the Preservation of Ancient Monuments, but worked out a well-conceived scheme for both the conservation of buildings which had escaped destruction and the exploration of the treasures of antiquity buried in sites where everything above ground had perished. Both duties—conservation and exploration—were entrusted to a skilled Director-General of Archaeology, aided by a staff of expert assistants in the provinces, and supplied liberally with funds. The Department, thus organized in a manner far superior to the crude arrangements previously in operation, has done admirable work, and its reports become more and more interesting every year. The field for research is practically unlimited, and it is impossible to imagine a time when the Director-General should have nothing left to do. The scientific study of the antiquities of India was for many years confined almost exclusively to European scholars, but since about the beginning of the current century numerous Indian-born students have recognized that the investigation of the history of their native land should not be abandoned to foreigners, and have been doing their duty in making additions to the world's store of historical knowledge.

Resignation of Lord Curzon. Lord Curzon, having been reappointed Viceroy and Governor-General after a brief visit to Europe in the summer of 1904, during which his place was occupied by Lord Ampthill, Governor of Madras, resigned office late in 1905. His retirement was due to a controversy concerning the position and duties of the Commander-in-Chief in India. The Home Government having accepted the opinion of Lord Kitchener and rejected that of the Viceroy, the latter was bound to resign. The Commander-in-Chief in India now combines the duties of executive command of the army in all its departments with those of military member of Council or

War Minister. Lord Curzon held that arrangement to be opposed to the recognized principle that in all well-conducted states the military should be subordinate to the civil authority. Much might be said on both sides of the dispute.

Lord Minto II: sedition. The nobleman chosen to succeed Lord Curzon in 1905 was the Earl of Minto, great-grandson of the half-forgotten Governor-General who had done such excellent service during the Napoleonic wars a century earlier (*ante*, p. 293). His period of rule is marked chiefly by two things namely—grave unrest resulting in many atrocious crimes; and secondly, important reforms in the machinery of the government of India.

Lord Minto met the dangers and difficulties of his situation with quiet courage, and did not allow himself to be turned from his course even by a wicked attempt made upon his life. The crimes of the secret conspirators, who foolishly thought to destroy the British supremacy by means of the murder of individual officials, were at their height in 1908 and 1909. It cannot be said that the conspiracy has been wholly rooted out even now (1914), but since 1912 the outrages have been fewer. The new laws needed to check new forms of crime were duly passed. They include provisions for the regulation of seditious publications, which must remain in force as long as the necessity exists. The Government would prefer, if possible, to maintain Sir Thomas Metcalfe's policy of an absolutely free press (*ante*, p. 312), but the safety of the Empire must be the first consideration.

Lord Minto rightly decided that the crimes of a small gang of conspirators, acting in concert with foreign anarchists, should not deter him from carrying out the reforms in the Indian constitution which appeared to be desirable on their merits. The repression of crime is a matter to be dealt with by a good system of police; reforms in the framework of the government of India are a separate affair, and rendered necessary by reasons of permanent validity.

The term 'constitution'. The idea of a 'constitution' is unfamiliar to Indian thought. Although in very ancient times we hear of communities governed by tribal assemblies, practically all the governments mentioned in the long course of Indian history were of one type—that of absolute monarchy. Whatever the race of the monarch might be, his will was supreme and free from control by laws or customs binding him. In the United Kingdom the case is different. For centuries past the power of the King and his ministers has been controlled by a body of law and usage regulating the relations of the Executive with Parliament, the people, and the judges, and defining more or less strictly the limits of action of the several authorities concerned in governing the country. That whole body of law and usage, vague in many respects, is spoken of as the 'English constitution'.

Growth of an Indian 'constitution'. A somewhat similar body of law and usage has been gradually growing up in India during the British Period. It mostly consists of positive law based on Acts of Parliament or on royal proclamations and charters. We may take it as beginning with Lord North's Regulating Act of 1773 (*ante*, p. 264). The next important stage is marked by Pitt's India Act of 1784, which fixed the relations between the Home or British Government and the Government in India. Further changes were made by the charters granted to the East India Company in 1793, 1813, 1833, and 1853. The greatest change of all was made when Queen Victoria by Act of Parliament and Proclamation took over the government of India in 1858 (*ante*, p. 330). The Governor-General and the Governors of Madras and Bombay had always been assisted by small Councils. The growth of the Indian 'constitution' since 1858 has been mainly directed to the expansion of those Councils, and the consequent limitation of the arbitrary power of the Executive. Laws were made by the Governor-General's Executive Council until 1853, and bore the name of Regulations until 1833, since which time they have been called Acts. Separate Legislative Councils, for the sole purpose of making laws, have gradually come into existence, and steps have been taken to make them less dependent on the Executive Government.

Lord Minto's reforms. The reforms of Lord Minto's time concerned both the Executive and the Legislative Councils. Both have been much enlarged, and the Governor or Lieutenant-Governor of each of the larger provinces either has now or soon will have an Executive Council, such as the Governors of Madras and Bombay always have had. Men of Indian birth have been admitted to the Executive Councils of the Supreme and local Governments, as well as to the Council of India, which advises the Secretary of State in London, and are thus entrusted with the innermost secrets of government.

Arrangements have been made for the election of members to the Legislative Councils, and the new rules allow much greater freedom of discussion than that formerly permitted. Each important province now has a Legislative Council of its own, and can make its own local laws. The reformed Councils are reported to work well.

Lord Hardinge of Penshurst. In November 1910, Lord Minto was succeeded by Lord Hardinge of Penshurst, a distinguished Foreign Office official and a grandson of the Governor-General who defeated the Sikhs in 1846 (*ante*, p. 316). All India was horrified on December 22, 1912, when a gang of criminals threw a bomb at the Viceroy as he was making a state entry into Delhi, and wounded him seriously, killing the attendant at his side. The perpetrators of the crime escaped in the confusion.

The visit of Their Majesties. The great event of Lord Hardinge's Viceroyalty is the visit to India of Their Majesties, the King-Emperor George V and his consort Queen Mary, which lasted from December 2, 1911, to January 10, 1912. On December 12 Their Majesties held a solemn Darbar at Delhi, and received the willing homage of princes and people, to whom they announced their coronation. His Majesty then took occasion to proclaim the revision of the boundaries of Bengal and the removal of the official capital from Calcutta to Delhi, as well as other measures of importance. Opinions may and do differ concerning the merits of the two principal changes proclaimed at the Coronation Darbar, but no difference of opinion can exist respecting the immense significance of the royal visit, and the reality of the loyal, reverential enthusiasm with which Their Majesties were greeted by high and low.

Now, in 1914, when the nations of the world are tearing each other to pieces in the most tragic war known to history, the King's enemies have been taught the supreme worth of India's heartfelt loyalty. The Victoria Cross awarded to more than one sepoy, and the many gallant deeds wrought in Europe, Asia, and Africa by all ranks of the Indian Army, whether Hindu, Musalman, or Sikh, testify to a real brotherhood in arms between the European and the Indian, and warrant a confident expectation that, to use His Majesty's words, greater unity and concord may in the future govern the daily relations of the public and private lives of his Indian subjects.

Conclusion. My story, brought down almost to the moment of publication, is now ended.

I would fain hope that the reforms announced from time to time by His Majesty or his advisers, may produce the beneficial effects intended; that each succeeding Viceroy, as he takes up the heavy burden of his office, may be granted the wisdom needed for the government of an empire unlike any which the world has seen; and that all the various peoples of India may give their rulers that loyal support without which progressive government is impossible.

My young readers will, I trust, ponder aright the lessons of history, and do all that lies in their power to further the peace, prosperity, and honour of their country, as well as of the still vaster empire with which its fortunes are so closely united.

INDIA UNDER THE CROWN

Some Leading Dates

A.D.	(For list of Viceroys see next page).
1859.	The Rent Act (x of 1859).
1860.	Indian Penal Code.
1861.	Councils Act; Civil Service of India Act; Chartered High Courts.
1863.	Amīr Dost Muhammad died; Sher Ali acc.
1866.	Orissa famine.
1869.	Suez Canal opened.
1875–6.	Visit of H.R.H. the Prince of Wales.
1876.	Quetta occupied.
1877 (Jan. 1).	Proclamation of Queen Victoria as Empress of India.
1877, 1878.	Famine in Southern and Western India.
1878–80.	Second Afghan war.
1885.	Panjdeh affair; third Burmese war.
1886 (Jan. 1).	Annexation of Upper Burma.
1895.	Chitrāl expedition.
1896.	Plague broke out at Bombay.
1898.	Tirāh expedition.
1899.	Gold standard introduced.
1900.	Famine.
1901.	Death of Queen-Empress Victoria; Edward VII acc.; death of Amīr Abdurrahmān; Amīr (King) Habībullah acc.
1904.	Tibet expedition; Universities Act.
1905.	Partition of Bengal.
1909.	Sedition; Indian Councils Act.
1911.	Visit of Their Majesties; Coronation Darbār.
1912.	Attempt on life of Lord Hardinge.
1914.	The Great War: India's help.

EAST INDIA COMPANY

1600 (December 31). Queen Elizabeth's charter.
1661. Charter of Charles II.
1708. Final fusion of rival Companies.
1773. Regulating Act (Governor-General of Bengal).
1784. Pitt's India Act ('Board of Control').
1793. Charter renewed.
1813. „ „ (India trade thrown open).

1833 Charter renewed. (Company's trading functions abolished; China trade thrown open).
1853. „ „ (Competition for Civil Service).
1858. Government of India Act (Direct government by Crown; Queen's Proclamation).
1874. Formal dissolution of the Company.

GOVERNORS-GENERAL

I. *Governors-General of Bengal or of Fort William* (*Regulating Act of* 1773).

(*Temporary and officiating in italics.*)

1774 (October). Warren Hastings, Esq. (Right Honourable).
1785 (February 1). *Sir John Macpherson.*
1786 (September). Earl (Marquess) Cornwallis.
1793 (August). Sir John Shore (Lord Teignmouth).
1798 (March). *Sir Alured Clarke.*
1798 (May). Earl of Mornington (Marquess Wellesley).
1805 (July 30). Marquess Cornwallis (for second time).
1805 (October 5). *Sir George Barlow.*
1807. Baron (Earl of) Minto I.
1813 (October 4). Earl of Moira (Marquess of Hastings).
1823 (January 1). *John Adam, Esq.*
1823. (August 1). Baron (Earl) Amherst.
1828 (March 8). *William Butterworth Bayley, Esq.*
1828 (July). Lord William Cavendish-Bentinck.

II. *Governors-General of India* (*Charter Act of* 1833).

1833. Lord William Cavendish-Bentinck.
1835 (March 20). *Sir Charles* (*Lord*) *Metcalfe.*
1837 (March 1). Baron (Earl of) Auckland.
1842. Baron (Earl of) Ellenborough.
1844. Sir Henry (Viscount) Hardinge.
1848. Earl (Marquess) of Dalhousie.
1856. Viscount (Earl) Canning.

III. *Governors-General and Viceroys* (*Queen's Proclamation*).

1858 (November 1). Earl Canning.
1862. Earl of Elgin I.
1863. *Sir Robert Napier* (*Lord Napier of Magdala*).
1863. *Sir William Denison.*

1864. Sir John (Lord) Lawrence.
1869. Earl of Mayo.
  1872. *Sir John Strachey.*
  1872. *Lord Napier of Merchistoun.*
1872. Baron (Earl of) Northbrook.
1876. Baron (Earl of) Lytton.
1880. Marquess of Ripon.
1884. Earl of Dufferin (Marquess of Dufferin and Ava).
1888. Marquess of Lansdowne.
1894. Earl of Elgin II.
1898 (Jan. 6). Baron (Earl) Curzon of Kedleston.
  1904. *Lord Ampthill.*
1904. Baron (Earl) Curzon of Kedleston (reappointed).
1905. Earl of Minto II.
1910. Baron Hardinge of Penshurst.

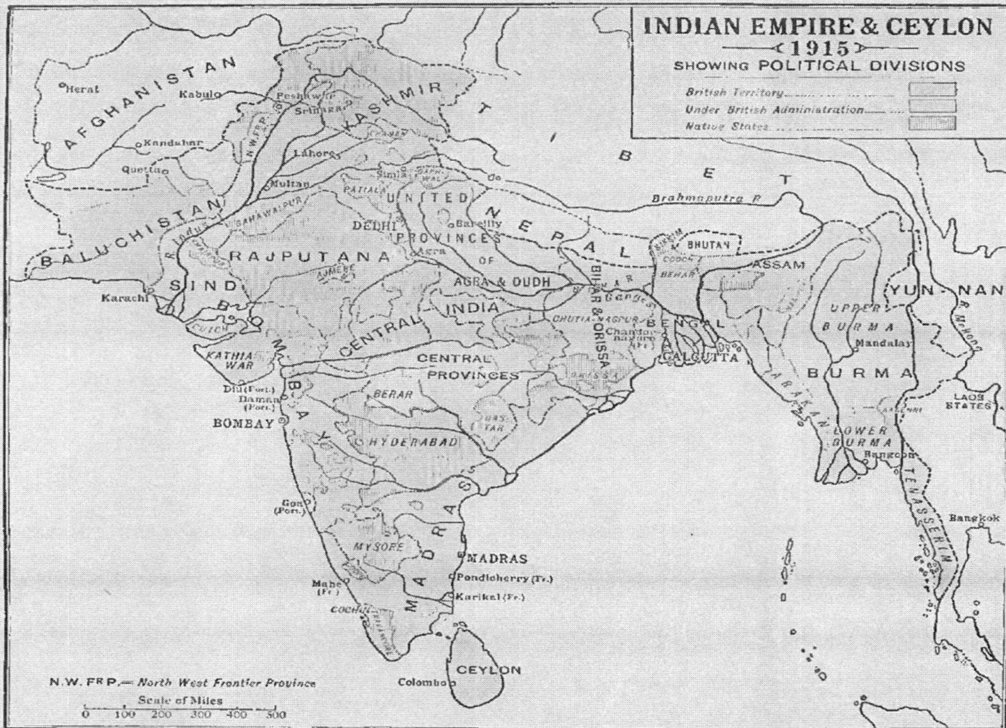
INDIAN EMPIRE & CEYLON
1915
SHOWING POLITICAL DIVISIONS
British Territory
Under British Administration
Native States
AFGHANISTAN
Herat
Kabul
Kandahar
Quetta
BALUCHISTAN
Peshawar
Srinagar
KASHMIR
N.W.FRP.
Lahore
Multan
Simla
PATIALA
TIBET
Brahmaputra R.
UNITED PROVINCES OF AGRA & OUDH
Bareilly
Agra
DELHI
NEPAL
SIKKIM
BHUTAN
COOCH BEHAR
ASSAM
RAJPUTANA
AJMERE
SIND
Karachi
R. Indus
BAHAWALPUR
CUTCH
KATHIAWAR
BOMBAY
Diu (Port.)
Daman (Port.)
CENTRAL INDIA
CENTRAL PROVINCES
BERAR
HYDERABAD
BIHAR & ORISSA
CHUTIA NAGPUR
Chandernagore (Fr.)
BENGAL
CALCUTTA
Goa (Port.)
MADRAS
MYSORE
Mahe (Fr.)
COCHIN
TRAVANCORE
Pondicherry (Fr.)
Karikal (Fr.)
CEYLON
Colombo
YUN-NAN
R. Mekong
UPPER BURMA
Mandalay
BURMA
ARAKAN
LOWER BURMA
Rangoon
LAOS STATES
TENASSERIM
Bangkok
N.W. FRP.— North West Frontier Province
Scale of Miles
0 100 200 300 400 500
GEORGE PHILIP & SON, LTD.